America's Painted Ladies

Elizabeth Pomada
and
Michael Larsen

Photographs by
Douglas Keister

AMERICA'S PAINTED LADIES®

*The Ultimate Celebration
of Our Victorians*

Viking Studio Books
NEW YORK

Photograph Credits

All of the photographs in the book are by Douglas Keister with the following exceptions: Arquitectonica: Norman McGrath; Union Hotel and Victorian Annex, Los Alamos interiors: Steve Underwood; 5332 Magazine Street, New Orleans, gryphon; 636 Arabella Street, New Orleans, harpsichord; 2142 Sedgwick, Chicago, gate sketches, and newel-post sketches; 315 East Lake, Waupaca, WI, front detail; Garth Mansion, Hannibal, MO, exterior; Ventura, CA church detail: Michael Larsen.

(Frontispiece) Detail of the entrance hall of The Mark Twain House, Hartford, Connecticut. The entire hall is illustrated on page 32.

(Page 10) Detail of the entrance to the John Mills house, Malone, New York. The entire house is illustrated on the jacket of this book and on page 44.

DUTTON STUDIO BOOKS

Published by the Penguin Group
Penguin Books USA Inc., 375 Hudson Street,
New York, New York 10014, U.S.A.

Penguin Books Ltd, 27 Wrights Lane,
London W8 5TZ, England,

Penguin Books Australia Ltd, Ringwood,
Victoria, Australia

Penguin Books Canada Ltd, 2801 John Street,
Markham, Ontario, Canada L3R 1B4

Penguin Books (N.Z.) Ltd, 182-190 Wairau Road,
Auckland 10, New Zealand

Penguin Books Ltd, Registered Offices:
Harmondsworth, Middlesex, England

First published by Viking Studio Books, an imprint of Penguin Books USA Inc.

First printing of this paperback edition, October, 1994
10   9   8   7

Library of Congress
Catalog Card Number: 92-71070

Printed and bound by Dai Nippon Printing Co., Hong Kong, Ltd.
Book designed by Kingsley Parker

ISBN: 0 14 02.3857 3

This book is dedicated to
our friend and editor Cyril I. Nelson,
whose leap of faith made the Painted Ladies books possible
and who has done so much to make them as beautiful as
the houses they seek to immortalize;
to the homeowners, colorists, and architects
whose artistry the book helps preserve;
and to The Victorian Network
for telling us about these gifts to posterity.

Contents

Acknowledgments

Like Will Rogers, who never met a man he didn't like, we have found that people who create and enjoy the Painted Ladies are a pleasure to know. These American beauties seem to bring out the best in the people who design, paint, own, and love them.

The homeowners in this book have pride, enthusiasm, and an eagerness to help. The Ladies have always generated positive energy. Indeed, without The Victorian Network, *America's Painted Ladies* would not have all of the houses it has.

Although Michael and Doug got along well, Michael and Elizabeth were not happy being apart for weeks at a time. Michael and Doug were energized by making instant friends around the country, seeing the gorgeous landscape, and finding unexpected houses. Elizabeth enjoyed meeting homeowners over the phone. We were all sustained by the hundreds of people around the country who did what they could for us, who answered questions, and who guided us around town, faxed maps, fed us, and put us up for the night. We've thanked separately the hundreds of you who sent photographs, but we hope that everyone in The Victorian Network, named and unnamed, will accept our deepest thanks.

Special thanks to:

Bruce Bradbury and Paul Duchscherer of Bradbury & Bradbury and James Martin of The Color People, who alerted their clients to our search; to Bob Buckter, who sent lists; and again to Bruce and Paul for their helpful comments about the transparencies; to editors Adele Horwitz, Jerry Gross, and copyeditor Margaret Ritchie.

Beverly Zell, Mark Twain House, Hartford, Connecticut; John Burrows, our scout in Boston; Tom and Martha Welch, Boston; Mrs. A. Klein, Eatham, Massachusetts; Carolyn Flaherty of *Victorian Homes* and Suzanne La Rosa of *The Old-House Journal* in Brooklyn, New York, for printing our request for houses. In New York: Mary Kay Gallagher, Brooklyn, Robert Selkowitz, Rosendale; Carol Wells Shepard, Saratoga Springs Preservation Foundation; Jennifer Haskell, 1890 House, Cortland; James Ryan and the staff at Olana, Hudson; Lynn Vaughan, Historic Albany Foundation, Albany; Juanita Bass, Bridgewater; Steve Maher, New Berlin; Near Westside Neighborhood Association, Oneida; Elaine DiBiase, Elmira, for her gift; Craig Breack, NYSHO, Wellsville; Helen Breitbeck, Oswego Heritage Foundation, Oswego; Carol Holchberg, Buffalo Restoration Association; and Michael Hall in Jamestown, for taking us around.

New Jersey: Jay and Marianne Schatz, The Abbey, Cape May, Nancy and Will Kahane, The Blue Amber Motel, Cape May, for their valiant efforts to find us rooms when the town was full; Nancy Streathearn, The Willows, Morristown. Pennsylvania: Michael Hardy, University City Historical Society, Philadelphia; Joedda Sampson, Pittsburgh; Charles Uhl, Pittsburgh; Judy Snyder, the Victorian Society of America, Philadelphia; Roger Moss and Gail Caskey Winkler, Philadelphia; Dick & Kim Fornof and Denny and Vicky McNair, Oil City.

Constance Bond, *Smithsonian* magazine, Washington, D.C.; Delaware: John Stevens, Dover; Michael Real at The Towers in Milford for his hospitality. North Carolina: Mark Sullivan at Historic Behania Society, Winston-Salem; Earl and Yolanda Miller, Greensboro, North Carolina; Doug Bebber, Asheville; Ken Land and Bill Wise, Winston-Salem; Chris Yetter, Raleigh. Georgia: Alan Fort, Savannah; Ron and Karen Horvath, Coleman House, Swainsboro, for their hospitality and a new way of looking at Painted Ladies; Debbie McCord, Shellmont B & B, Atlanta; Windell and Jan Keith, Atlanta; Eileen Segrest, Atlanta. Barbara Stagg, Historic Rugby, Tennessee; Debbie Richards, for making Louisville, Kentucky, memorable. Florida: Ruby Rivais and Frank McGinley, Pensacola; Carmel Modica, Seaside. Louisiana: Louis Aubert for showing us New Orleans; Lawrence Jennings, New Orleans; Bryce and Elroy Eckhardt, New Orleans, for their gift of music; Lloyd Sensat and Gene Cizek, who also took us around New Orleans; Stephanie Richards, New Orleans Preservation Resource Center; Patsy Torres, San Francisco Plantation, Reserve. Alabama: Anne Sieller Crutcher, Mobile Historical Development Commission; Edie Jones, Selma. Mississippi: Greg Campbell, Jackson; Nancy Bell, Vicksburg; Jo Pratt, Belle of the Bends B & B, Vicksburg, for a tour of the town. Arkansas: Carl Miller, Little Rock; Mark Christ, AHPP, Little Rock; Becky Witsell, for showing us Little Rock; Ned Shank and Crescent Dragonwagon for the lovely rooms and delicious food at the Dairy Hollow Farm, Eureka Springs; Carol Greer and June Westphal, Eureka Springs; Jack Strout, Eureka Springs.

Craig Bobby, Lakewood, Ohio, the most passionate house hunter we know; Iowa: preservationist Patrice Beam, our trusty scout, for showing us Des Moines; Alice Ersepke, Stone Cliff Manor B & B in Dubuque, for her hospitality; Julie Gross, Dubuque; Allen Nelson, Red Oak; Robert Pachek, Council Bluffs. Illinois: Fred Straus, Chicago, who runs the Painted Ladies contest; Don Miller, Elgin; Carol Kelm, Oak Park; John Wasik, Chicago; Marshall Segal for his hospitality; Sharon Ewing, Algonquin; Nancy Krueger, for taking us around Champaign and Urbana; Kathleen Webster, Galena. Indiana: John Tripi for showing us Wabash; Donald Urban, Fort Wayne; Dennis West, Indianapolis; Chris and Jennifer Bundy for their hospitality and taking us around Salem. Missouri: John Kirchdoerfer, St. Louis; Linda Underwood, househunter, St. Louis. Michigan: Judy Stull, Howell, for making sure we visited Grand Rapids and Coldwater; Tom and Lauretta Oxenham at the Wing Museum in Coldwater; Stan Smith, Ann Arbor; color consultant Neil Heidemann in St. Paul, Minnesota, for the tour. Wisconsin: Judith Knuth, Milwaukee. Doug Boilesen and Sharon Orlando and the Keister family in Lincoln, Nebraska, for their hospitality. Marcia Epstein, Lawrence, Kansas. Loren McCrosky, North Dakota Historical Society, Bismarck. Texas: Ed Meza, Sherman, for bringing the Painted Ladies museum show to Sherman and for showing us Sherman and Denison; Betty Baker, Bonnie Franks, and Doris Fox, Austin; Keith Downing, Dallas; Vaughn and

Bonnie Franks for their hospitality in their lovely Honorable Mention Bonnynook Bed and Breakfast Inn in Waxahachie; David Bush of the Galveston Historical Foundation for a tour. Colorado: James Martin for showing us Denver, and for his hospitality; Ron Neeley and Lance McDonald, Telluride; Barbara Morris, Ouray; Ken Marlin, Silverton; Roxanne Eflin, Preservation Office, Aspen, for her booklet on Aspen. New Mexico: James Jereb, Santa Fe, for his hospitality; Judee Gay Williams for guiding us around Las Vegas. Nevada: Andrea Daily Taylor, Virginia City. Montana: Harriet Malloy, Helena; Cathy Goetz, Bozeman; Alan Matthews, Missoula; color consultant Kitty Wargny in Butte, for showing us around; Mark Reavis, Butte. Washington: Ann Farrar, Bellingham; Paul Boyer, Port Townsend Visitor's Center. Oregon: Linda Dodson, Albany Visitor's Association; Roz Clark Kearny, Albany. California: Mark Carter, for putting us up at the Hotel Carter in Eureka; Ken Torbert of the Gingerbread Mansion, Ferndale, for a tour; color consultant Joe Adamo and David John Modell, Architectural Design, San Francisco; Paul Lee and George Skinner, Oakland; Christine Lyons and Greg Beatty, Alameda; author and Alameda Historical Museum curator George Gunn for showing us the town; Jim Stockton, Jack House and Gardens, San Luis Obispo; Dick Langdon, the Victorian Annex, Los Alamos; Alan Curl, for his tour of Riverside; Murray Burns and Planaria Price, Eastlake Inn, Los Angeles; Tim and Deborah Sakech, Dana Point, publishers of *The Official Guide to American Historic Inns*; Norm and Laverne Fisher of Fisher Photo.

Special mention to the traveler's friends: America's roads, which we found excellent; Super 8 Motels—clean, reasonable, all the same, all different; fast-food salad bars, an early sign of the greening of America; the "Today Show," *USA Today, The New York Times*, and local papers; National Public Radio, which made it possible to hear classical music while passing through Dickenson, North Dakota, and other locations deep in the heartland; Doug's cassette deck, which made it possible to enjoy 1960s jazz and rock; and Mozart and Bach, who provided music to match the splendor of the landscape (if only they could have been inspired by it!). Bach, the Master Builder, created with sound the same beauty, elegance, warmth, humanity, color, harmony, vitality, richness of design, and exhilaration that the Victorian architects and builders created with wood.

Special thanks also to our always encouraging family and friends: Rita Pomada; Alberta Cooper; Charles Pomada; Susan Sheeley; Alan and Carolyn Sheeley; Bill and Cyndi Meardy; Ray and Maryann Larsen; Carol and Don Kosterka; Kat, Chris, Eric, and Carol Larsen; Phil Herwegh; Diana and Denny Nolan; Ernie and Phil Germain; Fran Ames; Miriam and Will, Steve and Marta Vultaggio; and for her help and friendship, Antonia Anderson.

Introduction—Riding the Victorian Rainbow

Welcome to the class of 1991, America's Victorian Rainbow. It's been said that painting a house is the most intimate act that you can perform in public. *America's Painted Ladies* is a series of intimate acts that is helping to transform Victorian America.

In the early seventies, San Francisco homeowners started painting their Victorians in three or more contrasting colors. *Painted Ladies,* the authors' first book about these colorful Victorians, ignited a trend the authors called The Colorist Movement.

During the fourteen years since *Painted Ladies* was published in 1978, The Colorist Movement has continued to gather momentum. A growing number of homeowners around the country have been rescuing Painted Ladies-in-waiting from destruction and bringing them back to life with love, paint, and imagination. They have been transforming their plain-vanilla Victorians into a dazzling polychrome rainbow that stretches from coast to coast.

Homeowners are creating more Painted Ladies in more places than ever. The Victorian Network—homeowners, colorists, painters, craftspeople, architects, historians, preservationists, city planners, Victorian magazines, and house buffs nationwide, who play an essential part in the creation of these books—sent photos from all fifty states. Thanks in large part to their kindness, *America's Painted Ladies* contains the biggest and finest collection of buildings yet: 258 original and Neo-Victorians in 162 cities in forty-four states and the District of Columbia.

With a few exceptions in brick, the homes that you are about to enjoy are the most beautifully painted Victorians that we could find based on hundreds of letters and four trips that took Michael and Douglas more than forty thousand miles to forty-seven states. As always, our goal was to create a book as beautiful as the houses in it.

America's Painted Ladies is a tribute to the spirit, creativity, and imagination of the American people. Besides being a celebration of history, color, and architecture, the book is also a celebration of people: their humor, their pride, their passion, their courage, and their triumphs. They have shared their ideas on how restoring their homes has changed their lives and their communities.

The book starts in the East where the importance of tradition dictates a conservative approach to color. The farther west the houses are, the freer homeowners feel to adorn their homes with their favorite colors. Along the way, you will also see north-to-south variations in color: the hotter the clime, the lighter the colors. .

The Canvas Battlefield

"In the United States, it would seem that diversities of style and strong contrasts of architectural design are a perfectly natural occurrence."
— Nineteenth-century architect Calvert Vaux

Although the words *Painted Lady* are generic for a multicolored Victorian, the phrase was not used for a Victorian until *Painted Ladies,* the first book in the series, was published in 1978. This makes it strange to discuss whether a building is an "authentic" or "original" Painted Lady.

The three criteria for a Painted Lady are still:
• That the Victorian building be a balanced, felicitous blend of color and architecture;
• That the house be painted in three or more contrasting colors;
• That color be used to bring out the decorative ruffles and flourishes.

Because of their beauty, craftsmanship, inexhaustible variety, the quality of the materials that went into them, and their sheer numbers, Victorians are the greatest gift of America's architectural heritage.

Part of the reason is what constitutes a Victorian. The Victorian era lasted from 1837 to 1901, the years of Queen Victoria's reign. In America, these sixty-four years also encompassed a uniquely rich mélange of architectural styles, most of which are included in *America's Painted Ladies:*
• Greek Revival, 1820–1860 (not usually considered Victorian), the simple Greek temple look, a popular symbol of the democratic ideal (see 2016–20 Burgundy in New Orleans, page 101);
• Gothic Revival, 1830–1860, used for cottages and castles; the cottages (see Ithaca, New York, page 51) have steeply pitched roofs and gingerbread hanging from the gables;
• Italian or Tuscan Villa, 1830–1880, in which a square tower overlooks an asymmetrical but simple façade (see Wilmette, Illinois, page 151);
• Italianate, 1840–1880, with its bracketed eaves, a flat or bay-windowed façade, and perhaps a porch (see Austin, Texas, page 184);
• Chateauesque, 1860–1890, large-scale stone construction with steep roofs and a wealth of decorative details (see Saratoga Springs, New York, page 40);
• Second Empire, 1860–1890, a mansard roof with dormer windows above, an Italian villa or Italianate below (see New Berlin, New York, page 48);
• Stick, 1860–1890, buildings outlined in strips of

wood with the façade of the building highlighted with decorative "stick work" (see Albany, Oregon, page 226);

• Eastlake, 1870–1890, named for the English arbiter of taste Charles Locke Eastlake, an ornamental style that combines a profusion of light decorative elements with heavy architectural elements (see Lincoln, Nebraska, page 177);

• Colonial Revival, 1870–1920, with its larger-scale mixture of previous Colonial styles (see 217 East 19th Street, Brooklyn, page 34);

• Queen Anne, 1880–1900, the ultimate, anything-goes Victorian, offering an endlessly varied array of decorations, colors, and materials (see Malone, New York, page 44).

The artful blending of architectural elements painstakingly picked out has produced these winners of battles on canvas that Isaac H. Hobbs, the author of *Hobbs' Architecture,* wrote about in 1876: "Designing a building is like a battle upon canvas of color, each part striving for supremacy.... Give each [element] its just due, and they will all be quiet; no wrangling; but one beautiful, peaceful, harmonious assemblage, all coming forward with their little gifts, giving them quietly and freely."

Making an Art Out of Necessity

"Many who want to do what will be considered in good taste are puzzled to know what colors to use, and how to direct their painter so as to give him a tolerably clear idea of what they want."

—E. Rossiter and F. Wright,
Modern House Painter, 1882

The Painted Ladies are reviving a Victorian tradition. The proud, ambitious Victorians who built these homes embellished them with many colors. In *Victorian Exterior Decoration: How to Paint Your Nineteenth-Century American House Historically,* Roger Moss and Gail Caskey Winkler include an 1871 color card from the Harrison Brothers paint company that has forty-two colors. This color revolution was made possible because of nineteenth-century advances, including the standardization of paint manufacturing; lithography, which made color charts possible; and railroads, which transported the paint.

In *The Devil's Dictionary,* Ambrose Bierce defined painting as "The art of protecting flat surfaces from the weather and exposing them to the critic." Color is still an extremely emotional issue in preservation. Homeowners in this book have endured the anger of neighbors who are aghast at their choice of colors (sometimes because they're looking at the primer) or who believe that "It's always been white," even though examining old photographs or scraping the house to find the original colors usually proves it wasn't.

There are three approaches to painting a Victorian:

• The scientific approach, in which you scrape the building, determine what the original colors were through microanalysis (the eye cannot judge paint that has been in the dark for a century), and reproduce them;

• The historical approach, in which you learn what colors houses like yours were painted when they were built and use those colors;

• The "boutique" approach, in which you use whatever hues you choose.

We don't favor one of these approaches over the others, but we do favor giving homeowners the freedom of expression to choose the approach they prefer.

The desire for historic re-creation, restoring a house as closely as possible to the way it originally looked inside and out, is admirable. But most homeowners are more comfortable with Victorian revival style, which enables them to capture the spirit of Victorian color and décor and adapt it to their own tastes. Instead of following someone else's ideas, they enjoy using their homes to make their own artistic statements, a sentiment the Victorians would agree with.

An editorial in *The Baltimore Sun* in October 1991 took the Town Council of Sykesville, Maryland, to task for considering the possibility of developing a palette of approved colors. The editorial suggested that the Town Council study the Painted Ladies books and concluded with this recommendation: "We urge the Sykesville Town Council not to make the mistake of passing restrictions that will unduly prohibit residents from showing their pride in colors." Amen.

Most homeowners are guided by good taste and peer pressure, and because they don't want to have to live with a mistake that's two stories high, they tend to err on the side of caution. The Israeli statesman Abba Eban absolved the others when he said, "Mistakes are the ornament of freedom." A hundred years from now, it won't matter what colors today's homeowners choose for their homes. What will matter is that they cared enough about their homes to protect them for posterity.

Meanwhile, homeowners pay for the work and live with the results, and it's not a once-in-a-lifetime decision. In most climates, Victorians have to be repainted every five to ten years. This enables homeowners to give their Painted Ladies a new outfit every time they paint. In Grand Rapids, Michigan, Don and Dan Steenwyk change the color scheme on their architecture office every six years.

Steven Aardweg wrote from the Philadelphia suburb of Bryn Mawr, "I've changed color schemes so frequently my neighbor joked I must belong to the 'House Color of the Month Club.' When people move into the neighborhood, I stop by with a hello, a handshake, and my Painted Ladies books. My ultimate neighborhood fantasy would be an enclave of Painted Ladies right here on the Main Line!" Steven is a man after our own hearts. If, as one journalist remarked, we are evangelists of color, Steven is our first missionary. Go get 'em, Steven!

Homeowners have told us that their houses spoke to them and told them what colors to paint them. We once heard about a homeowner who had to stop listening. His house told him how to paint it, but when he got finished, it told him to buy the house next door.

Permission Granted

At first, we thought that The Colorist Movement was a revolution, but actually it's an evolution. Jo Pratt, the owner of the Belle of the Bends B&B, noticed the evolution in the use of color in Natchez, Mississippi. Over the last decade, homeowners have gone from all white to two colors to three colors. In this, they've echoed the evolution that we have noticed around the country. First, homeowners change to another color from the one color that the house has "always" been painted (that is, as long as they can remember). Then they become more daring and add a second color. Then they are finally ready to take the leap of artistic faith and pick out details with one or more additional colors.

Trendsetters are eager to try new ideas. But most homeowners need time and a sense of permission to allow themselves to risk the disapproval of their friends and neighbors by plunging into the uncertain world of multicolor paint schemes.

They receive permission by looking at books and at houses that have been polychromed, and by working out the color scheme for their own home. This usually involves "swatching," trying colors out on part of the house and on passersby, who are always ready with advice.

Although some homeowners throw caution to the winds when choosing colors, most, including those in San Francisco, are conservative about color. As many of the homeowners in this book found out the hard way, making any kind of statement takes courage.

Inside Jobs

"The parlour…gives out again, like a dried flower warmed in the hand, its essential quality, a rich ease."
—Joyce Cary, *To Be a Pilgrim*

Writing in *Victorian Sampler*, Debra Anton noted that "The current revival of the Victorian style is something that the Victorians would have appreciated. Theirs was an age that embraced many historical styles in home decoration as part of a desire to recapture 'the good old days,' while simultaneously putting its own ebullient stamp on each revival. Their joy in decorating their homes was absolute."

We have learned that our readers want to open the doors to the Painted Ladies and take a peek at what is inside. In keeping with the Victorian spirit of eclecticism, the interiors in the book are a wonderful mix of old and new.

The German architect Mies van der Rohe believed that "Less is more." Most of the interiors in this book are a testament to the belief that less is a bore. In the 1878 volume *The House Beautiful*, Clarence Cook wrote about "the ornament of life—casts, pictures, engravings, bronzes, books [as the] chief nourishers in life's feast." This elegance born of new prosperity gave a room life and character as homeowners sought to achieve the Victorian ideal: a cultured life centered on the family. Then as now, cocooning was a way of life. Most of the homeowners whose interiors you will see revel in clutter and eclecticism, the hallmarks of High Victorian decor.

In 1922, Charlie Chaplin designed a "California Gothic" mansion for himself. According to an article in *Architectural Digest*, "With his constant gallivanting around the world, the…house never really felt lived in; for months at a time, it sat unoccupied.…Actress Ina Claire quipped when she first visited the large, stark mansion, 'It isn't home, but it's much.'" *America's Painted Ladies* is fortunate to be able to include four remarkable museum interiors that are home and much: Mark Twain's steamboat fantasy in Hartford, Connecticut; Frederic Church's masterpiece, Olana, overlooking the Hudson River; the fabulous San Francisco Plantation in Reserve, Louisiana; and the Villa Montezuma in San Diego, with its radiant stained glass.

Murphy's Law of Restoration

Restoring a Victorian proves Murphy's law of restoration: "Restoring a Victorian will cost twice as much and take twice as long as the estimates." It's a major undertaking that requires all of the creative, physical, and financial resources that most homeowners can bring to the challenge. For them, restoring a Victorian means never having to say you're solvent.

Whether or not these houses are considered landmarks, and many are, homeowners are making landmarks out of them through their unceasing efforts to restore them and make them beautiful inside and out.

Perpetual Motion

The original idea for this book was to shoot the interiors of the houses in *Daughters of Painted Ladies*. Our editor, Cyril Nelson, thought that the book should also have some new houses. But when *Victorian Homes* and *The Old-House Journal* were kind enough to print a request for photos of houses, we received enough photos to create an entirely new book.

While they were in a Manhattan taxi, Doug and Michael saw a bumper sticker that read, "I never get lost. Everyone tells me where to go!" In fact, we became prisoners of our mail. The Victorian Network told us where to go so well that we could not afford the luxury of exploring the country for houses.

Did we miss houses that should have been in the book? You bet! Judy Stull of Howell, Michigan, provided one example. We weren't planning to go to Grand Rapids or Coldwater, but Judy insisted we go, and the result is the inclusion of five buildings in Grand Rapids and two in Coldwater, one of which is the cover girl for the 1993 *Painted Ladies Calendar*. We'll never know all the houses we missed, but with your help, we'll include those that we can next time.

Finding and shooting interiors was a catch-as-catch-can affair. We began each of our four trips with a list of houses. But between the uncertainty of how long it would take to shoot a house, what unexpected houses we might find, and how long it would take to drive to the next house, we could give homeowners only overnight warning of our arrival. So sometimes we wouldn't be able to get in, or a B&B would have guests in its rooms, or we would find a new house and no one would be home. With forty-six states to drive to, it was always shoot and run, so we had to shoot what we found and push on.

We weren't always able to shoot houses in the best light or weather or before the paint was too badly weathered. The choices of what to photograph and the choices the three of us made with Cyril Nelson of what to include in the book were subjective and would probably have been different at another time.

Eye of the Beholder
One thing that has changed since 1986 is how we look at Victorians. The buildings in the book go beyond the Victorian styles listed above. For example, Frederic Church's magnificent home, Olana, is Moorish Revival. We have also been seduced by transitional buildings such as Stone Cliff Manor, a bed and breakfast in Dubuque, Iowa, which has Queen Anne, Colonial Revival, Italianate, and rusticated elements.

When we look at a simple Queen Anne/Colonial Revival/Arts and Crafts building such as 455 Marlborough Road in Brooklyn, we have to bring different expectations to it. It won't have the exuberant decoration that implores owners: "Paint my parts in many colors." Such a house creates a challenge for the homeowner, who has to use color to make up for its simplicity.

The stronger the architecture is, the subtler the colors can be. The simpler the architecture is, the more compelling the colors and their placement must be.

If this book proves anything, it's that our interests are eclectic. Consider, for instance, the Arts and Industries Building of the Smithsonian Institution in Washington, D.C., built in 1879–1881. Ornamenting this massive

The Smithsonian Institution, Washington, D.C.

brick museum are glazed bricks in bright baby blue, beige, yellow, red, and black. The roof had colored tiles, but they're gone, and nobody remembers what color they were. The Washington architectural firm of Cluss & Schulze did the exterior design. Part of the ceiling is beautifully painted, so the next time you visit the Smithsonian, be sure to look up.

Home, Sweet Home
"Ah! There is nothing like staying at home for real comfort."
        —Jane Austen, *Emma*

*"**The human need for richly nurturing surroundings is so pervasive and so fundamental that wherever we are—at home, at work, on the road or on vacation and away from it all—we have to have places around us that nourish our eyes, our ears and all our senses simultaneously to be able to flourish as human beings and feel at home with ourselves.**"*
  —Tony Hiss, author of *The Experience of Place*

After one of our slide shows, a nice lady came up to us and said that she thought that Painted Ladies were prostitutes. Michael assured her that they all had hearts of gold leaf. Gold leaf is only one of the reasons why this is the golden age of Victorian restoration.

Why is there such interest in Victorians now? In *The Use of History*, A. L. Rowse suggests one reason: "... a building expresses the needs, the character of the age." We live in an age of pressing and depressing concerns, in a stressful, uncertain world being transformed by technology, the globalization of business and culture, and historic political changes.

In such a world, these shrines to craftsmanship and individuality are reassuringly old. Victorians are imbued with enduring beauty and the beauty of enduring. We need the beauty, warmth, security, creativity, humanity, vitality, individuality, and human scale of these wonderful buildings more than ever. We need Victorians as much as they need us.

This explains why Neo-Victorians are sprouting up across the country, a trend within a trend that we salute with a section on Neo-Victorians at the end of the book. That is why the town of Mashpee, Massachusetts, turned a moribund shopping mall built in the fifties into Mashpee Commons, a nineteenth-century downtown with homes, shops, and sidewalks.

Architect Cecilia Reese Bullock is the founder and president of Historical Replications in Jackson, Mississippi, which sells floor plans for Victorians. In explaining why people stay at B&Bs and want to live in Victorians, she said, "People stay in gracious homes that remind them of the past. They want to duplicate that feeling and at least give the illusion of having some firm roots in a mobile society. A grandiose house from another era helps them make a nostalgic statement filled with traditional values."

Debra Anton observes that the Victorian age introduced the words "Home, Sweet Home," and the Victorians lived by those words. The homes in this book are a tribute to a lifestyle that has gained growing appeal as America lurches toward the millennium.

Victorians improve their owners' quality of life because, more than houses from any other period, Victorians symbolize what a home should be: a refuge; a source of food, shelter, love, pride, pleasure, and entertainment; and part of a community.

The homeowners in this book love their homes because they have a past; they have space, character, and spirit; they're comforting and nurturing for the body, mind, and spirit; and they provide a sense of continuity, security, and contentment.

Someone once said of a couple she knew that they lived in a beautiful little apartment overlooking the rent. One way to beat paying rent is to buy a house, and around the country, there are still great buys to be had on Victorians, especially if homeowners are willing to build "sweat equity" by restoring their houses.

Social observers detect a new level of neighborhood concern and community involvement, especially in questions about school, home, and family security. Restoring and maintaining a Victorian helps to foster a spirit of community.

Up Color

What caused the Painted Ladies to flourish?

The age of black-and-white is over. This is the age of color. Consumers want what they buy to be colorful. Color creates an aura of youth, fun, excitement, and desirability. The relentless flood of color images on television and in movies and magazines has created the need for the visual stimulation of color.

The most important factor fostering The Colorist Movement is that the desire to create a Painted Lady is contagious. Painted Ladies are labors of love that generate goodwill and positive energy. They are proof of the transforming power of beauty. At first, they were isolated beacons of color that transformed the homeowners who painted them. The homeowners started taking pride in their homes. They started sweeping the streets and forming neighborhood organizations. When the sky didn't fall and their neighbors got used to the idea, they wanted Painted Ladies of their own.

Painted Ladies make people look up. They make people more aware of and eager for color, and not just on Victorians but on all styles of architecture, and not just on exteriors but in interiors as well.

After the museum show of images from *Daughters of Painted Ladies* ran at the Red River Historical Museum in Sherman, Texas, curator Ed Meza reported that residents started painting their buildings regardless of what style they were. "We've got the fever," he reported gleefully.

Canadian architect Witold Rybczynski, author of the marvelous book *Home: A Short History of an Idea*, observes in *The Most Beautiful House in the World*, "Buildings must survive the ravages not only of time but also of fashion." Architecture evolves as a series of reactions against the prevailing style. Architects are once again using color and ornamentation.

Bernardo Fort-Brescia, a passionate modernist architect from Peru, has said, "I look at a house as a canvas," and "I use color to reenforce the concept of the building, to emphasize the intent of the architecture." This is what color consultants do with Victorians.

Bernardo and his wife, Laurinda Spear, are partners in Arquitectonica, a Miami architectural firm that, as a story in the *San Francisco Examiner* commented, "revolutionized architecture around the world in barely a decade.... Color is the chief ornament, wielded the way a billboard artist would use it—to be seen clearly even from swiftly passing cars. Their façades are virtually abstract paintings, designed to arrest the eye but not to intimidate viewers." The "sky court" that rises from the twelfth to the seventeenth floors of Atlantis, their award-winning 1982 condominium complex, is a thrilling example of the firm's work. We think of it as a contemporary Painted Lady.

The Colors of Money

Greenbacks also help spread The Colorist Movement. Tax incentives make it attractive to own and rehabilitate Victorians.

Making a Victorian beautiful adds to its value. If you are trying to sell your house, a tasteful paint job will give it "curb appeal" to potential buyers. You probably won't be able to double the price of the house, as a San Francisco homeowner did after his house had received a Bob Buckter color scheme, but the increase in the woodenware—merchandise a general store would have sold a century ago.

The restoration of the gas station with a five-color paint job made a tremendous difference in the prosperity of the town, since it drew antique car buffs on their way to and from the car shows in the next town to photograph their vintage cars in front of the period gas pumps. The textile factory that had become slum housing was turned into shops.

Local people began to talk about "The Easter House" on Main Street. Strangers stopped her to ask, "Why Pink?" "To each, I gave my little speech about how things were improving and how the colors alerted them to positive changes. Rainbow colors and historic preservation sparked a rural renaissance here."

These colors are brighter than most homeowners would want, and they have provoked some angry reactions, but Karen is undaunted: "Taking a rundown, neglected building and painting it and polishing it, making it useful and desirable, that is a thrill. So is painting unnoticed trim in vivid colors to awaken others to the exuberant sense of fun these buildings projected in their prime, then renting the completed buildings as stores or middle-class housing, thereby ensuring the survival of the buildings because they have once again become financially viable. I am having the time of my life doing something important: historic preservation in rainbow colors."

Public convenience, Shartlesville, Pennsylvania.

Victorian storefront, Shartlesville.

A bench in Shartlesville.

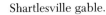

Shartlesville gable.

Riding the Crest

America is riding the crest of a wave of interest in Victorian culture.

Rodger Tate in Great Falls, Virginia, has observed that architectural salvage stores are closing in his area because fewer Victorians are being torn down.

In *Nineteenth Century*, the magazine of the Victorian Society of America, Executive Director Judy Snyder noted these highly visible signs of Victoriana:

• Disneyland's Main Street is Victorian;

• The set for Bill Cosby's TV show is a Brooklyn brownstone (Did you know that Brooklyn has more Victorians than San Francisco? If they had been built with wood instead of brownstone, The Colorist Movement might have started in Brooklyn instead of San Francisco!);

• The Victoria's Secret chain (Judy wonders when she sees the "Victoria's Secret lingerie catalogues feature romantically clad models lounging in nineteenth-century surroundings.... just who is this Victoria with such a sexy secret? Are they using the name because it plays on the perceived mores of the period or because the word 'Victoria' sells in 1991?");

• A strong national interest in nineteenth-century arts and crafts like dollhouses, which are being turned into miniature Painted Ladies, and quilts.

Jan Stehlick of Dorchester, Nebraska, won the 1990 Rainbow Challenge of the Nebraska State Quilters Guild with *Remember the House on the Hill*, her elaborate rendering of a Victorian mansion with a reflection in the tiny window of a modest cabin. This 1896 Queen Anne in Buffalo, New York, appeared in *Daughters of Painted Ladies*. The 30″ by 40″ quilt is made of 300 pieces of antique and hand-dyed fabric and lace, hand- and machine-quilted, with whimsical appliqué and such touches as doors that open.

But beyond these outward signs of the interest in Victoriana lies a far more extraordinary reality. Today, Victorian America is a country within a country, a culture within a culture, that:

• Contains millions of residential, commercial, religious, and institutional buildings that are restored, maintained, used, and enjoyed by tens of millions of Americans and foreign visitors;

• Keeps preservation organizations and government agencies busy fighting a perpetual battle against the greed, ignorance, and ambition of those who would destroy the Victorians;

• Generates hundreds of billions of dollars a year in real-estate sales, taxes, public and private restoration efforts, maintenance, tourism, antiques and home furnishings, and Victorian hobbies, crafts, merchandise, and media. (The story of how Queen Victoria conquered America after her forebears lost it may be a book idea.)

Remember the House on the Hill, a quilt by Jan Stehlick.

Old Houses—New Jobs

One hopeful sign for America's future is the entrepreneurial explosion that is starting to transform American business. Victorians are creating their share of entrepreneurs: thousands of businesses, including a burgeoning number of color designers, that help homeowners restore, decorate, and maintain their homes. Indeed, it's been suggested that a thorough restoration of a home generates more work than building a new house.

The Victorian entrepreneurs have helped spark a national revival of period arts and crafts. But there is something different and inspiring about this new generation of entrepreneurs. Like the homeowners they serve, they love what they do, so they bring to their callings a positive attitude toward their craft, their customers, their communities, and the environment. Dedication, responsiveness, and social responsibility are the hallmarks of this new breed of women and men.

Artistic License is a unique guild of such top-quality craftspersons in the San Francisco Bay Area. They are represented in this book by the work of five of their members: Bob Buckter, Larry Boyce, Bruce Bradbury, Paul Duchscherer, and David John Modell. Artistic License will be the subject of the authors' next book.

Out of the Ashes

The Colorist Movement is also a preservation movement. Many of the homes in these books were saved from demolition or were fixer-uppers when they were bought.

Peter Remillard House, Preservation Park, Oakland, California.

In *Historic Preservation*, the magazine of the National Trust for Historic Preservation, J. Jackson Walter noted that "historic preservation is a multibillion-dollar industry having an enormous impact on American society." One example is the Main Street program that has restored and revitalized more than six hundred downtowns with the help of federal funding.

On a small scale, California offers two examples of saving Victorians and using them in new ways. Between its social problems, the catastrophe of the 1989 Loma Prieta earthquake, and the devastating 1991 fire in the Oakland Hills, Oakland has endured more than its share of major problems. But the rebuilding of downtown Oakland and Preservation Park testifies to the city's commitment to the future.

Preservation Park is a restored Victorian office complex in the heart of downtown Oakland at 14th Street and Martin Luther King, Jr., Way. Sixteen endangered Victorians have been rescued from the wrecking ball. Eleven have been moved into a beautifully landscaped park. There are forty-two tenants, 65 percent nonprofit and 35 percent small creative businesses. All of the buildings in Preservation Park are wheelchair-accessible and close to Bay Area Rapid Transit and the Convention Center.

The Peter Remillard House at 654 13th Street was built on this site in 1887 for the founder of the Remillard Brick Company, the biggest brick maker in California. Remillard's daughter was still a leader in the business community in the 1960s. The Remillard houses the East Bay Perinatal Organization.

Saved by Love and Anger

In Southern California, Oxnard's graceful Heritage Square revitalizes the city's historic past with a six-year preservation project that is bringing new economic and cultural life to downtown Oxnard.

In *The Greek Passion* by Nikos Kazantzakis, one of the characters says, "Without a great deal of love or anger, nothing gets done in the world." When Dennis Matthews learned that the city planned to tear down two turn-of-the-century homes and a historic church for a parking lot, he swung into action, working with the redevelopment agency and the city council. Dennis planned carefully to save these homes and bring other historically significant endangered homes downtown to transform the area. Heritage Square cost the city $5.3 million, but residents also contributed $3 million. Now there are shops, offices, restaurants, a museum, and a cultural-arts complex that bring people back into what was formerly a rundown area.

The crowning jewel in Heritage Square is the Petit House, which was moved to its present site. Built in 1896 for Justin Petit, with ornamentation by Herman Anlauf, the house was the first farm residence in Ventura County with electricity. Gary Blum, one of Justin Petit's great-grandsons, restored the building, which now houses an architectural landscaping firm. Main Street Architects in Ventura did most of the restoration and called in Bob Buckter to design colors for the buildings in the square, which was still a work in progress when we arrived.

The Queen Is Dead, Long Live the Architecture

"*Yankee Enterprise has no sympathy for the picturesque.*"

—Jasper Cropsey, an artist of the
Hudson River School

America's Victorian buildings are a priceless, irreplaceable part of our heritage. Nineteenth-century wealth and ambition created a twentieth-century treasure. But despite their valiant efforts, the thousands of community, state, national, and governmental organizations charged with protecting Victorians are often no match for individuals, developers, and institutions that put their immediate interests ahead of the long-range, abstract values of preservation. Painted Ladies-in-waiting, a mute constituency unable to speak for themselves, are being destroyed or remuddled or surrounded by new buildings that destroy their context and diminish their value. (*Remuddled* is a preservationist term for remodeling gone awry.)

How do we assess the intangible value of preserving century-old buildings?

How do we convince a developer, a church, a university, or the government that a white elephant is worth saving?

Petit House, Heritage Square, Oxnard, California.

How do we show the growing numbers of new-comers from other cultures who neither know nor care about Victorians that they shouldn't demolish or remuddle these houses for profit or to suit their passing needs?

At a time when eighty-seven languages are spoken in the public schools of Los Angeles, the United States has become a world unto itself. One of the challenges this multicultural mosaic presents is educating newcomers as well as new generations of Americans about the value of preservation.

In another century, these buildings will be even more valuable historically, culturally, and esthetically than they are now. Preserving them is more important than indulging the destructive desires of owners who don't appreciate them and won't be around in a century to regret their follies.

Not all the Victorians in America can be saved, nor should they be. The rights of an owner of a building are transitory; the rights of the public to benefit from the building as part of our architectural heritage are lasting. But what about the rights of the Victorians?

The goal of the following Bill of Rights is to strike a balance between the inevitably conflicting desires for preservation, progress, and property rights. It is meant to offer people concerned about preservation a basis for discussion and action in their communities.

If you agree with the Bill of Rights, feel free to print

it in your newsletters and brochures and to change it to fit your circumstances. We will welcome your ideas for changes. These suggestions are not meant to stop needed change but to prevent Victorians from becoming victims of unjustified harm.

A Victorian building is a unique link binding our past to our future. Once destroyed, its history, beauty, and craftsmanship cannot be replaced. The value of a Victorian as a source of continuity and as a part of America's architectural heritage will always grow.

Color applied with affection and artistry helps make people aware of how remarkable these buildings are, but Victorians need and deserve a Bill of Rights to help protect them from neglect.

A Bill of Rights for Victorian Buildings

Just as trees are part of our natural environment, Victorian buildings are part of our cultural environment. A Victorian recognized for its architecture or history is entitled to certain inalienable rights:

A Victorian has the right to survive, unless preservationists agree that it is not worth saving.

A Victorian has the right to retain its original façade.

A Victorian interior has the right to survive without alteration except for the addition of such modern amenities as kitchen and bathroom fixtures, heating, electricity, and other changes that meet building-code requirements. Such changes will be made with minimum alterations to the building and with the goal of preserving the architectural integrity of the building.

A Victorian has the right not to be stripped of its original woodwork, stained glass, and fixtures. If original woodwork or fixtures are removed, the owner is obligated to document them and store them in the building in good condition and pass them on to new owners as part of the deed, to permit restoration in the future.

A Victorian has the right to a complete documentation, illustrated when possible with photographs and video, of its history and the alterations done to the building. An owner is obligated to keep the history up to date. When the building is sold, the seller is obligated to give a copy of the documentation to the next owner as part of the deed to the building.

A Victorian has the right to be maintained inside and out with the same love and pride with which it was built.

A Victorian has the right to be used for whatever purpose will require the least alteration and enable it to be maintained in the best condition.

A Victorian has the right to remain on its original site. If a Victorian cannot remain on its original site, it has the right to be moved to a site as close in location and character as possible to its original site.

A Victorian has the right to retain its visual context. If a new building is to be added near a Victorian, the new building must be appropriate in character and scale to its surroundings.

A Victorian has the right to have its value understood and appreciated by the community. This can be accomplished if individuals, business and nonprofit organizations, and all levels of government will strive to:

• create a preservation board with the power to protect Victorians and Victorian neighborhoods;

• give landmark status to deserving buildings and districts to help protect them;

• establish and carry out a master preservation plan for the community;

• encourage preservation and preservation groups;

• have the history of our architectural heritage and the value of preserving it taught in schools and textbooks at all levels;

• give annual awards for restoration and preservation efforts;

• support the founding and maintaining of house museums with paid staff or volunteers from preservation groups;

• commission a history and a photographic inventory of the buildings in the community;

• support tourism, including house tours, a walking map of Victorians, and a booklet or book about the community's Victorians;

• assist homeowners researching the history of their homes;

• establish interior and exterior maintenance standards and the means to enforce them;

• provide information and financial assistance on restoration and maintenance;

• buy the house and sell it to someone who will care for the Victorian, if the current owner can't or won't take care of it;

• calculate periodically the economic value of Victorians to the community through jobs, taxes, tourism, merchandise, the business generated through restoration and maintenance, changes in ownership, and appraised value;

• discourage developers from destroying Victorians.

These rights are to be protected with a spirit of community, a sense of fairness, and a recognition of personal rights along with the need to balance them against the enduring value of the community's architectural heritage. Preservation is only possible with the continuing passionate assistance of those who care about making what is of enduring value from the past a gift from the present to the future.

Although a cabinet-level official for preservation is an appealing idea, these rights are not intended to stop needed change nor (heaven help us!) to generate more bureaucracy.

It was not a bureaucracy that enabled The Colorist Movement to spread from one city to fifty states, and it was not a bureaucracy that sent pictures of houses in every state for this book. Mostly, it was homeowners who love Victorians and understand their value.

Saving the Best for the Rest

America is only as good as its people, and Victorians bring out the best in their owners. Restoring a Victorian is a labor of love that inspires others to restore theirs. If someone had told Michael when he was driving a taxi around San Francisco in 1973 that, because he fell in love with the Painted Ladies, people around the country would be inspired to paint their houses, he wouldn't have believed it.

But all over the country, homeowners have told us that the books gave them the courage to paint their houses and inspired them with the ideas for doing it. These restorations were especially touching in towns where the restorers were the first people to paint their houses and had to overcome the hostility of neighbors who didn't understand what they were doing.

Restoring a Victorian is a perfect metaphor for restoring America. Those who preserve a Victorian with love and respect are preserving a slice of America. They are helping to save our heritage by keeping it alive and flourishing for future generations.

One of the greatest challenges that individuals and institutions face is how to maintain a spirit of renewal, a sense of ambition, optimism, open-mindedness, and compassion. The Colorist Movement is one of the most hopeful signs of renewal in America.

Victorian America is helping to lead us into the future by helping us to appreciate our past. Our rediscovery of Victorian America is making history by allowing us to embrace our heritage, and to balance change and tradition. Preserving our Victorian architectural heritage is helping us to preserve what is best about us and about America.

Wide Open Spaces

To understand how beautiful, vast, and empty the United States is, you have to see it for yourself. People are leaving big cities because of the problems and the people they confront in city life. But outside the big cities, there's a world of room. West of Chicago, the landscape becomes more and more empty until you reach the California coast.

If the 5.5 billion people on the planet were standing next to each other, everyone having two square feet on which to stand, do you know how much space they would take up? Just eight hundred square miles, the size of Jacksonville, Florida. The United States has less than one twentieth of the world's population. It's empty out there, folks, and dotted with small towns offering beautiful, empty, cheap Victorians that are waiting to be restored with loving hands.

Victorians can be turned into B&Bs, restaurants, and offices like some of the buildings in this book. Adaptive reuse has rescued thousands of dilapidated damsels-in-distress and has given them and their owners a new way of life. Victorian America is a cornucopia of opportunity.

Only You

This book was made possible not because we decided to find the most beautiful Painted Ladies in fifty states, but because The Victorian Network told us where they were. The only hope we have of finding all of the best Painted Ladies in the United States is in The Victorian Network's helping us find them.

We have already started a file for the next national Painted Ladies book, but meanwhile we are doing a *Painted Ladies Calendar* every year. So don't hide your colors under a bushel! If your house has enough gingerbread to absorb three or more contrasting colors, please send us duplicate snapshots of the exterior, the most interesting detail, the interiors of rooms in any period or artistic style, and information about your house as soon as it is finished.

We are the singers; your houses are the song. Make us the instruments of your artistry.

If you know of other houses in your town or anywhere else, please send photos of these, too, or their addresses. Churches, institutions, and commercial buildings are especially hard to find because we can't count on their owners' reading *The Old-House Journal* or *Victorian Homes* or even knowing what a Painted Lady is.

Gazing Through the Polychrome Crystal Ball

You who care about Victorians, homeowners who lavish care on them, we the authors, and Dutton Studio Books are in the service of an idea: Victorians are worth preserving and beautifying. What we are doing is important. How important only time will tell.

You can't stop an idea whose time has come. The Painted Ladies books are like the proverbial pebbles dropped in a pond. They have already made far greater ripples than anyone thought they would.

As the number of tourists interested in history increases, the number of Victorians adapted for use as B&Bs, restaurants, and stores will grow to accommodate them. This will create more Painted Ladies, because businesses housed in Victorians have both the means and the incentive to become Painted Ladies.

Because of local interest, the rise in tourism, and the growing value of old homes, preservation is going global. People around the world are becoming more aware that preservation makes dollars as well as sense.

As soon as we find enough beautifully colored houses around the world, we hope to do a book about how different cultures use color on their homes.

A century from now, today's color schemes will be regarded as the early period of The Colorist

Movement. The finest of today's Painted Ladies will be regarded as old masters (mistresses?). The work of the leading color consultants will hang on museum walls.

But while the artistry with which Victorians are painted will continue to evolve in ways nobody can imagine, it will continue to become more creative both in colors and the way they are used. Gold leaf and faux finishes will go national once homeowners absorb the exquisite artistry of the homes in *The Painted Ladies Revisited*. We're eagerly looking forward to seeing your future efforts.

Some day, an enterprising soul will start a special-interest group (SIG), an electronic bulletin board so that homeowners around the country can discuss painting and preservation questions.

Homeowners will soon have computers that will enable them to experiment with colors and placement. Once these computers are in general use, someone will start an SIG so that homeowners can look at color designs being done around the country and exchange advice. Color consulting by modem is also coming.

In the next century, technology will catch up with nature, and homeowners will be able to create crystal-clear three-dimensional, holographic images of their houses, showing how colors will actually look on their houses in different lights. Then they can print out these images and have the paint store match them.

The only prediction that we can make with absolute confidence is that the universal need for beauty, decoration, self-expression, and a sense of community will sustain The Colorist Movement. Some day, perhaps, homeowners will turn Victorian America into a vast polychrome garden with irresistibly beautiful flowers that you gather with your eyes. Imagine what it would be like to experience America if every Victorian in the country were restored and beautifully painted. A worthy goal for the next millennium.

A Note About the Captions

Captions include the address, the year the house was built, and the architectural style of the house. We mention the architect and the color designer when we know who they were. Some owners preferred to remain anonymous. The paint colors are often included.

Associations, B&Bs, color consultants, craftspersons, museums, painters, reception halls, restaurants, and suppliers are listed in the resource sections at the back of the book.

Beyond this information, we tried to include what you would want to know about the history, the owners, and the painting and decorating of the houses, and what you would enjoy learning about them.

THE NORTHEAST

This section includes two of our favorite houses: the Mark Twain House in Hartford, Connecticut, and Frederic Church's masterpiece, Olana, overlooking the Hudson River in New York State. A writer's house and an artist's house, both the best of their kind in the country.

New York was the most surprising state. Driving through the beautiful countryside photographing houses was like unwrapping one present after another. With twenty houses in fifteen towns, New York has leaped into the forefront of states with Painted Ladies. Only California has more. New York highlights include:

• The Christmas House, a polychrome extravaganza in Elmira designed by colorist Paul Murphy.
• Turback's in Ithaca, which came back from a fire more beautiful than it was when it appeared in *Daughters of Painted Ladies*.
• The Pink House in Wellsville, the only house in the book still owned by the family that built it.
• John Mills's home in Malone, New York, a small town near the Canadian border, an unlikely spot to find a cover house.

And of course, no photographic safari for Painted Ladies would be complete without a stop at the ultimate Victorian resort, Cape May, New Jersey. We found three seaside beauties, all B&Bs, to share with you, including Angel of the Sea, the first Painted Lady that was torn asunder and (almost) put back together again.

MAINE
SEARSPORT

The Carriage House Inn, 120 East Main Street, Route 1. The inn, which overlooks Penobscot Bay, was built in 1874 by Yankee clipper-ship Captain John McGilvery. (In 1885, one-tenth of all full-rigged sailing ships sailing under the American flag were commanded by Searsport's 286 captains.) During World War II, army officers were garrisoned here, and later, the house served as the retreat of artist Waldo Pierce, who was visited here by Ernest Hemingway.

Cathy and Brad Bradbury chose a delicate scheme of Colonial Revival ivory, Rookwood blue green, and Rookwood red to give their Second Empire mansion a nautical air, and it graces the cover of the 1992 Maine publicity brochure. Other homeowners in the small seaside town are also giving their Victorians a polychrome facelift. The inn is on the National Register of Historic Places.

VERMONT
WILLIAMSTOWN

Rosewood Inn B&B, Main Street, Route 14. Rose tones and blues highlight the Rosewood Inn, a surprising Steamboat Gothic Queen Anne mansion built in 1898 by granite merchant George Beckett, whose ancestor came to America on the *Mayflower*. The Beckett family lived here until the 1930s, and two owners later, in 1987, John and Elaine Laveroni turned it into an inn. They modulated the original polychrome scheme using historic colors and polished the original woodwork still gracing the comfortable Victorian interior. They cheerfully see to the constant upkeep because "our old lady always seems to need loving care."

NEW HAMPSHIRE
HANOVER

3½ North Park. California has definitely influenced the restoration of this charming 1884 Queen Anne cottage in Hanover, home of Dartmouth College. The house was built for merchant Frank Webster Davison, a cousin of John D. Rockefeller, and remained in the family until 1982, when it was a lodge for Dartmouth students. Melanie and Richard Podoluc bought the house in 1985, and fell in love with a color scheme in *Daughters of Painted Ladies*. After major restoration "that will probably never be complete," Bob Buckter created the color scheme of three grays, navy blue, burgundy, white, and gold leaf in 1989. A regional treat: The polychrome slate roof from nearby Vermont. Doug Keister's Sinar camera almost caught a flurry of bats on their nocturnal excursion from the attic.

MASSACHUSETTS
NEW BEDFORD

100 Hawthorn Street. Fancy-cut shingles, a striped roof, and crowned chimneys were the final touches on the careful restoration of this handsome multigabled 1888 Queen Anne, built by merchant John Tabor and his wife, Annie. The sixteen-room, nine-thousand-square-foot house has been lovingly restored over a ten-year period, starting with the stripping of asbestos shingles and a cheap oil-base cream paint on all the turned poplar wood on the interior. Slate-blend roof shingles were put on the 4,500-square-foot rooftop in a striped pattern.

When the asbestos siding was removed, three gables revealed tree-of-life designs, and much of the house was covered with clapboard and fancy-cut shingles. These have been replaced. But the house objected to the new roof and new plumbing. The copper weather vane refuses to point north. So Anne Desnoyers keeps holy water on hand for that unexplainable occurrence. The Desnoyers painted the house in three shades of green, ivory, and harvest gold in 1991. The garden has been designed to reflect the shape of the house. Note the gazebo built and painted to harmonize with the house. It's the entrance to Anne's chiropractic office in the basement.

27

PITTSFIELD

169 Pomeroy. The golden glow of evening burnishes the unusual design elements on this 1875 French Second Empire home nestled in the Berkshires. Local architect William Rathburn used his signature design of distinctive concave or bell-like curved roof slopes on the home, regarded as the best example of its kind in the state.

Lydia Littlefield of Egremont, Massachusetts, chose the five autumnal, historically authentic colors. Restoration—including interior papers from Bradbury & Bradbury—has been a long-term project for Alice and George Wislocki, who were facing a battle to prevent an overwhelming apartment complex from being plunked down next door, destroying the natural context of the house.

CONNECTICUT
WINDSOR

The Charles R. Hart House, 1046 Windsor Avenue. Inspired by an Aspen cottage in *Daughters of Painted Ladies*, the former innkeepers adorned this striking B&B with ten colors that rise from "the earth to the sky." There are times when the blues on the gable match the sky. At first, the town reacted as if a bomb had been dropped, but response to the overall restoration has been enthusiastic. When Bob and Dorothy McAllister bought the house in 1990, they became instant fans.

The Charles R. Hart House was built in Connecticut's oldest town in the early 1860s as a farmhouse. In 1889 and 1890, James Hutchinson updated his home with Queen Anne embellishments. When Charles R. Hart, a Hartford merchant, bought the place in 1896, he added Colonial Revival details on the front.

When Jane and Lon Pelton of Clearwood Builders, the previous owners, restored the place over a period of several years, they were intrigued to see that the house itself provided them with information about its past and its architectural details.

For example, a small porch at the rear of the house had been enclosed for use as a sunroom by one owner. The Peltons decided to replace it with a traditional Victorian porch. On the ground under the sunroom, they found a piece of shaped board, the original design of all the lattice work under both this porch and the large front and side porches. Inside, the house is a time capsule from 1896, from the Lincrusta walls in the foyer to the lighting fixtures.

RHODE ISLAND
PROVIDENCE

89–91 Parade. Here's a welcoming house bedecked with a built-in bouquet of sunflowers on the gables and bandboards. One hundred thousand dollars was lavished on exterior restoration of the historic 1882 Benjamin E. Arnold House, a Queen Anne on the same block as 77 and 81 Parade, which appeared in *Daughters of Painted Ladies*.

The two-family, twenty-eight-room house had been reduced to being a rooming house shielded by aluminum siding, so restoration was long and hard. The house is in the Armory District, and the Providence Preservation Society Revolving Fund helped with plans and advice. One of the owners says that if you're restoring a Victorian, you need the patience of a saint. Now this flowery refuge has been divided into six condominiums.

(*Overleaf and right*) The Mark Twain House, 77 Forest Street. To see The Mark Twain House is to love it. One of the finest Victorian museums in the country, it is an outstanding example of constructional polychrome and of how just one accent color can make a house "pop."

"The place I live in must have my heart and soul, my eyes to see with." In 1874, Samuel Clemens prodded architect Edward Tuckerman Potter to create "one of the oddest buildings raised in this state as a dwelling, if not the whole country." Described as "part steamboat, part medieval castle and part cuckoo clock," the nineteen-room brick residence, in multicolor brick, blue slate, white concrete, and black and vermilion paint, is also decorated with brick, laid in varying angles and projections; festooned with window boxes, porches, spindles, and brackets; the whole topped with a hexagonally shaped slate roof. The striped awnings are a Victorian tradition.

Here Twain wrote eight books, including *The Adventures of Huckleberry Finn*, *The Adventures of Tom Sawyer*, and *A Connecticut Yankee in King Arthur's Court*.

The spectacular entrance hall also reflects Twain's beloved steamboat style with its silver-stenciled panels, native American textile patterns on the ceiling and walls, and tiles and stained-glass windows designed by Louis Comfort Tiffany in 1881.

"How ugly, tasteless, repulsive are all the domestic interiors I have ever seen in Europe compared with the perfect taste of this ground floor, with its delicious dream of harmonious color, and its all-prevailing spirit of peace and serenity and deep contentments." This was Twain's feeling about the library, which was used as the family parlor.

Twain purchased most of the furnishings on European jaunts. Daughter Suzy bought her father the rocker on one side of the fireplace, and Olivia, his wife whose fortune paid for the house, favored the silk Venetian chair for knitting and reading. The oak fireplace mantel, a richly designed work of art, was carved for Ayton Castle in Scotland in 1869. The glass-enclosed conservatory offers a secluded bower bathed in light and quiet.

The billiard room on the third floor was Twain's study, his tranquil retreat. Everything you see here is as it was in 1881, with pipes and billiard cues decorating the ceiling. The writer's desk faces the wall just to the right of the front of this photo, put there to prevent the author from staring out a window or daydreaming. Bret Harte, General William T. Sherman, and actor Henry Irving were among the guests who challenged Twain to a game of billiards.

In 1896, Twain wrote, "To us, our house was not unsentient matter—it had a heart, and a soul, and eyes to see us with; and approvals, and solicitudes, and deep sympathies; it was of us, and we were in its confidence, and lived in its grace and in the peace of its benediction. We never came home from an absence that its face did not light up and speak out its eloquent welcome—and we could not enter it unmoved." This is an eloquent rendering of sentiments felt by many Victorian homeowners. Mark Twain is also a presence in Elmira, New York, and his hometown, Hannibal, Missouri.

NEW YORK
BROOKLYN

217 East 19th Street. In 1989, Rose McGuinness and Nancy Franklin, the owners of this 1901 Colonial Revival home, which has been in several commercials and movies, asked San Francisco color consultant Bob Buckter for an elegant, dramatic color scheme. They wanted something sunny that wouldn't stick out like a sore thumb. The sculpted swan's neck pediment has been deftly picked out in a peachy six-color scheme highlighted by cinnamon and melon, with a hearty sprinkling of gold leaf.

Merchant Will Ryan had paid a Mr. Ackerson to build the house at a cost of $10,000, plus $2,500 for the lot. Mahogany pillars in the parlor, polished oak walls in the dining room, and bird's-eye maple in the billiard room attest to Mr. Ryan's good taste and open pocketbook.

Rose McGuinness remarked, "The house makes me feel very happy when I look at it. My neighbor says she enjoys it more than I do because she sees it more than I do"—a good reminder of the social value of color and architecture.

455 Marlborough Road. After renovating the interior of this smashing 1903 transitional Queen Anne/Colonial Revival/Arts and Crafts home for eight years, the owners painted the house as the culmination of what they wanted the house to be. They looked at pictures of houses they liked on their travels, and one of the owners concluded, "No one would know me better than I. I would work for a long time on what I call the Final Touch." To accent the brick red, apple green, the tawny gold, they took a favorite sweater to the paint store to match the teal blue and finished the house in 1991. This warm dollhouse is an outstanding example of how to use color to compensate for the lack of decoration.

NYACK

(Opposite) 1 La Veta Road. A flower garden of colors—rose, geranium, old rose, and accents of iris and daffodil, spring green, and a creamy white—were prescribed by mail by Santa Cruz color consultant Doni Tunheim of Fresh Façades. A lumber magnate named Perry built his Hudson River–front Queen Anne in 1900 on the site of an earlier home. In 1991, an appeals court decreed that the eighteen-room mansion had not been, as required by the contract, delivered "vacant," since it was reportedly inhabited by an apple-cheeked ghost in Revolutionary War garb. The owners insist that they have transformed it from horrific to holy. Today, it's a "ray of joy" on the street.

HUDSON

Olana State Historic Site. RD 2, one mile south of the Rip Van Winkle Bridge on Route 9G. "I can say, as the good woman did about her mock turtle soup, 'I made it out of my own head.'" So mused Hudson River School artist Frederic Edwin Church about Olana, the home he designed. Built on a bluff with panoramic views of the majestic Hudson River and the Catskill Mountains, the Moorish-style Italianate villa and its surrounding estate remain today much as they were at the time the artist designed them in 1870. One of America's premier landscape painters, Church's art depicts nineteenth-century American attitudes toward life and nature. For Church, Olana was a work of art, a refuge from the cares and pressures of an ever-encroaching world. It was judged to be one of the best examples of domestic and artistic architecture of its period and was designed to look like a hilltop village.

"A feudal castle which I am building under the modest name of a dwelling house absorbs all my time and attention. I am obliged to watch it so closely, for having undertaken to get my architecture from Persia where I have never been, nor any of my friends either, I am obliged to imagine Persian architecture, then embody it on paper and explain it to a lot of mechanics." The multicolor-tiled front doorway could be the entrance to a mosque. The color, variety, and intricacy of the designs that frame the second-floor windows in brick, wood, English Minton tile, and stone are dazzling.

The court hall was a room used by the family and their guests for entertainment and visiting. Church designed it as the visual and structural center of the house. A Persian garden of colors—turquoise, rose, salmon, green, and violet—enliven the stencils designed by the artist.

The colors spring from this room to successive spaces, where they blossom on walls and ceilings. Church used the same palette in his painting *El Khasne*, which hangs in the sitting room. Sumptuous fabrics and exotic furnishings together with a well-stocked library and "modern" comforts create an interior conducive to artistic and intellectual endeavor.

Church designed and built the studio addition between 1888 and 1891. This project provided him with an artistic outlet when arthritis prevented him from painting. As a home and as a work of art, Olana combined the two major interests of the artist's life for more than thirty years. His photographs enable curators to replicate the world he lived in. The upkeep on this massive treasure is perpetual, eased and challenged by the existence of Church's own stencils, molds, sketches, and pigments. On the one hand, the curators have the tools needed to maintain the house exactly as Church wanted it. On the other hand, the artist's legacy is a constant presence demanding devotion to perfection.

Today, Olana remains a testament to ninteenth-century life and ideas. Visitors take away the sense of a life lived out of the world, yet forward looking, uniting the artist's spiritual, intellectual, and physical life. With its extravagant wealth of color and decoration, Olana rises over the Hudson as one of America's most spectacular Victorians.

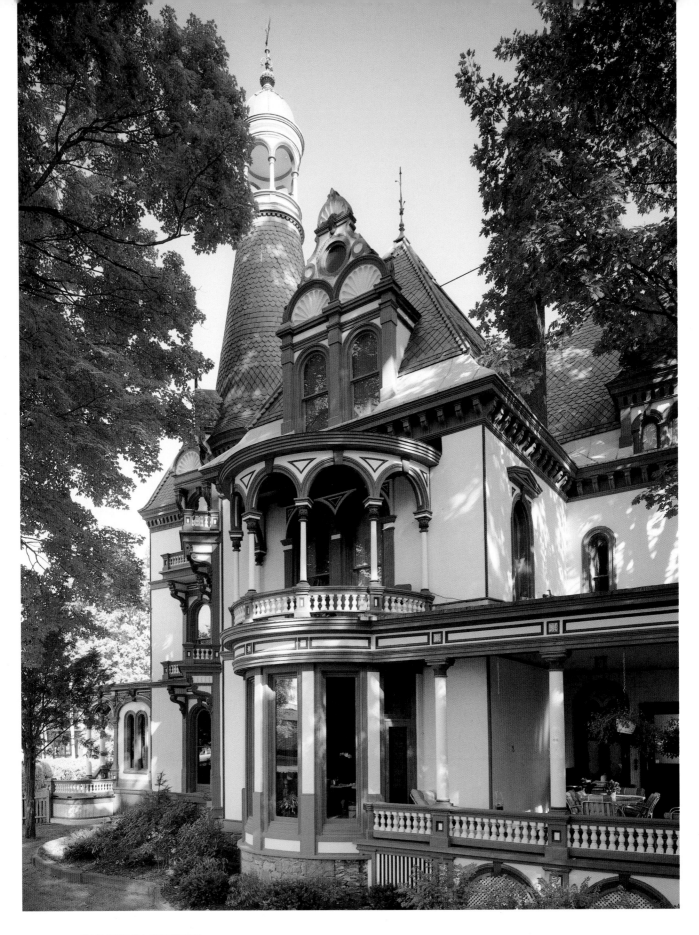

SARATOGA SPRINGS

The Batcheller Mansion, 20 Circular Drive. Mineral springs and a thoroughbred racetrack made Saratoga Springs one of the country's leading society resorts. By the second half of the nineteenth century, some of the grandest hotels and finest Victorian homes in the nation had been built in Saratoga. Designed by architects Nichols and Hacott of Albany, Kasr-el-Nouzha, or House of Pleasure, a flamboyant French Renaissance–style Queen Anne, was built for George S. Batcheller in 1873. It blended features of French chateaux with minarets and was the first private home in the United States to have its design patented. Much of the finely detailed woodwork and window glass remain. The exterior polychrome treatment echoes the original colors.

49 West Main Street at Quaker Street. "Restoring homes is a passion" for Bill and Judith Dieffenbach. Bill feels that "The rewards of restoration are the satisfaction of creating something that's tangible and not having to wonder if you made a meaningful impact. This is like a piece of living history that you get to sleep in."

Naturalist Franklin T. Pember built this handsome Second Empire home in 1873 and added Queen Anne touches for his mother in 1891. The Pembers paid for a sewer system for the whole town and built the opera house, now gone, and the Pember Museum of Natural History, which is still operating.

When the Dieffenbachs bought the house, it had been empty and trashed for two years. The house was filled with structural problems, rot, mold, and junk. "So many new door frames had been cut into some rooms that two entire sides of the house had no support other than clapboards, plaster, and possibly a mystical force emanating from the core of the earth." Bill's insistence on using only lumber, fixtures, and plumbing made before 1900 necessitated spending large amounts of time salvaging old buildings for materials and rooting through basements and garages. But they also discovered the layout for the original Victorian gardens hand-drawn on a piece of wood inside a wall.

The porch had not yet been replaced when these photographs were taken, so Bill painted the paper covering the middle band of shingles! The placement was determined by Mr. Pember himself, in 1891, but his ten colors were altered to "Grand Canyon" colors that change with the changing light and weather to emphasize the workmanship of the building. The house took so long to finish that some neighbors got to like, and prefer, the plain, loud, pink primer.

Bill's advice on restoration: "Do not listen to modern contractors. Consult craftsmen with preservation experience, other homeowners, old-house societies, and *The Old-House Journal*. Do not be afraid to jump in, even if you don't know what you're doing. If you did you would never take it on. Ignorance leads to adventure if not exactly bliss."

MALONE

100 Elm Street. "In regard to the Adirondacks," Thoreau said, "the question is not what you look at, but what you see." Malone is located high in the Adirondack Mountains near the Canadian border. This dazzling Queen Anne was designed in 1881 for Archamides Russell by Wells S. Dickinson, called a "master-spirit of his age." All of the exterior and interior decorative wood was local timber milled in Malone.

The Painted Ladies books were the inspiration for the ten historical colors owner John Mills chose when painting in 1989. The color scheme was a collaboration between John, local architect Mark Camens, and painter Paul Horan of Cambridge, Massachusetts. The fifty stained-glass windows helped suggest blues, reds, and golds. John says, "We just enhanced what the people who built the house had done when they called it 'Queen of the May' in honor of its completion date."

Painters under the direction of Paul Horan took four and a half months to prepare for and apply the 40 gallons of primer and 110 gallons of oil-based gloss paint, highlighting the garlands, medallions, cornice friezes, and decorative stenciled cutouts, balusters, and sunbursts. When asked what are the joys and hazards of restoring a Victorian, Mills replied, "The joy is the result—the hazards are in discovering the unexpected."

510 Main Street. The ribbons on the straw hats flanking the doorway of this charming Stick-style home reflect the tasty colors on this 1874 Queen Anne. A doctor named Carpenter built the house for himself when he returned from the Civil War. Owner Tanna Abell had a hard time explaining to the painter what kind of colors she wanted, but when she said she wanted something to make passersby "smile when they walked by," he understood.

Now the only problem she has in the house is the candles. Every time she places them in the front parlor, one of them tips slightly to one side or the other. "Sometimes I feel that Dr. Carpenter comes back and tips the candles just to see me keep returning to straighten them. I feel that he is pleased to be sharing his house with our large, energetic brood."

426 Broad Street. Classic colors emphasize the Moorish details on this stately mansion. James Bennett, part owner in a lumber mill, built an Italianate in 1872. His widow sold it to James Bates in 1881. Bates added a French Second Empire exterior and a Renaissance Revival interior.

In 1984, when Paul and Marcia Newsom bought it, the Bennett/Bates home was broken up into five remuddled apartments. They lived in two apartments and spent a year and a half researching before they started work. They talked to a woman who had lived in the house in the teens and twenties, and who gave them pictures of the house before it was modernized.

Outside, the scars of a frieze and brackets and shadow lines of the original porches made rebuilding possible. Paul used a microscope to determine the three original colors on the house and then used almost the same colors to give the house the "ambience" of the original. The Newsoms made and painted the frieze before replacing it on the house.

Bradbury & Bradbury wallpaper echoes the stained glass and fine woods in the imposing front door.

In the dining room, the wallpaper and ceiling treatment designed by Paul Duchscherer unifies the room, although the change in the direction of the flooring near the far end of the Bokhara rug shows where the original library ended. The original cherry woodwork and all but the Victorian Rococo Revival gentleman's chair, the Colonial Revival lamp table, and the rosewood and walnut burl Edwardian sideboard are Renaissance Revival. The jeweled parlor lighting fixture of the Aesthetic Movement, made about 1875, complements the nine stained-glass windows. The marbleized slate mantel to the right of the dining-room table is the only one remaining of the original eleven. Bachelder's drawing of the battlefield at Gettysburg, 1864, is a family piece, and the celery dish on the table was painted by Paul's great-grandmother.

Paul's advice to homeowners is to take notes and make checklists, with the dates of the innumerable inspections, then pass the inspection notes to the next generation of owners, since, "After all, you're only the custodian for a while. And don't just march to the beat of a different drummer, *be* the different drummer."

BRIDGEWATER

The White House Berries Inn Restaurant and B&B, Route 8 at Route 20. A house rarely reflects the spirit of the owner perfectly, but this breath-of-spring color scheme captures the spirit of its cheery proprietor, Juanita Bass. People drive from miles around for her soul food and Yankee dinners served with hush puppies, black-eyed peas, and lots of love.

Juanita spent thirty years buying and selling antiques and raising six children. She still has a little antiques shop behind the restaurant and says, "I feel I've come a long way since my great-grandfather was a slave in Virginia. He came north and settled in this area. So here I am!" Her father, Everett Holmes, the first black mayor in New York State, was elected by write-in votes.

Juanita bought this 1874 Italianate built by Dr. H. Bailey a few years ago and went to work polishing and primping. She remembered it when there was a sign on the door that read: "White House. Berries for sale." It was the first house in the village with electricity and indoor plumbing. The original marble mantelpieces, light fixtures, and grain-painted woodwork have survived. The oldest tulip tree in Oneida County still blooms in the front yard.

A visit to her daughter in San Francisco inspired the five colors: teal, gray green, mauve, pink, and white. The next Halloween, a young trick-or-treater came to the door and said, "Hey, lady, I love your house." "Then I knew I had done the right thing. More and more Victorian homeowners are daring to do what we have done with colors. We love it."

Main Street, Route 8. Two different Painted Ladies fans, including a man who called his own beautiful home Wysteria Gardens, alerted us to this explosive outburst of color on a country road. The frilly tiara of cast iron on the roof and the frothy necklace circling the piazza of this jewelbox Mansard mansion are matched in splendor by the selection of pinks on this unsung treasure, which was empty and on the market when it was photographed.

A master cabinetmaker and undertaker named David H. White was paid a dollar a day to build the house for Captain Charles Harris in 1860. The mansard roof is slate, the massive doors are oak and chestnut, and handcrafted spindles line two winding interior staircases. There's also a hidden room off the dining room said to have been a stop on the underground railroad for transporting slaves to freedom. (The railroad tracks are about four hundred feet from the rear of the house.)

When the present owners discovered it, it was VOV—Vacant, Open, and Vandalized—with "refuse from when time began, and plaster ceilings, where they hadn't fallen down, hung so low we had to duck to walk through. Family and friends thought we were crazy. Our mothers tried to convince us to think things over more carefully. But love is blind, and we went on our way, pulling down plaster, repairing ceilings, plumbing, roofs, porches, and gingerbread." Once the house was in perfect shape, they painted it themselves in geisha pink, bud pink, and dewberry. Then their business prevented them from moving in, so when we saw it, they were looking for someone to love the house as much as they do.

CORTLAND

27 North Church Street. W. J. Greenman, founder of the Cortland Door and Screen Company, ordered this Queen Anne mansion from the George F. Barber Cottage Souvenir No. 2 catalog in 1896. John Harrison served as builder. With an interior paneled in bird's-eye maple, the house cost $1,000. Duplicates of the house are in Mobile, Alabama, and Winona, Illinois, but the handsome color scheme, designed with the advice of curators at The 1890 House Museum and Center for Victorian Arts in Cortland, is unique.

ITHACA

(*Opposite*) Turback's, 919 Elmira Road. Tobacco farmer Thomas Jefferson Williams hired local carpenters to build Sunnygables from local pine in 1851. The gingerbread was made by hand. The first bathroom in Ithaca was installed during remodeling in 1875. Cornell graduate Michael Turback bought one of America's stellar Gothic Revival houses in 1968, restored it, and turned it into a restaurant featuring New York State specialties.

Shortly after the house appeared in *Daughters of Painted Ladies*, the place went up in flames, Turback, buoyed by an outpouring of concern from friends and patrons, duplicated the complex architecture and gingerbread detail from the first story up, opening up a second story under the roof. Carol Wells Shepard, who once wrote, "I'm sure I will die some day looking out my car windows at architecture instead of road," provided the glowing historically authentic color scheme. Three colors were used, with a fourth on the gable ends, but the building details were more accentuated.

CORTLAND

The Fitzgerald House, 39 Tompkins Street. L. J. Fitzgerald, President of the Cortland Wagon Company, built this Queen Anne in 1885 of cherry clapboard. At the time, it was cited as one of the most perfect examples of the Queen Anne style in New York. The last Fitzgerald daughter lived there alone with her maid until she died in the 1950s.

After surviving years as a fraternity house, it appeared on the cover of Roger Moss's classic *Victorian Exterior Decoration* as a fine example of High Victorian color. It had been painted in the late 1970s or early 1980s with a Federal Block grant of $22,000 to arrest deterioration. But it was a sloppy job. Only three sides were finished.

By the time the present owner, Mark Haig, took over in 1988, there were forty-two football players living in the house, staging keg parties for three hundred people. After several hundred thousand dollars' worth of interior and exterior restoration, including a finishing paint touch-up and the installation of 150 spindles in six designs on the front porch, the place was leased to a sorority.

ELMIRA

The Christmas House, 361 Maple Avenue. "Many a small thing has been made large by the right kind of advertising," wrote Mark Twain, and Elmira has made itself a tourist destination by calling itself "Mark Twain Country." Twain summered here at his in-laws' home during the 1870s and 1880s and is buried here. Elmira also boasts the largest National Register district of Victorian homes in New York State.

The Christmas House, an imposing late Queen Anne, was built in 1894 by architects Pierce & Bickford for lumberman Justus Harris, who sold it to politician Daniel Sheehan in 1904. Elaine DiBiase opened her Christmas store in 1983 in a white elephant. In December 1988, color consultant Paul Murphy suggested that the building would be perfect as a Painted Lady. "I had never heard of Painted Ladies and December is not the time to talk to me about anything but surviving to January," Elaine remembers, "but Paul returned with the books. I took one look at them and said 'We'll do it.'

"He wanted bright red and green, and when he painted the first section, I almost had a stroke. It was modified to the present fifteen colors. Even so, the neighbors on the right side came over and pleaded, 'You're not going to paint our side like that also, are you?,' and others called the district councilman to see if there were city ordinances stipulating the number of colors. But when it was completed, we had a dedication by the mayor and invited the neighborhood, and now it sometimes looks drab to me!"

520 West Water Street. Financier Wilber W. Fish moved into this handsome Second Empire home in 1879, four years after its construction, and his son Edwin lived here until 1945. One owner later in 1972, Jim and Judy Frandsen moved in. Restoration and upgrading of the interior took twelve years, then they decided it was time to tackle the exterior. *Painted Ladies* inspired the choice of polychrome, and when the slate roof was refinished, red tiles were inserted with new curved-to-match gray tiles from the New York–Vermont border.

When they realized that it was difficult to mix paint to match colored pencil sketches, they painted different combinations of colors on different sections of the house as tests. Friends insisted they would sue for the accident they were going to have in front of the house trying to keep up-to-date with the color combinations. Others wondered whether the house would be a patchwork of multicolor. The three blues, gray, and red combination inspired many in the area to paint their homes.

The phenomenal front parlor with its original fabric wallcovering, done by W. & J. Sloane & Co. of New York City in the 1890s, is unique. Turkish exhibits at the Philadelphia Centennial Exposition in 1876 and the Turkish Bazaar at the 1893 World's Columbian Exposition in Chicago were wildly popular. The original silk tufted in gold satin still covers the ceiling. The remaining silk wall panels have been repaired, after having been ripped by Edwin Fish for the insertion of a ticker-tape machine.

The original valances over the windows and fireplace are Eastlake. The antique parlor set in an identical Eastlake design are a happy accident. The furnishings are family heirlooms gathered on trips. The child's rocker and doll are from Judy's mother.

BATH

16 Pulteney Square West. Cruise blue, seacrest green, golden tan, and moss rose bedeck this 1880s Stick cottage in an upstate New York town founded in 1793. According to colorist Paul Murphy, the peak forms an *A* for "alpha" and the circle around the horseshoe center window, an *O* for "omega." It may be Greek to us, but Paul is as creative with symbolism as he is with paint.

ADDISON

Church of the Redeemer, 7 Front Street at Wall Street. The doorway of this small 1860 Episcopal church makes a joyful noise unto the community. Color consultant Paul Murphy added a dark gray pinstripe to the "preordained" pale gray background, then used light green-blue accents that will match the brand-new copper on the recently rebuilt steeple as it weathers. A milky blue accent brings out the major architectural features.

WELLSVILLE

The Pink House, 193 West State Street. No less than five different fans submitted pictures of this frothy confection for this book. After Edwin Bradford Hall (a descendant of a member of the original Plymouth Colony) and his bride Antoinette fell in love with Italian castles while on their honeymoon on Lake Como, he designed and built this delicious towered Italianate villa in 1869–1870 with the help of architects Henry Searle & Sons. The fourth generation of the family still summers at The Pink House, making this the only Victorian in the book still in use by the family that built it.

Hall mixed the pink with a zinc-base formula in his drugstore, and although different shades have been applied over the years, the basic design of pink and white with gray, and maroon sashes remains. The stencils, fringe, and tassels on the exterior provide a unique frosting.

Ghost stories about the house abound and are based on two tragic misfortunes. Mrs. Hall's sister drowned herself in the town's millpond in 1858 before the Halls' marriage. Gossip averred that she was in love with Hall, but he married her sister instead. Years later, Mr. Hall's two-year-old granddaughter drowned in front of him in the fountain pool in the circular driveway—he was too infirm to rescue her—so the pond is now filled in with flowers.

The front parlor looks today as it did in the 1880s with its carved double wooden arches centered by a globular finial; hand-carved-to-order pilasters of calla lilies, ivy, and birds; elaborate gold-leaf cornices over the double arches and windows; and mirrors and pier glasses in matching gold. Hall purchased the white marble mantel and the attached four-foot alabaster vases in Italy. His pierced-brass chandeliers still form patterns in the pier glasses. The French clock was bought on the Halls' honeymoon. The painting of the girl to the left of the mantel is of three-year old Fanny Hall Carpenter, the grandmother of present owner, Julian Woelfel. The pale blue chairs were painted with gilt and flowers by Aunt Louise, who also painted the pale blue satin on the chairs at the back of the photograph.

A music alcove was added to the living room in the late 1870s. The two circular stained-glass windows portray luxuriant tropical blossoms and the Florida Everglades, a favorite winter getaway.

Throughout the house, the arched ash doors have panels and molding of curly maple and cherry and flourishes of hand-carved black walnut. Most of the paintings are by family members. Fanny Hall Carpenter did the one over the piano. Her daughter Lillian did many others. The photographs on the tables are also of family members. The old rocker with the dragon on its back is a family favorite.

JAMESTOWN

304 Main Street. Color consultant Michael C. Hall brought new life to this 1876 Italianate commercial building with deep sage green, deep pewter, twilight taupe, and a rich maroon—all historical colors. He feels that when designing a row of Victorian commercial buildings, it is important that no one color design dominate. This building is on the right in a row of three.

To Hall, "Exterior color designing is an emotional confrontation with history. It breathes new life into long-neglected and abused buildings. Never, in recent times, have people become more aware of their architectural history than when they are painting eighty-nine spindles in three color tones. It is at moments like this when craftsmanship and appreciation meet head-on. To view a carved rosette emerge from under six coats of poorly applied white paint is like a Renoir painting being discovered behind a paint-by-numbers print."

PENNSYLVANIA
PITTSBURGH

1317 Sheffield Street. A brilliant blue wakes up the brick façade of this downtown Pittsburgh rowhouse, where urban renewal is bringing the city back to life. Artist Lisa Blackson, the owner of this turn-of-the-century rowhouse in the Historic Manchester District, used to live in San Francisco. She wanted something to perk up the neighborhood, and although the Manchester Citizens Corporation advocates only historical colors, she had already painted a mural on her garage in back, so her neighbors knew she was a free spirit. She used the Pantone Matching System color deck to create three colors to dress up her home: shrimp coral, teal for the insets, and cerulean blue.

WEST NEWTON

(*Opposite and left*) 906 Vine Street. A dollhouse painted to match the "big" house, a brass firepole from the attic to the second floor, and fire-eating dragons on the lamp posts make Whispering Amethyst fun for the six Hope children. Banker William McCune purchased the 1887 Stick-style house for $600 and a gold watch.

A century later, Carol Hope received this house, with a big red bow on the door, as a Christmas present from her veterinarian husband. Carol worked closely with Paul Hook and Company Construction as the restoration and renovation continued. She chose serene, cool colors—four blues, three purples, and pink—to bring out the wonderful feeling of her new home. The town was so pleased that they used a photograph of the house as part of a promotion for residential development. Carol's advice for taking on an old house is to really love the house and have a very strong marriage.

OIL CITY

Jonathan H. Hutchinson Funeral Home, 201 Bissell Avenue. Steep hills on the northwestern edge of Pennsylvania have given this little nineteenth-century oil boomtown an inaccessibility that has preserved its Victorians. The Jonathan H. Hutchinson Funeral Home, a Queen Anne/Colonial Revival mansion built in 1899 for oilman Thomas B. Simpson, is notable for its octagonal tower capped with dome and finial and the cut-granite section on the first floor around the tower. The Hutchinson family, including six sons and a daughter, moved into the eighteen-room house in 1979, after a thorough restoration.

One son, Eric Hutchinson, a color consultant, designed the blue color scheme for a house that was suffering from what he calls "white blight" or "the Casa Blanca blahs." The name of the paint, Summer Haze, served as the inspiration for the four-color design, which was to simulate the blue sky and clouds on a bright summer day. To Eric, "These wonderful masterpieces undoubtedly deserve a better destiny than cloaks of white and gray. Let winter succumb to spring!"

PHILADELPHIA

3733 Lancaster Avenue. Jayne Hairstyling, located in a storefront in a commercial brick 1878 Italianate in Historic Powelton Village, got a fanciful new look when Jayne's husband decided to paint it in 1990.

Dennis Aufiery is an artist and color consultant, and he approached the project as he would a painting. He wanted the façade to have a quality of light, a sense of life. The birdhouse was added as a way of extending that sense of life—a gesture of inviting nature into the city. After he restored the façade, he replaced the asphalt roof with a Victorian handmade tin roof. Then, during a two-month period, he painted the entire front himself. He used fourteen colors—mauves, purples, blues, and greens, close in value and hue—to create a neon effect.

NEW JERSEY
CAPE MAY

(*Opposite*) The Abbey, 606 Columbia. Cape May became a resort two hundred years ago, but it took on a Victorian air when much of the town was rebuilt in the ornate styles of that period after a fire in the 1870s. Fashion passed it by after the turn of the century, allowing "protective neglect" to save it for posterity. Today, there are six hundred Victorians in a two-square-mile area, and it is again a thriving seaside resort filled with delightfully painted homes and B&Bs. A National Historic Landmark City, Cape May is the reigning queen of Victorian resorts.

Jay and Marianne Schatz, the hospitable owners of The Abbey, an 1869 towered villa B&B that appeared in *Daughters of Painted Ladies*, once told us why they had chosen the colors of a five-dollar bill as their color scheme: pale green, dark green, cream (and bittersweet red). They said that if they had simply papered the place with five-dollar bills, both the cost and the effect would have been the same. They have to repaint every three to five years. No wonder painters call the seashore "a hostile atmosphere."

Stephen Decatur Button, who designed The Abbey for Pennsylvania coal baron John B. McCreary, also designed the Second Empire cottage behind it for his son George in 1873. When this lace-edged Mansard-roofed home became part of The Abbey, it had been converted to five apartments, and a major restoration was needed. When it came time to paint, the Schatzes used the same color scheme, reversing the importance of the greens, a Victorian approach to painting neighboring houses.

(*Overleaf*) Angel of the Sea, 5 Trenton Street. Winner of the 1990 National Trust for Historic Preservation Award for B&Bs, Angel of the Sea has been sliced in half and moved three different times. Now it's the largest Victorian structure facing the sea in Cape May.

Philadelphian William Weightman built the mansion as a summer cottage in 1850. His son, William, Jr., cut the building in half and moved it to the oceanfront in 1882 and added the elaborate towers and decorations. When the storm of 1962 spared the home, it was saved from demolition and moved to a short-lived college complex as dormitories.

John and Barbara Girton bought both parts in 1989 and moved them back to the ocean. After two years of restoration, they connected the two parts with a porch and painted their Angel pink, nutmeg, white, and two grays. The Historic Preservation Committee of the town approved this scheme out of the four different color renderings supplied by the paint company. Wood ceilings, wainscoting, and Victorian bathroom fixtures remained intact. To restoration architect John Oliveri, the Angel of the Sea "is close to being the way it was when it was first moved in 1881. It was a dream come true for us."

The Linda Lee, 725 Columbia Avenue. This irresistible Gothic Revival cottage, the John Beniset House, was built in 1872, one of several speculative buildings built by Peter McCollum. The second owner, a Philadelphia banker named Porter, named the house after his daughter, Linda Lee. The ruby etched glass around the front door glows in the evening light. The house looks as if it had been kissed by the morning sunlight. In a nineteenth-century tome called *The Weekend Book*, the authors assert that "There are three arts—painting, music, and ornamental pastry-making; of which last, architecture is a subdivision." They might have been thinking of this delicious confection when they wrote that.

DELAWARE
MILFORD

(*Left, opposite, and overleaf*) The Towers, 101 Northwest Front Street. "Enjoy the grace and elegance of a bygone era" is the motto of this grand bed and breakfast. This National Register house was built in 1783 by Dr. John Wallace, the stepfather of John LoFland, "The Milford Bard," a well-known poet in the area and a friend of Edgar Allan Poe, who was a frequent visitor. The Towers was remodeled in Steamboat Gothic style in 1891 by Rhoda Roudebush, the governor's daughter. Both dates have been immortalized on the chimney.

Rhoda spent four years turning a simple residence into a towering extravaganza with ten types of gingerbread outside and more than five miles of cherry and walnut paneling inside. A craftsman imported from Italy created the stained glass, which is still intact. Upstairs, the wainscoting has alternate panels of cherry, walnut, and chestnut. Although the house was abandoned, moldy, and sinking into Delaware's sandy soil, Michael Real and Mark Springer couldn't resist saving it and restoring it to its High Victorian glory. While stripping wallpaper off a wall, they found that it had been covered in gold leaf. Other surprises kept workmen on their toes as Michael tackled the interior while Mark worked on the exterior.

Twelve pastels, including purple, yellow, lavender, pink, and blue, were drawn from the stained-glass windows to give the bulky structure eye appeal. For a while, the citizens of Milford, a historic river town on the Mispillion River, close to the Atlantic Ocean and Delaware and Rehoboth Bays, panicked when they saw the house garbed in a Pepto-Bismol pink primer. A front-page interview with Mark in the local paper enabled residents to relax, as he explained that what they were seeing was the gaudy primer, and that he was planning a traditional mauve treatment.

Bob Buckter, the noted San Francisco color designer, has told us that people get more upset when they see the prime coat, or the samples of swatching that don't seem to come together, than they do when they see the finished, harmonious color scheme.

The Adams German tile fireplace in the music room is what convinced Michael and Mark to buy the house. The sycamore coffered ceiling is outstanding. Note also the walnut columns on the right leading to the hall. The grand piano in the music room, the warm cherry woodwork in the front parlor, and the French collectibles add charm to The Towers' eclectic, romantic decor. The walnut dining table reflects the fine cherry paneling on the ceiling.

THE SOUTH

From the Chesapeake Bay to the southernmost tip of the continental United States, from below sea level in New Orleans to the Brigadoon of the Ozarks, Eureka Springs, the pace in the South is slower, easier. Virginia combines beauty and history as does no other state. The richness of the rolling hills and the state's past make it well worth a visit. Mount Vernon, Monticello, and Williamsburg provide three of the finest glimpses of early American history in the country.

Key West attracts visitors with its Caribbean colors and evocative past. Vicksburg and Natchez beckon with their Civil War remembrances, their abiding link with the Mississippi, and their living reminders of a splendid architectural heritage from days gone with the wind.

We made some great discoveries on this trip. In Charleston, we found the Saracen Restaurant, a unique elaborate Moorish fantasy in polychrome stone. Savannah's Gingerbread Mansion has shed its creamy Greek Revival lace mantle for a classy eleven-color coat of many colors. Ron Horvath's painstaking restoration of the Coleman House in Swainsboro, Georgia, is a model of loving attention to detail. Louisiana's astonishing San Francisco Plantation makes us wonder how many other plantations were not just faux marble white.

If southern colors seem pale, remember, as color designer Louis Aubert explained about "The Big Easy," "The color palette tends to be on the soft side because of the very bright light of New Orleans. We share the same latitude as Cairo, Egypt." Louis Aubert provided another interesting note on color in the South when he explained that most of the black cast-iron bedecking balconies and fences in New Orleans was originally green. The color darkened with age, and then the owners would tell the painters, "Just do it as it is." Since the paint looked pretty black by then, that is what they got. Now, of course, people say, "Paint it green? But it's always been black!"

MARYLAND
BALTIMORE

1906 Mount Royal Terrace. James Gamble is an unsung hero of The Colorist Movement. In 1975, he wanted to paint his princely 1884 Italianate brick rowhouse in natural colors, so he chose dark hunter green, dark tobacco brown, and harvest yellow, with white sashes and window trim.

His neighbors were so irate at both the choice and the number of colors that they took their grievance to the local historical society, which threatened to take James to court, but he was adamant and they finally let him alone.

Three years later, when *Painted Ladies* came out, someone from the society brought James a copy and told him he was right; many of the original Victorians had been painted in polychrome. The book quotes the April 1885 *California Architects and Builders News:* "One of the principal ingredients of this style is to cover the buildings, when finished, with a bountiful supply of paint, using more colors by far than the tailor who designed Joseph's Coat.... Red, yellow, chocolate, orange, everything that is loud is in fashion, and the entire exterior is so gay that a Virginia creeper or a wisteria would be bold, indeed, if it dare set leaf or tendril there. If the upper stories are not of red or blue...they are painted up into uncouth panels of yellow and brown, while gables and dormers are adorned not with tasteful and picturesque designs, but with monotonous sunbursts and flaming fans done in loud tints." Maybe it was this quote that convinced the society.

A painting tip: James painted the house with Martin's Epoxy in 1975, and when we photographed it in 1991, it was still in excellent condition.

73

VIRGINIA
ARLINGTON

1506 North Nicholas Street. Anna Dale Sullivan, a colorist and the author of a regional guide, *The Old House Source-book*, now out of print, used delicate colors to make her charming cottage come to life. Anna chose grayed blue-green shingles with warm white trim, light gray shutters, and terra-cotta on sashes and fish-scale to harmonize with the slate, stone, and brick used in the neighborhood. Early spring dogwood creates a lovely frame for the house.

Barney T. Noland built his home in 1892 in the Fostoria section of Arlington, and his daughter still lived in her gift from him, a "honeymoon cottage" across the street, when the Sullivans moved into the Noland house in 1972. The Sullivans were able to buy some of the original furnishings from the daughter's estate.

ALEXANDRIA

216–220 South Fayette Street. Termites are responsible for The Sisters, a stately line of Italianate rowhouses in Historic Alexandria. S. B. Stoutenburgh built three houses on Fayette Street in 1889 and added two more in 1890. By 1977, the exteriors had been "colonialized" with recessed door-ways, shutters, and press-board siding over Brick-Tex siding.

In 1987, termites were discovered, and since renovations were in order, the owners decided to do it right. By the time they had finished the restoration of their house and were ready to paint, so were two of their neighbors. They all cooperated to make the row look its best, using the yellow trim to provide continuity. Their historically authentic colors make a simple but pleasing statement.

RAPIDAN

Eastern View B&B, 22283 Clarks Mountain Road. Eastern View is a felicitous blend of three architectural periods. The central part of the house was built about 1839. The left side of the house was added in a Federal style in 1850. The owner at that time, Dr. David Pannill, was a friend of Zachary Taylor. Extensive renovation and an addition with Victorian ruffles and flourishes occurred in 1875.

More than a century later, restoration was a challenge, with rewards that included finding surprises such as old photographs behind the mantel, the names of the original workers on the house, a hidden fireplace, a hidden staircase, and a message from J. S. Goode under the molding: "He that believeth not will be damned." The colors—warm white, red-brown sumac, valley green, Charleston green, and a darker green—are as close to the original as possible.

Owner Paul Murphy, a restoration contractor and consultant, feels that "There's a lot more sentiment among Americans now for things historic. Most of my clients would prefer to live in an old house that's been restored rather than something that has no charm or character to it." Eastern View has a special character: a benign ghost who walks around carrying a candle.

RICHMOND

1113, 1211–1215, and 1405 West Main Street. Richmond has a fine collection of Victorians in traditional colors. But several blocks of commercial, turn-of-the-century buildings on West Main Street have erupted in delightful, vibrant pastels. Eck Enterprises owns sixty buildings in Richmond, and Hilda Eck's suggestion for making these buildings succeed, after restoration, was to make them bright, something people would notice, something to make people happy. Ed Eck's cousin, Foster Maegher, a color designer in Los Angeles whose work appeared in *Painted Ladies*, also offered advice.

The Ecks really enjoy bringing buildings back to life. After the façades have been restored, they blow up photographs and test colors, deciding first on a field of color, then on a trim color, and then they embellish them with accent colors. Often, "field application" inspires changes in the colors or their weights. The Ecks look at the block as a whole, as well as individual buildings, and they use design elements and lighting to create dramatic façades. On the 1200 block, the seven buildings were each given different colors, but, as in Alexandria, they are held together with the linen-cream trim color. Plans for more buildings are in the works.

PETERSBURG

269 High Street. Dusty rose, soft cream, a judicious touch of carmine red, and a crowning tiara add grace and stature to this late 1880s Second Empire home built by B.A. Traylor for fire department captain Thomas C. Elliott, Jr. When Moses Long, an educator, restoration advocate, and contractor painted the house in 1990, after doing the blue one across the street, the colors were approved by the Petersburg Historic Review Board.

Long slowly buys houses that need help, restores them, and rents or sells them as residences and commercial properties. If he had his way, he would restore the whole inner city of Petersburg. The Appomattox River has reopened for riverboats from the Old Town to Williamsburg and Jamestown to the ocean, and Petersburgers are working together to restore the area.

NORTH CAROLINA
GREENSBORO

The Olive-Smith House, 715 Walker Avenue. Businessman J. C. Olive and his wife built this picturesque Queen Anne in 1892 for $5,000, and the house remained in the family until 1989, when Terry McKinney and Ron Jump bought it from the Olives' grandson, Colonel Irving Smith. A third of the furnishings stayed with the house as links to the past.

The new owners spent eighteen months restoring their home and won the Most Important Historic Property Award for 1991 with a nine-color historical color scheme. Ron believes that "A house is meant to be used. We wanted it to be comfortable so people can come and feel as if they can sit down."

The gentleman's parlor was a masculine room enjoyed by Colonel Smith. The round table with faux graining, the rose chair, and the navy velvet rocker are original to the house, as are the curtain rings. The unusual L-shaped bookcase is burled walnut lined with bird's-eye maple. The three American horseracing prints were found at a bookseller's stall along the banks of the Seine in Paris.

Terry and Ron continue the Victorian practice of moving furniture with the seasons. In winter, the seating in the parlor faces the fireplace. In summer, it is moved in front of the fireplace and faces the window so that one can enjoy the outside.

The patented 1924 Hotpoint Automatic Electric stove is the star of the kitchen. Note also the complete set of mixing bowls on the top shelf and the Richards grindstone on the counter, both dating from the early 1900s.

A cousin created the faux-marble fireplace surround in the child's bedroom. The clock, a Jermone double-decker with oak works, belonged to Terry's father. Ron's father made the cradle. As a child, Terry wore the blue jacket that's on the doll. The little boy's and girl's shoes and the buttonhook were found under the floor of a house Ron and Terry were helping a friend dismantle.

130 West End Boulevard. Henry Poindexter, a prominent Winston-Salem merchant, built this haughty Queen Anne in 1892. The house remained in the family until the last of his ten children died in 1976. They all remained single, because their father said that if they married, they would not inherit the family wealth. In 1977, the house was sold to an insurance company that wanted the land, but not the house. The company gave the house to the Crystal Towers Neighborhood Association, which incorporated so the gift would be a tax write-off.

The association asked for proposals so they could give the house away. Michael and Penny Hazen won, moved the house three blocks away, and moved in in 1978. It took a year of red tape to get loans released so they could put in heat and electricity and start to renovate.

The Historical Properties Commission in Raleigh did a paint analysis to determine the original colors. The Hazens matched them by computer, using Munsell color chips, and painted the house in 1990. The yellow, dark green, gray-green, and red are brighter than the Hazens anticipated, and the neighbors either hate it or love it. We think that if Poindexter could have seen it glistening in the spring rain as this photo captures it, he might be pleased enough to let his children get married.

225 West End Boulevard. The original owner of this 1895 Stick-style home ran a hardware store and sold figs from the trees to pay his yearly taxes. The trees still bear fruit.

Mary Ann Zotto, the present owner, bought a house that had been brought back to life after it had been condemned. Mary Ann is a painter (canvases, not houses) who grew up in Texas, Antigua, and Mexico, so her house, artwork, clothing, and garden show the influence of a tropical palette. When this photograph was taken, there were only seven colors. By the winter of 1992, there were fifteen. Yellow, yellow orange, orange, red orange, Nile green, and others were added to different shades of plum, raspberry, periwinkle, blue, teal, and pink. Three more colors are planned for spring 1993.

Mary Ann explained, "In my artwork, if I put a color on a canvas, I have a little personal rule that although I may reduce it, I cannot totally eliminate it. So each succeeding color must take into consideration all the previous colors chosen. This allows some pleasing although unlikely combinations that you might not consider if you just sat down to select them to look good to begin with. I am using this device in my choice of house colors. Just about any hue will work with another one—the challenge is to pay attention to the particular value or tint or saturation of your choices."

SOUTH CAROLINA
CHARLESTON

(Above and overleaf) Saracen Restaurant, 141 East Bay Street. And now for something different. When Michael discovered this gem, he didn't see a Painted Lady, but he did see a polychrome stone sculpture too beautiful not to photograph. Architect A. J. Downing, in his *Treatise on the Theory & Practice of Landscape Gardening,* wrote, "The Saracenic, or Moorish style, rich in fanciful decoration, is striking and picturesque in its detail, and is worthy of the attention of the wealthy amateur."

Tonalities of stone and exquisite design demand further investigation of the extraordinary interior created by the owner Ms. Charlie Farrell. The multicolor interior, in which a stained-glass skylight in a starry sky reigns above filigree-work windows, faux finishes galore, Arabic arches, frescoes, and wonderful woods and stenciling, is also a beautifully executed work of art.

Architect Francis D. Lee designed the Farmers Exchange Bank in 1854 in a mélange of Gothic, Hindu, Moorish, and Persian styles. At the time, this eclectic combination, influenced by England's Brighton Pavilion, was described as Saracen.

After years of being abandoned and surviving the threat of destruction for a parking lot, Saracen is a restaurant in which you can feast on Charlie's fine continental cuisine. Electric lights have been installed above the skylight, since a second story has been installed in the building. Saracen is listed as a National Historical Landmark and is the only building of its kind in the United States.

GEORGIA
NEWNAN

64 College Avenue. John and Binka Bone are commercial pilots with high-tech jobs. They feel that coming home to Newnan and the "high-touch" feeling of their Victorian cottage is truly a step back in time. They also have a Model A Ford for rides in another era.

Inspired by the restoration of Newnan's magnificent Parrot-Camp-Soucy Home, which appeared in *Daughters of Painted Ladies*, the Bones decided to gussy up their 1893 Queen Anne. They worked with interior decorator Don Walls to plan the exterior color scheme.

While taking into account the interior colors and the jewel-toned windows, Walls "felt that the deep red would say to everyone what the people were about. The house sits close to the street, and I felt that the body should be rich but deep to help make the house recede where a lighter body would allow it to come forward visibly too much. Also, the darker color would show less dirt and keep this pristine appearance more easily. The color scheme is sensitive to the Victorian period but compatible with the current owners for the 1990s."

The Bones affectionately refer to their home, which is in Historic Newnan and on the National Register, as "The Money Trap."

SWAINSBORO

Coleman House B&B, 323 North Main Street. The Coleman House, a Queen Anne and the largest house in Emanuel County, was built in 1890 by James Amascus "Tobe" Coleman, who served in the Civil War. "Tobe" became a merchant and the first president of the Citizen's Bank of Swainsboro.

When Ron and Karen Horvath took over, major renovation and restoration were needed. Fifteen period bathrooms had to be installed. Every single finish board in the 10,000-square-foot house had to be stripped of modern, nonhistorical plaster and varnish. The ninety-eight windows had to be removed and recorded. The 2,000-square-foot piazza with its five hundred spindles had to be restored. In 1991, the house, a model of loving attention to detail, was nominated for an award from the Georgia Trust for Historic Preservation.

Nine historically authentic colors had to be carefully applied to the exterior, but there were neighborhood residents who didn't forgive Ron for the colors.

The mahogany chairs in the parlor are Eastlake. The 1860 settee still has its original silk upholstery. The 1890 pump organ is played at parties. The house has eleven original fireplaces with bric-a-brac overmantels and beveled glass mirrors. In the dining room, the mantel displays part of Ron's clock collection. That's an 1830 Vienna Regulator over the settee. Kevin Wynott makes the silk Victorian floral arrangements to order.

Karen Horvath enjoys sharing her quilt collection with guests. This relatively new quilt, a Star variation, is on a bed from the Coleman family found at an auction. The clocks are miniature Vienna Regulators. The Standing Rembrandt–baselamp has a shade handmade with antique laces by a friend in Fort Lauderdale. The Art Nouveau crystal shades on the far side of the bed are signed by Quiselle, a craftsman in the Tiffany glass workshop. The trunk, with "J. C. Coleman" stenciled on the side, was found at a yard sale.

A conversation corner in the hallway shows off the wonderful woodwork in the house and two early-1900s French bordello chairs from Louisiana. The clock is eight feet tall, one of the tallest Vienna Regulators ever made. On the marble table is a turn-of-the-century banquet lamp and a rare small blue German perfume lamp inlaid in silver, with a ball that heats the perfume to scent the room.

Karen Horvath hung five rooms with Bradbury & Bradbury wallpapers. The view of the entryway emphasizes the original intricate wooden room divider with Moorish symbols. The spools on the divider had been whittled and then screwed together. Since Mr. Coleman owned a sawmill, all but four of the rooms are made of tongue-and-groove boards. The house is made entirely of heart pine. Each room on the first floor has a decorative corner transom and baseboard blocks with a wheat motif. A Princess Di doll greets visitors, lit by a 1910 lamp with a reverse-painted shade.

208 Adams Street. In 1820, Thomas Whaley built a small two-over-two (two rooms over two rooms) home which was purchased by Reverend Edmund M. Pendleton in 1853. After a few changes, Richard A. Graves purchased the place in 1880. The family owned it until 1983, and as Nancy Stevens explained, "Every time a Sears Roebuck catalog came out, they added a room." When Nancy bought it, the house had been vacant for fifteen years. Friends told her that she should immediately buy a hardware store and marry a carpenter. Instead, her first chore was to evict the inhabitants: ticks, lizards, king snakes, wasps, and "dirt dobbers." She immediately got Rocky Mountain spotted fever. There are still a few lizards, and she lets the snakes have the right of way when they slither in front of the lawn mower. In restoring the house, she found Dr. Pendleton's letters from 1834 to the middle of the Civil War behind the walls. Tom Roberts, her Ace Hardware Man, was wonderfully helpful in identifying what-cha-ma-callits and thing-a-ma-jigs and showing her how to use them.

When it came time to paint, he helped mix colors to order. It took many gallons to test, but only five for the siding—and forty for the primer. "A friend of mine had volunteered to help paint the primer," Nancy recalled. "He said it would be real easy. You'd open the can, set it on the ground within ten feet of the house, and stand back. The house would suck it up itself."

The colors are close to the original ones. "Apparently, my ghost is guiding me," Nancy says. In some of the interior rooms, when she began to scrape, she discovered the colors that she chose are those that were used in the first place. And this is what happened on the exterior as well.

SAVANNAH

211 East Bolton Street. The Victorian section of Savannah is on the upswing, with many potentially beautiful derelicts being purchased and restored. This lovely 1898 Queen Anne, twin to a house across the street that burned down, is a kit house, similar to one that appeared in *American Home Builders Catalog,* which offered houses shipped by rail from New England.

It was badly vandalized when Larry Paquin and George Holitik II bought it, and they are proud of the work they've done. George studied historic preservation at the Savannah College of Art and Design. Both spent time in the Bay Area and were inspired by the architecture and the colors, and both are interested in art and interior design. They feel restoring their home is like painting the Golden Gate Bridge—once you finish one end of it, you have to start painting the other end again.

The enclosed second-floor porch, which made Larry laugh when he first saw it, is now an orchid conservatory. Reed green, almond, Yosemite blue and Navarro red, with butterscotch yellow, brighten the façade. Even the new picket fence was done in four colors by the owners, who say, "We learned that it's amazing the contortions the body can get into trying to reach odd spots. I even used a lineman's pole-climbing belt to keep me from falling." Their advice: "Take your time and don't rush."

(Opposite and left) The Gingerbread Mansion, 1921 Bull Street. This Steamboat dreamboat Gothic, built in 1899 by merchant Cord Asendorf, was one of our favorites in *Daughters of Painted Ladies.* We told the story of how Mr. Asendorf's daughter protested the creamy tricolor coat the new owners had dressed the house in—insisting that the house "had always been white," and forgetting that photographs taken at the turn of the century show a polychrome paint job. Jan Galloway spent the summers of 1989 and 1990 adorning the house with eleven colors that carried the interior theme of greens, mauves, and burgundies outdoors. She chose the colors from the tile work in the fireplace surrounds. This new scheme is closer in its shadings of lights and darks to the original than the creamy one in *Daughters.* The Galloways offer home tours; The Gingerbread Mansion is a popular choice for weddings and parties.

FLORIDA
KEY WEST

First Union National Bank of Florida, 422 Front Street. Key West dances to a different beat, mixing Old Havana with New England, and painting in hot-weather Caribbean pastels. This unique multicolor brick building, built in 1891 and still used as a bank, could easily be in the Piazza San Marco. The Doge's Palace has a similar balcony. It took five years to hand-carve the mahogany balcony, which was made in Cuba. Inside, the teller windows are of rod iron, and the original ledgers from 1891 are on display. John Ruskin made this style fashionable in the 1890s and labeled it Venetian Gothic. Detractors call it "streaky bacon."

Colours Key West, 410 Fleming Street. Built in 1887 by Francisco Marlo, a prominent cigarmaker, this Caribbean "conch" home recalls the charm of yesteryear with fourteen-foot ceilings, chandeliers, polished wood floors, and graceful verandahs. The town advisory board raised its eyebrows when James Remes added peach to his yellow-and-white scheme, but he convinced them that this was historically appropriate for the architecture. After eight years of hard work, James advises restorers to have plenty of funds and remember that cheap paints always fail.

Discovered in 1513 by Spanish Explorer Juan Ponce de León, *Florida* means "land of flowers." The tropical garden at Colours Key West, an "adult liberal" guest house, includes an aviary of Australian finches.

1400 Duvall. Key West is the end of the road, the tip of America. The Southernmost House in the Continental United States is also called *Casa Caya Hueso* ("Key West House"). It was built by Judge Vining Harris, who was married to Florida Curry, daughter of Florida's first millionaire, who salvaged reef-wrecked ships. Constructed over four years, from 1896 to 1900, the house cost the princely sum of $240,000.

Hilario Ramos, Sr., restored the house to its original opulence as a residence in 1952, and his son, former State Representative Hilario Ramos, Jr., is responsible for introducing the Old Island Restoration Bill, which was adopted in 1963. Mr. Ramos's daughter, Matilde Generosa Ramos, saved the house when hotel developers threatened it with demolition. She remains vigilant, preserving it for the future.

For many, the island represents the dream of romance, the beauty of nature, the "last resort." This shot of continental America's Southernmost House could not have been taken without Doug Keister's tripod ladder. The pinks, greens, and palm trees add up to a quintessential Florida Painted Lady.

PENSACOLA

Pensacola Steamship Association, 101 South Alcaniz Street. Here on North Hill in Pensacola in 1781, the Spanish army under General Bernardo de Galvez defeated the English at Fort George and helped turn the tide of the American Revolution. Pensacola is known as the city of Five Flags because it's been governed by Spain, France, England, the Confederacy, and the United States.

This sedate little 1890 Queen Anne cottage with Gothic trim fits well with nearby Historic Pensacola Village, a popular tourist destination, which is helping to oversee the documentation and oral history of the West End Hill Property Owners' Association, funded by a state grant. Façade repairs were made, and authentic colors painted on, in 1976, before the building was taken over by the Pensacola Steamship Association.

811 North Spring Street. At the turn of the century, prominent Pensacolans built their houses on North Hill in a variety of styles ranging from Neoclassical to Spanish Revival. This stately 1902 Queen Anne is one of them. Today, the district is listed on the National Register of Historic Places, and North Hill is becoming a showplace for restoration and preservation.

The Leopold Mayer family, who built this house, lived in it until 1975. John and Marcia Priller, who own it now, worked with Classic Strokes painters to determine the five colors, which the Prillers found on the firehouse in *The Painted Ladies Revisited.* Now the Architectural Review Board recommends that others choose five coordinating colors similar to those chosen by the Prillers.

ALABAMA
MOBILE

Mauvilla Mansion, 1306 Dauphin Street. Spaniards founded a colony in Mobile in 1599, and the French celebrated their first Mardi Gras here in 1702, when Louis XIV thoughtfully sent a boatload of brides to the lonely young men garrisoned here. In 1763, the Union Jack was raised over the Fort, and then Mobile was sold to the United States as part of the Louisiana Purchase. It remains a lovely city of broad, quiet streets shaded with magnolias and live oaks.

Behind the demure façade of this 1871 Stick Italianate, once the Mauvilla Boardinghouse, lurks a potpourri of style and extravagance. The place was built by sheriff/banker Duncan Parker. It was originally painted rust, blue, and white with colored tiles but was whited out in the 1890s. The only Canary Islands palm in the city was planted in the front yard in 1910.

George Daniels, a Michigan professor of history, decided he had to move to the Gulf Coast. On a visit in 1979, he and his wife stepped inside the vacant, silently pleading house. Sheila said, "This is it!," and they moved in.

After making it livable, the Daniels painted it, as the Mauvilla Boardinghouse should be, mauve, with lavender, eggplant, white, and gray. At the time, the director of the Historic Commission wanted it stained in earth tones. There's a new commission, and several neighbors in the Dauphin Historic District have painted their homes to complement the Daniels' home.

Sheila's collections fill their home with an eclectic clutter that is Victorian in spirit. George explained that it's "a happy blend of things we like that look nice together. Unpredictability and the warmth of the colors provide the only continuity."

Frolicking cherubs and white billowing clouds welcome visitors to the Mauvilla Mansion. The ceiling and walls were designed and painted by Baltimore artist Christopher Winslow. The hallway features twins guarding a French curio cabinet filled with art glass and other treasures.

The hallway opens onto the green living room, an eclectic combination of French and Oriental furnishings that is Art Nouveau in feeling. Note the mid-nineteenth-century French screen and armoire and several Japanese and Chinese pieces of the same period. The theme of the room, lilies and lily pads, is echoed in the ceiling, painted by Christopher Winslow.

Mr. Oso, a black bear on rollerskates, is the butler of the house. In the background is an iron and marble dining table and French chairs acquired in Chicago. On one wall is an ornate 1850s gilded pier mirror with matching valances from a Mobile home. On the other wall are mirrored shelves holding art glass and oil paintings. The walls are hand-painted—Christopher Winslow's conception of golden palm trees, inspired by a room at the Villa Viscaya, a famous Florida mansion.

Everything in the "ladies parlor" celebrates the feminine, from the statues and a set of Gibsons on one wall to a pair of Victorian birds, discovered as a window display in Paducah, Kentucky, guarding their eggs. The collection of bronze and marble statues in the background are personal favorites, as are the Art Nouveau lamp and the 1850s bronze andirons.

In addition to housing Sheila's collection of nine hundred beaded bags, the guest room features a collection of antique bridal bouquets and Victorian nosegays. George custom-designed and constructed the bed himself. Unique wicker pieces include an Eiffel Tower lamp, a three-piece parlor set, a chaise longue, and a Victorian rocker.

VICKSBURG

(Opposite) In the serene parlor looking toward the dining room, guests are greeted by a pair of Mr. and Mrs. chairs from 1860; an 1860s Victorian clock and lamp; an 1840 marble-topped table; and a Dresden family picture. In the dining room, you can see an 1830 cherry table from Kentucky, an original gasolier chandelier, and an original fireplace and pier glass. There's an 1851 tree-of-life candelabra, and the Dresden china is a family heirloom. The Mona Lisa is an early British print.

The plasterwork on the ceiling was done by Bavarian artisans who came to the area in the 1850s. The grapeleaf pattern in the dining room is remarkable, and the carved cypress-wood molding around the windows and in the doorway is the only one of its kind in Vicksburg.

MISSISSIPPI
VICKSBURG

Belle of the Bends B&B, 508 Klein. The Klein's Landing section of Vicksburg was a boat-docking spot, and John A. Klein built four family homes on the land. He sold his first lot to someone outside the family in 1875; ice man Murray M. Smith and his wife, Kate, built this Italianate in 1876.

Later, the Yazoo River changed course, leaving the area high and dry. In 1903, the government rechanneled the river, and the lead boat in the opening celebration was the *Belle of the Bends*, which sank and was raised, sank, and was raised again. The captain of the *Belle of the Bends* was Jo Pratt's grandfather.

Jo and her husband, Wally Pratt, bought the Smith house, which had always been a single-family home, so it's better preserved than any in Vicksburg, with its mantels, fireplaces, and chandeliers intact. But renovation and restoration, including the final color work, continue. Robert Lee Tolliver (on the left) and Percy Shorter were just putting the finishing touches on the inviting doorway when we drove up.

Jo has used color on her rental homes. Over the last ten years, she has noticed an evolution from all white to two colors, and then to three colors. She chose basic colors of teal, persimmony rust, and beige to enhance the architecture.

NATCHEZ

708 North Union. Inspired by an article in *Victorian Homes* magazine, David and Julie Timm decided to revitalize their yellowing 1890 Queen Anne. Architect John Waycaster helped with the color design of yellow, brown, mauve, Natchez green, light blue-green, and white.

At one time, an "initiation" of first-graders consisted of running from the school next door to touch the house, because it is haunted. Ghosts still live in the house, but they haven't disturbed the Timms. Neighbors love the house, which is now a bright spot in this part of town. In 1835, a novelist wrote about Natchez plantation life, "The peculiarity of the dwellings of planters is evinced in hiding the prettiest cottage imaginable under the wild, gnarled limbs of forest trees, fringed with long black moss." He would surely approve of the greenery framing this house.

LOUISIANA
NEW ORLEANS

Casa de Felicidad, 716 Dumaine Street. "It has much the look of a stranger, with its high rooms and long dormered windows, its shingles and its planks crowded in among the rank of neighbors all of brick and tall enough to look down upon its insignificance," noted the *Daily Picayune* on September 9, 1874, in an article about this simple, sunny 1871 shotgun cottage. The *Picayune* went on to describe its two octoroon owners, François Lacroix and Cordeviolle: "Cordeviolle was a very flashy, elegant-looking fellow, a duelist and a 'blood' of the first water. Lacroix was more staid in his demeanor, but an artist, a maker of coats that passed muster before the severest tribunals of Europe, of trousers that made the dandies of Rotton Row or the *Champs Elysées* groan with envy. They were models of style, the expression of the esthetics of dress." Lacroix and Cordeviolle would feel right at home in their little cottage and at ease in the cozy garden behind it.

The shady garden and its gurgling fountain provide an oasis amid the heat and bustle of the French Quarter. The brick and stone create an aura of cool tranquility.

926 St. Peter Street. This enchanting shotgun cottage was set on one of the original 100 squares laid out between 1718 and 1822 to form the settlement of New Orleans, now known as the Vieux Carré or French Quarter. Smokey gray, ivory, and pigeon blood make this 1855–1860 home the quintessential Vieux Carré Creole cottage.

Living in a Victorian enables Barbara and Don Rusina to find comfort, to feel pride and a sense of accomplishment, and to know first hand how the past affects the present. They put a great deal of time, money, and energy into restoring their home and are concerned that some preservation societies hinder rather than help. Barbara feels that people don't always know the difference between renovation and remodeling, and that if more people would spread the word that money can be saved on taxes through restoration, more Victorians would be saved.

2034 Burgundy near Frenchman. The Count de Marigny, once the richest man in America, owned a large plantation, or faubourg, just outside the Vieux Carré. He subdivided his land into small lots and planned to duplicate the Champs Elysées in another part of town, the Elysian Fields. Thus the small Faubourg Marigny became the first suburb of New Orleans. This single shotgun cottage was built in the 1870s on what had once been the garden of a Creole house. When Jean Stastny and Mitchell Osborne bought it in 1975, they were urban pioneers in a downtrodden neighborhood, but they liked being close to the Quarter.

The house took ten years to clean up, restore, and remodel, and in 1985, after testing dozens of combinations, they painted the building in seven colors of rose, pink, blue, and gray. The unusual tulip design on the brackets was restored and emphasized. Two other buildings in town have copied the scheme.

Inside, the original marble mantel had been painted pink (the previous owner was a shrimper). The original lighting fixture of copper-coated brass, the moldings, and the medallions were intact but needed work. To make the house more livable, they broke down the walls between the first two rooms to make one big one, and put the kitchen in the next room and the bedroom in back. To help make New Orleans summers bearable, they built an L-shaped four by thirty-seven-foot-long lap pool along the side of the house.

The collections in the front room give the eclectic interior an air of Victorian profusion. The picture over the mantel is a poster from Mitchell's first book, *New Orleans, the Passing Parade*. (He is a photographer, and his second book is *Mardi Gras: A Celebration*.) Mitchell and Jean found the organ at an auction in Ohio for seventy dollars. The barber chair is a gussied-up antique, and the decanter on the coffee table is from Jean's great-grandfather's distillery, which was sold just before Prohibition to the company that makes Four Roses whiskey.

2016–2020 Burgundy. This fabulous find is the oldest Painted Lady that we know of, yet one of the most cheerful. Historically accurate colors were used on this vibrant New Orleans treasure, built in 1836 by Asher Moses Nathan, a Jewish merchant from Amsterdam. The house is transitional, from Creole cottage to Greek Revival, so the architectural details are Greek Revival and the floor plan is French, with no hallway. Although there are three doorways, it was a single shotgun cottage until 1890, when it was changed to a double.

When it was bought in 1976 by art specialist Lloyd Sensat and Eugene Cizek, a professor of architecture, the house was in terrible condition. Gene likes to preach urban renewal, so he practiced what he preached. Gene and Lloyd learned that bright Caribbean colors were popular in New Orleans before the arrival of the pale Greek Revival colors, and they used a French red, *gros rouge*, that was very popular in the 1830s. The bright yellow and Creole greenish tan were also popular, as were the indigo-blue shutters, which reflect light on the interior.

Free people of color were not allowed to marry whites at that time, but they could get a contract for cohabitation. Asher Nathan housed his mulatto family here, and the painting in the front parlor is of Nathan and his mulatto son done by Jules Lyon, who was famous here and in Paris. Everything else in the room, including the schoolteacher's desk and the drapery hangings, are from Louisiana except for the Charles X sofa with its mid-nineteenth-century antique silk. The chandelier is French and dates to the eighteenth century. The floors are local red pine. The owner after Nathan was Annette Tronchet, whose uncle was the attorney for Louis XVI of France and completed the Code Napoléon for the emperor.

(*Opposite*) In the bedroom, a Louisiana walnut and peeled-oak rocker, a cypress footstool, and a poplar-top table with stretchers of heart pine and oak legs were all made in Avoyelles Parish in the 1830s. Multicolor woods in furniture were another hallmark of the period. One of the quilts is from Louisiana; the other is from Andrew Jackson's Hermitage in Tennessee. French silk drapes the window and bed. The chandelier is from the Quadroon Ballroom, which is where Nathan and his amour may have met.

Lloyd and Gene are active in preservation and have created a remarkable Education Through Historic Preservation Program, which uses historic landmarks as learning tools for children, up to college level. Every year since 1977, they've had a project that takes place over the school year.

In 1991, they used their own home for a Tennessee Williams festival, in which students touring the house learned about the Faubourg Marigny; the house; the neighborhood; the arts, dress, and decorative arts; how they had evolved historically; and the leading figures during the history of the house. Their annual booklets are available by mail.

634 Louisa Street. This large yet still relatively simple Creole cottage is a little older than most (1890), with a wider, more defined verandah and more room for landscaping. It was built by an old sea captain and is now a private club.

Jackie McPherson chose country club cream, pomegranate red, sea green, and mandarin orange so the house would look warm and inviting amid the greenery. She has restored more than twenty award-winning historical buildings, which satisfies her love for fanciful, beautiful objects and provides a respite from her law practice.

5332–5334 Magazine Street. New Orleans is below sea level, so this home, with its classic New Orleans late-Victorian features, was built in 1903 on raised piers, using native swamp cypress and heart of pine. The house received a new coat of raspberry, teal, Wedgwood blue, pumpkin, and beige in 1991. Lou and Kim Harris consider their home an out-of-town sister to San Francisco's Painted Ladies.

Redoing one room at a time for fourteen years, the Harrises stripped and stained cypress, hung wall coverings, converted gas chandeliers, and did all the tasks necessary to change a good working-class house into one they consider an elegant Victorian lady. Jonathan Wallick Construction, a contractor specializing in period restoration, handled the structural work.

Lou painted the colorful arrays of trim about the friezes as well as the medallions on the ceilings. Kim stripped all the woodwork on the baseboards, the door frames and mantels, and in the circular staircase in the foyer. The Harrises' museum-quality collection of art glass inspired the use of Art Deco wallpapers. Paul Duchscherer of Bradbury & Bradbury was consulted in the selection and placement of their papers, and Denis Gauthier of New Orleans did the work. Joel Dyer did the faux marbling.

In the dining room, "Tiffany Shiffany" wallpaper by Philip Graff complements the Harrises' Art Nouveau furniture and their collection of Art Nouveau and Art Deco glass by Steuben, Daum, and Tiffany. The sideboard is quarter-sawn oak, and the table is nineteenth-century, made in New Orleans. The poster over the fireplace is by Jules Cheret; the portrait of Sarah Bernhardt is a lithograph by Paul Berthon. In the carved Indian shadowbox is a hand-illuminated biblical scene. A Gallé lamp is in the corner, and a La Verre Française lamp is on the server. The epergne is English, by Thomas Webb. Note the highly unusual painted globes and fringed English chandelier.

The Harrises learned how to apply gold leaf while repairing a pier glass and then continued to find new ways to use gold leaf and glossy paint. "A standard joke in this house," Kim noted, "is that there is no past tense of the verb to renovate."

In the front parlor, Lou painted the anaglypta (a kind of Lincrusta) on the walls orange to go with the Bradbury & Bradbury peacock frieze, then painted the ceiling molding in nine colors. The floor-to-ceiling pocket windows are covered with handmade Venetian lace hung from mid-Victorian repoussé brass and fabric cornices. Most of the furniture they found had to be restored.

The chairs are rosewood, Louis XVI Revival, with Italian fabric. The mahogany pedestal with gilt-bronze bust of Ophelia by Aizelin, the slag-glass bronze table lamp on the carved-teak table, and the shaped mahogany pedestal table with marble top are all finds. The gas wall brackets with crystal drops still work. There's a rare mid-1800s tea caddy table, with cannisters for holding tea, in front of the mirror. The nine-foot gold-leaf mirror is Renaissance Revival and was found in four pieces.

New Orleans instrument maker Charles Foster created this gorgeous French double harpsichord, a reproduction of an eighteenth-century harpsichord with three sets of strings. A painting by Watteau was the inspiration for the decoration of the top lid of the instrument.

(*Opposite and left*) 936 Arabella Street. Some call this the "Oh-my-God" house, because that's what people say when they drive by. Other sobriquets include the circus house, the carousel house, the Hansel-and-Gretel house, and "the croquet set." One neighbor said: "I don't need a cup of coffee in the morning anymore. I just open my door and look across the street."

Once a farmhouse for a sheep and goat truck farm on the outskirts of New Orleans, this 1887 Stick structure received a coat of twenty-two colors in 1991. The house has four main colors: sweet orange, blue clay, pagoda blue, and rosewood. The trim colors are rosewood, Prussian green, light Dutch blue, wild carrot, brilliant tangerine, Algerian red, brilliant blue (sign paint), blue-green (sign paint), wild plum, chrome yellow and Bryce blue (sign paint), gold, bright red and maroon (sign paint), process blue, light blue, reflex blue, light gray on the porch deck, and white.

Bryce Reveley, a textile conservator and harpist specializing in medieval and Renaissance music, is a museum curator. She supervised the renovation of the interior, keeping it as authentic as possible. Faux-marble columns, fireplace mantels and surrounds, and door frames add to the cool aura.

630 Pacific. If this alluring 1892 double-shotgun cottage looks familiar, it's because you saw its step-by-step restoration on the *This Old House* television show. Color consultant and interior-design specialist Louis J. Aubert transformed the house from being pale, peeling, and choked in white aluminum siding into one that is delicately graceful and alive. The four lavenders, gray, grape, and plum are authentic to the area. The striped porch, in Autumn Dusk and Melodious Mauve, took a lot of persuading on Louis's part, but is a long-lost New Orleans tradition.

The original owner worked in the South Pacific Railroad complex a block away and paid $1,800 for the house. Algiers Point is a National Register Historic District ninety blocks square that developed as a rail center just across the river from downtown New Orleans and the French Quarter. The area has been described as a nineteenth-century Mississippi River town peeking over the levee at the twentieth century. Owners Elvis and Jean Golden feel that their "challenge is to maintain our incredible small-town pace as we move toward the twenty-first century." To them, "A Victorian gives a sense of place in a very mobile world."

RESERVE

San Francisco Plantation, Highway 44. Built in 1856, this sensational National Historic Landmark is a galleried home that combines Creole style with Steamboat Gothic. It's the most decorative of the Plantation manors, built of plastered brick and topped off with a massive roof. The builder, Edmond Bozonier Marmillion, clung to the old ways for the interior floor plan, preferring Greek Revival style to Creole, while garnishing the outside of his house with copious ornamentation and Gothic Revival windows.

The extraordinary color scheme dates to 1856. The exterior stucco was and is painted in ochre-tinted lime wash, scored with white penciling to simulate stone blocks. The sun sometimes gives this wash a peach tint. The woodwork is light yellow-green with shutters and lattice painted a brilliant cerulean blue like the shutters on Burgundy Street in New Orleans. Star ornaments are picked out in brilliant yellow. There's a slightly darker yellow-green trim as well as grained and varnished doors and brilliant blue blinds encircling the building below the "umbrella roof." Cypress cisterns with fanciful copper roofs provided running water to the end rooms of the house.

The name San Francisco, here, has a French derivation, which is almost a pun. The builder's son, Valsin, lavished money on interior decoration until he found

himself, in the patois of the area, *sans fruscins*, without a penny. A later owner, Achille D. Bougère, corrupted the name to San Francisco in 1879. None of the original furnishings remained by the time the house was given to the public in 1974, so the decision was made to restore the house to its state in the few golden years just before the War Between the States, when the house had been at the height of its splendor.

The Marmillion household inventories noted the location of every piece of furniture each time the family held a significant social event. The restorers therefore knew what furniture they needed and where to put it. The restoration cost two million dollars and was completed in 1977. The house is famous for its fine painted ceilings, executed around 1860, and for the faux marbling and wood graining, now carefully restored.

Both gorgeous drawing rooms are furnished in an open Creole style. The painting and stenciling on walls and doors had been painted over, but the shadow of the original work showed through enough so it could be restored in an identical match. The ceiling frescoes were also covered over, but it was possible to re-create them also. The furniture is richly figured tropical rosewood in the style of John Henry Belter, the renowned New York cabinetmaker known for his technique of laminating rosewood veneers, which were steamed and pressed before being carved into the desired curved surfaces. The downriver parlor, or gentleman's room, in green, damask, and mahogany is impressive. The candelabra is a period piece.

The master bedroom is richly appointed in New Orleans rosewood, English chintz, and "Velvet Brussels" carpeting. Note the rare 1845 closestool, or *pot de chambre*, which contains a water tank and a flushing mechanism in the same case. The mosquito netting has been thrust aside to wait for evening. It is believed that Valsin occupied this room with his wife.

At one time, San Francisco Plantation looked at the Mississippi across an expanse of formal gardens, but time has brought the levee closer to the front door. Frances Parkinson Keyes put a ballroom on the third floor in her novel *Steamboat Gothic*, but this was truly fiction—the ladies couldn't possibly have gotten up the narrow staircase in their hoopskirts.

(*Opposite*) The upriver parlor is noted for the ceiling and frieze of exquisitely painted flowers, birds, jewels, and scrollwork. The blue fireplace is faux marble, and the purple walls are painted their original color. This was the room the ladies preferred. In summer, the furnishings are given "summer dress" to protect the gold leaf and the pale fabrics, with palmetto fronds under grass matting and muslin covering the pictures, chandeliers, and furniture. We shot these pictures the week before the summer dress was to go on (in the hour and a half before the museum opened).

ARKANSAS
LITTLE ROCK

The Hemingway House, 1720 South Arch Street. This distinguished 1896 Queen Anne is located in the Quapaw Quarter, where restoration and preservation are regarded as essential to the revitalization of the city. One of Little Rock's best examples of Queen Anne architecture, The Hemingway House was built for W. E. Hemingway, a justice of the Arkansas Supreme Court, and his wife, Helen, by architect Charles Thompson. Bob Buckter provided a color scheme of gray, white, dark blue, redwood, slate, sky blue, and gold leaf in 1983.

HELENA

The Tappan-Cunningham House, 727 Columbia. Mark Twain once wrote that "Helena occupies one of the prettiest situations on the river." When Ferdinand De Soto crossed the Mississippi in 1541, he found a thriving native culture, with large villages and fleets of 100 canoes in this area, where Crowley's Ridge and the Mississippi almost touch. Helena was also the cradle of delta blues, the music that grew out of rural life along the Mississippi.

In 1892, this Queen Anne, listed on the National Register, a reminder of the Gilded Age in Arkansas, replaced an earlier home destroyed by fire. Major Tappan, a farmer and a Confederate veteran, founded the Tappan Coal Company. His family lived in the house until 1987, and is still in the coal business in the same offices downtown.

Ernest and Cathy Cunningham bought the building in 1987 and painted it with the advice of Little Rock designer Becky Rogers Witsell in 1989. They used brick, pumpkin, gold, gray, cottage red, and green in syncopated rhythm on the exterior. Ernest has been a State Representative for twenty-three years and has served as a Speaker of the House. The Cunninghams have restored two other buildings in town and are active in Helena's exciting and ambitious preservation program. When they painted their home, one seventy-year-old lady said, "You know, it looks like one of those San Francisco houses."

Handford-Terry House, 658 Boswell. In 1888, merchants Charles and James Handford built two mirror-image Queen Annes across the street from each other in the second-oldest town in Arkansas. It's said that the builders went back and forth across the street building them at the same time. Even the mantels and fretwork are identical. The Handford-Terry House, which belonged to Charles Handford, is listed on the National Register.

Owners T. J. and Tommie Hively worked with architect Charles Witsell on the thorough restoration of their home. A period stairway and handrail were installed after this photograph was taken. A red roof has also been put on since, in the replacement of some faulty shingles, the owners found that the original wood shingles or shales had been painted red. Tommie says that to restore a Victorian, you have a lot of patience and be a little crazy.

Becky Rogers Witsell identified and mixed six colors—red, yellow, turquoise, orange, sky blue, and green—that are historically identical to the originals. The Witsells restored their own home, The Hanger House of Little Rock, which appeared in *Daughters of Painted Ladies.*

JONESBORO

The John Vernon Bell Home, 303 West Cherry Avenue. This adorable 1895 Queen Anne, which is on the National Register, is dressed in five historically authentic colors. Carol and Michael Dougan bought the place in 1973. They didn't like the original brown and olive but did want historical colors, so they had a coloring party, and their guests created color schemes on photocopies of the façade with Crayolas that matched historical paints.

They ended up with gold, yellow, terra-cotta, clay, and beige from Roger Moss's *Century of Color.* The horseshoe window on the second story is reminiscent of the house in Bath, New York, and it's possible that this is a catalog house, but no pattern has been found. Carol often tells people that no matter how busy she is, or how many stressful experiences she has taking her away from the house, when she opens the front door and walks into the hall, she feels as if she has pulled a warm blanket around herself.

EUREKA SPRINGS

The Purple House, 17 Benton Street. The Brigadoon of the Ozarks, preserved by neglect, is now on the National Register of Historic Places. Its motto is "moving forward and reaching back," and it's done just that. By beautifying its Victorian homes, restoring its mineral springs, and encouraging fine craftsmen, Eureka Springs has become a popular tourist mecca.

This 1881 Queen Anne cottage is near the healing spring around which Eureka Springs was built. It changed hands every few years, as people came and left the famous spa area, until the last owner's family bought it in the mid-1960s. Bill Taylor painted the house using sound historical principles and the laws of color harmonies he learned at the Dallas Art School. He used three shades of blue-gray, two of rose, two of blue-green, and two of purple. Keeping the same intensity in all nine colors and using colors that are all related make the color scheme work.

Crescent Cottage Inn, 211 Spring Street. Crescent Cottage, an 1881 Queen Anne pink, white, and chocolate confection, was the home of Powell Clayton, the first governor of Arkansas and founder of the Eureka Springs Improvement Company. Former owner Berenice Pereboom, who also restored The Rosalie, a favorite in *Daughters of Painted Ladies*, researched Victorian colors in San Francisco and did the color design in 1977. (The pink, white, and chocolate combination is like that on the Maxwell House in Georgetown, Colorado.) The scheme led to the founding of the Historic District Commission to prevent its ever happening again without permission, since all the other homes in town had been painted in white or earth tones. The increasing value of beautifully painted Victorian B&Bs is making people think twice about what's historical and what isn't.

Ron and Brenda Bell, who frequently greet their guests in Victorian garb, bought the place in 1983, restored it, filled it with their antique furnishings and collectibles, and turned it into a homey Victorian B&B, the third in town. In 1991, there were fifteen. Of the 750 homes in town, 200 of them are used for tourist lodging, and forty-five trolleys carry 400,000 people a year up and down the steep hills in a town that's part Carmel and part Switzerland. The Bells love knowing that they have saved a bit of history to be enjoyed by themselves and others in the future.

Cliff Cottage, 42 Armstrong Street. This frothy blue Eastlake cottage was built in 1890 for Mayor W. H. D. Brown. It was brought in by train and horse and wagon to the site, then enlarged by the enclosing of the back porch. Karen Kinsel, a native of Arkansas, had always wanted to live in Eureka Springs when she grew up. She went to college, studied real estate, and became the first Century 21 broker in Eureka Springs.

Mr. Brown's home had changed hands many times and had been white until the former owners decided to paint it red and white in the 1970s. It became a tourist lodging and a hot-dog stand, and when Karen bought it, the first thing to go was the red-and-white color scheme, inside and out.

Bill Taylor, a mason and landscape architect who used to own 17 Benton, helped with the placement and matching of her colors of four shades of Deep Pool aqua and Chippendale Rose. With small-scale jewels like this, it's no wonder that the town is on the National Register of Historic Places.

The Pearl Tatman House, 256 Spring Street. In 1890, Pearl Tatman, the first woman doctor in Arkansas, built what is one of the most photographed homes in Eureka Springs, a Queen Anne with a Steamboat spirit. Jim and Lucilla Garrett, the former owners, converted the house into tourist lodgings and painted the house in two pinks, two blues, and black, "the first outrageous color scheme in Eureka." Jim and Priscilla Bowie bought the house in 1990 and celebrated by renewing their marriage vows in Victorian costume. Now they rent the house to visitors. When we arrived, they were just finishing restoring the house across the street into suites to be called Miss Priscilla's.

THE MIDWEST

America's heartland encompasses more Painted Ladies than any other section of the book. The Midwest has sixty-three houses in forty-three towns in eleven states.

Generalizing about such a large and varied part of the country, running from Ohio to Oklahoma to Minnesota, is difficult. But two abiding, contradictory images remain etched in the memory. We traveled through endless miles of beautiful, rich farmland and saw what looked like more than enough corn to feed the world.

But scattered through the landscape like almost empty husks are towns that fate has not been kind to. Lack of opportunity has driven young people into the cities, leaving their hometowns with abandoned Victorians, Painted Ladies-in-waiting mutely imploring passersby for help.

At a time when urban problems are worsening, these homes are an inexpensive alternative that presents entrepreneurial opportunities for B&Bs, offices, and restaurants. Sufficient civic passion could transform some of these towns into Victorian retreats like Galena, the Cape May of Illinois.

Waiting to regale you in the Midwest are:

• Sunny O'Neil's Christmas treat in Mount Vernon, Ohio.

• Tusculum Avenue in Cincinnati, one of the most colorful streets in America.

• The cover girl for the 1993 *Painted Ladies Calendar* and the Wing museum in Coldwater, Michigan, a town which, like Grand Rapids, we were not planning to visit until Judy Stull in Howell, Michigan, told us about it.

• Two of the eight homes Wanda Bengoechea moved to the cornfields outside of Champaign, Illinois, to save them from demolition.

• Marshall Segal's remarkable exterior and interior restoration of his home in Chicago.

• Outstanding work by two colorists, James Jereb in Wilmette, Illinois, and James Martin in Lincoln, Nebraska.

And three B&BS:

• The Allyn Mansion Inn in Delavan, Wisconsin.

• Stone Cliff Manor in Dubuque, Iowa.

• The Garth Woodside Mansion in Mark Twain's hometown, Hannibal, Missouri.

For the Midwest, the nineteenth century was the Colonial period. So the area is blessed with a magnificent Victorian heritage as well as fertile farmland. Let us hope that they will both receive the tender loving care they need.

OHIO
CLEVELAND

(Overleaf and right) 3340 Archwood. Real-estate mogul Oscar Kroehle bought and moved the 1870 Italianate Doubleday house "on great greased timbers" in 1901. He got his start as a baker and is known for being the first to sell wrapped bread. Today, after major restoration, his home is on the National Register and is the pride of the Brooklyn Centre Historic District. Note the cast-iron filigree on the panels of the front door. Raymond Benjamin and Frederick Hauret used dollhouse colors of plum, two greens, and rose to create an immensely appealing design.

We found out about this house from one of America's most passionate Victorian buffs, Craig Bobby. Craig is an amateur photographer who since 1987 has taken thirty-five hundred photographs of Victorians in eighty towns in eleven states. He explains that he "has always been an incurable romantic—and these buildings are nearly all that remain of a period often referred to as the 'Romantic Age.' Also, these buildings represent the only time in history that Architecture merged wholly with Art." We have received twenty-five photographs of houses in eight towns from Craig over the years, and he is responsible for the discovery of six of the thirteen houses selected in Ohio. The state should give him a medal, better still, a grant to spend his life documenting the state's Victorians. Now what we need are forty-nine more Craig Bobbys!

LAKEWOOD

The Heckenberg House, 1568 Grace Street between Franklin and Madison. This glorious 1893 Queen Anne is another Craig Bobby discovery. Harvey Heckenberg, secretary-treasurer of the National Carbide Company, which became Union Carbide, built this balloon-construction house out of southern yellow pine for $23,000. His ex-wife lived there until 1960. The house and furniture were then sold for $12,000.

The interior retains its original woodwork, light fixtures, and plumbing, but as owners Jonathan Boylan and Marianne Ludwig explained, "The challenge to us is to be able to continue to maintain it, using the same materials and craftsmanship. Large windows, spacious porches, and beautiful woods spoil a person for more modern construction." They painted their proud grand dame in 1984, working with Jay Gardner of Local Color to choose Grace Rose, putty, brick red, hunter green, and gold. The Heckenberg House is on the National Register.

VERMILION

The Captain Gilchrist Guest House, 5662 Huron Street. Located on the banks of Lake Erie at the foot of the Vermilion River, the "Venice of Northern Ohio" or "Fisherman's Dream" is an increasingly popular tourist town. In the 1860s, the Gilchrists, a shipping and lumber family, moved to Vermilion.

The house, later an inn, was restored, painted, and turned into a B&B by the owners, Dan and Laura Roth of Roth Commercial Art Design. They used peach blossom, white, dark coral American Beauty, light coral, and Tinkerbell blue on the house, and alternated red and yellow with dark green on the carved tulips. They decided on the body color and picked corresponding complementary colors as the painting progressed, "which drove our painters crazy and made for some repainting as we changed our minds upon seeing how the colors worked together. It cost a

little more in paint and time but achieved the results we were after. If we had worked strictly from color samples, we would not have been able to take into consideration the result of shadows on

soffits, etc." The Roths have another Painted Lady two blocks away and find joy in watching a house that has slept quietly for a hundred years suddenly stand out and be noticed.

HUDSON

142 South Main Street. This extraordinary 1880s Gothic Revival, with its pierced bargeboards and romantic octagonal tower, is in a "New England village" founded by Connecticut religious leader

and millionaire David Hudson in 1799. John Brown grew up here, and the town served as a stop on the underground railway. Hudson's concern about preservation dates to 1907, when the town voted to have electrical and telephone wires

installed underground. It was so pretty that millionaire John D. Rockefeller used to have his chauffeur drive him to Hudson from Cleveland just so he could sit on a park bench eating an ice cream cone and listening to the clock-tower chimes on the village green.

When Richard and Amy McCormick moved in, they became part of the preservation program to keep Hudson a "living community." They're slowly restoring the house as well as the property. After having the missing wood trim duplicated and put back, they worked with the projects office of the Cuyahoga County Archives to determine authentic color combinations and decked their home in brown tones: Mojave beige, toffee, ivory, and dark red. Like the lush greenery around it, the colors embrace the house, creating an organic blend of color, setting, and architecture.

119

WADSWORTH

The Ephraim Hunsberger House, 295 College Street. Extensive restoration and repairs have turned a depressing 1883 white elephant into a charming polychrome Queen Anne. Because Mr. Hunsberger was a founder of the first Mennonite college, the house was the scene of Mennonite church services in the mid-nineteenth century.

Elaine Brown worked with her father, a retired decorator, on the interior papering and restoration and the exterior colors. Scars of the original gingerbread were found when the mineral-fiber siding was stripped from the narrow wood-lath siding, so Tom Brown traced it, and a woodworking friend cut the pieces for him on a jigsaw.

The house has been nominated for the National Historic Register, and the City Chamber of Commerce gave the Browns an award for the Best Restoration of 1990. The local newspaper headline read: "Browns' Hard Work Puts Old House 'In The Pink.'"

NEW PHILADELPHIA

422 North Broadway. Merchant S. S. Urfer built this subtle but elegant Queen Anne in 1884. The Gundys bought it in 1989, and since Len Gundy is a third-generation contractor, they worked extra hard on the restoration of their new home.

Len observed that "You cannot duplicate the 'feel' of a Victorian with today's designs and materials. On the Fourth of July, when the front yards of North Broadway fill with families to watch the annual parade, and our front porch is crowded with family and friends, it's like stepping back in time."

Inspiration for the colors came from the Devoe Paint Company's *Exterior Decoration*, published in 1885. Bright beetroot, deep jungle green, king's blue, otter brown, leafy bower, shadowy evergreen, and flat black—all given zest with a splash of gold leaf jewelry—show how bewitching a historically correct Painted Lady can be.

MOUNT VERNON

600 North Main Street. Sunny O'Neil has been well known as an authority on Victorian Christmas traditions since she wrote *The Gift of Christmas Past* in 1980. Her home reflects her continuing research into the Victorian period. Her Second Empire house, built in 1855 for Mark Curtis, is decorated for Christmas all year round. The cherry red bows on the Christmas wreaths bring out the two reds, two blues, white, and black on the handsome façade, even in summer, when that striped awning is needed for shade.

Sunny travels to present workshops on dried-flower arranging and Victorian décor at the Smithsonian. The shop in her home, where she gives tours, displays Christmas decorations as well as dried-flower arrangements and pressed-flower pictures. At the same time, the O'Neils use the house as a home that can be overrun by four grandchildren.

The dining-room wallpaper, light and rosy because the room is dark, is not a historical replica but reminds Sunny of one in the Harriet Beecher Stowe house in Hartford, Connecticut. A silver epergne filled with silk and dried flowers centers a white lace tablecloth over a red cloth. Through the hall door, you can see the front hall and the staircase decorated with a garland of dried flowers.

CINCINNATI

332–338 Tusculum Avenue. This trio of 1886 working-class Stick structures lines one of the most colorful streets in America. In the 1980s, two blocks of homes were scheduled to be torn down to widen Columbia Parkway. Neighborhood residents banded together and went to Washington, D.C., to save the district. The seventeen homes are now on local and National Historic Registers.

All three owners moved in about the same time, had children, tackled the restoration, and decided to paint at about the same time. They all had different ideas, but there were no clashing colors. The Columbia-Tusculum District has become an architectural and artistic point of interest in Cincinnati.

When Terry and Adrienne Cox, the owners of 332 (on the right) moved in in 1987, the neighborhood was depressed. The house had aluminum siding, and there was no porch. They had always wanted a Cape Cod home, so they chose the colors and painted the house themselves in red, white, blue, and gold in the summers of 1990 and 1991.

Pat and Bernie Dwertman of 338 had to rebuild the back porch, too, and did it in redwood with tongue-and-groove flooring and ceiling. They stopped counting an endless stack of receipts at about $15,000 so they could enjoy the porch more. Bernie wanted a real car stopper, and Pat was a little timid at first, but the more color swatches she combed through, the braver she became. She wanted either an orange house or a purple one. But Rick Michilak in 334 chose purple first, so she tested colors and ended up with coral, white, blue-purple, goldenrod, and crocus.

The Michilaks designed their ten-color scheme of lavender, dark purple, teal, mint green, off-white, tan, deep yellow, sky blue, hot pink, and red pink, then painted it themselves over two summers. They recommend hiring professionals to do the work. Ever since a college visit to San Francisco, they had wanted to live in a Painted Lady. To them, a Victorian is more work than a new house, but there's far more personal reward. They love their home; their neighborhood, which is being painted creatively; and the gawkers who drive by on weekends and point.

MOUNT VERNON

(Opposite) The Russell-Cooper House, 115 East Gambier. "Our spirits are tied to America's past, and this is our way of giving something back," innkeeper Tim Tyler explained on earning the 1989 Outstanding Achievement Award from the Association of American Historic Inns.

He and Maureen moved to Mount Vernon, a quintessential small town, in 1987 and spent nine months removing old paint, wallpaper, and "eight layers of linoleum and tar paper." The interior has been restored to its High Victorian elegance and includes original 1829 random-width hardwood floors, five staircases, an embossed tin dining-room ceiling, embossed paper ceilings, Lincrusta dadoes, picture and chair rails, and original Russell-Cooper furnishings from 1750 to 1930.

Surgeon John W. Russell bought the 1829 house, built as a four-room one-and-a-half-story dwelling, in 1854 and left it to his daughter Anna and her husband, Civil War Congressman William C. Cooper, in 1887. By 1895, they had transformed the exterior into an imposing Victorian, adding the round columns with incised decorations, the ornate finials, and the wooden balustrade. A small museum in the hallway pays homage to the Russell-Coopers. The completion of this restoration led directly to the formation of the Knox County Renaissance Foundation, whose purpose is the preservation and development of the area's architectural heritage.

Myra hand-mixed dozens of colors before choosing the final five. The close-ups show the many color swatches the owner went through before painting. The mailbox is all that's left of her last Victorian, a B&B on the other side of town. She was forced out of her home when the two houses on both sides of hers were sold and all five were demolished for a parking lot. Myra sold or gave the hardwood floors, doors, balusters, fireplaces, cabinets, lights, and floorboards to homeowners who would cherish them.

CINCINNATI

(Opposite) 217 Lorraine Avenue. When Myra Griffin moved in in 1986, this high-contrast 1885 Queen Anne was covered with a gray stucco-like substance that allowed the architectural trim to show. She was still painting the porch spindles when this photograph was taken.

Mr. Jergen of Jergen's Hand Cream lived next door and built this and the house next door as wedding presents for his daughters. The neighborhood, the Gaslight Historic District, was built when a tramway began so the rich could live at the top of the hill. The gaslights on the street still work.

2816 North Main Street. Porticoes, porches, and projecting pavilions make this stunning brick Queen Anne home a wonder to behold. It stands on the tallest hill in "Flag City, USA." Charles Henry Bigelow, part owner of a planing mill, built it in 1883, and his family lived here until 1947, when it was sold to Eden Bricker for $18,150. The exquisite interior woodwork, the grand curving butternut staircase with a "pulpit" on the first landing, and the enormous black combination safe at the bottom of the back stairs are still in mint condition.

The house was built when gas was so bountiful there was a gas well on the property. There are seven gas fireplaces (now converted) and a profusion of gas lamps now converted to electricity. The original Oriental brass light in the newel post is a dragon that breathed fire when the gas was lit. Bigelow's son Philip was said to have used the house as part of the underground railroad, and there's still a secret room in the attic.

Eden Bricker was known for his wines and jellies; he also penciled the date on the door to the tool shed every time he mowed the yard or shoveled snow, leaving a strange but interesting record of his life. The Bricker family lived here until 1988, when Ed and Janice Sartore moved in and restored the exterior.

They painted the house in cracker cream, cottage red, village green, and lighter green in 1989, picking out the lovely woodwork, thus highlighting a wonderful study in Victorian architectural excess. The Sartores had lived in a brick ranch house before moving in and Janice wrote, "There is nothing to be compared with living in our present home. With its sound structure, spaciousness, incredible woodwork, floors, and elegance, this grand old home can hardly be compared to the modern homes of today. Our Painted Lady is very precious and irreplaceable to us."

TOLEDO

2109 Scottwood Avenue. Basically Queen Anne in style, the 1902 Arthur Sieben House has a number of touches and details, such as the fanciful twin turrets on the side of the house, which are common in the French Chalet style. The stone porch, with its scrolled wooden arches and carved exterior appliqué, is also notable. Mr. Wachter, the architect of the Toledo Museum of Art, is said to have built this as his residence.

The previous owner had decided that she wanted a Painted Lady after a trip to San Francisco and created an eleven-color scheme with a main color, mouse gray, that matched the stone in the front porch. Cottage red, turquoise, rose pink, bench green, and makeup pink are accent colors. The house appeared on the cover of *Toledo Magazine* and is a proud part of the Old West End Historic District, the largest group of Victorian homes in Ohio. The motto of the homeowners in the area is "Never criticize your neighbor's house, because we love our houses as much as our spouses."

2115 Scottwood Avenue. The solid elements of this doorway look like a house unto themselves. This house, too, is in the twenty-five-block-square Old West End, which Frank Lloyd Wright studied when planning the Oak Park project in Illinois.

Linda Kalzymarek restored her twenty-five-room 1910 Edwardian duplex during a year of hard labor and found a twenty-dollar McKinley gold coin in the joints. Linda restores old homes for a living and knows that restoration must be a labor of love. To her, houses should be happy places—and all of hers have happy colors. She used eleven tones of purple with green and cream on this one. Linda is restoring all ten houses in the 1400 block of Huron Street, and she promises that it will be the most colorful block in Ohio.

409 East Clinton Street. Ed and Judy Stull used turn-of-the-century photographs of their 1895 Queen Anne/Stick home to guide them in their two-year restoration of the exterior, with its delectable curved porch. Paint scrapings determined the original paint colors—Kentucky bluegrass, forest green, sandstone, and cottage red— and the photographs helped with color placement.

This immaculate and impeccably detailed house was purchased from the estate of the Monroe family, the original builders, because the Stulls decided to save it and restore its dignity. They spent eight years working on the interior, doing everything they could themselves. For a while, they lived, slept, and had a baby boy, named Ryan, in one room because the rest of the house had been gutted.

They believe that people who restore Victorians should take their time, work carefully, and know what they're doing before they do it. Ed credits the Painted Ladies books for lending support and encouragement during his work, since they were often shown to skeptical onlookers as testimony for the contrasting yet authentic colors. The "Tinker Toy House" has received local and state preservation awards. Best of all, it's sparked awareness and historical restoration in Howell.

GRAND RAPIDS

303 Madison Avenue Southeast. The restrained feminine color scheme and the exuberant relief decoration over the windows and porch fascia on this 1883 Queen Anne impart the air of a grande dame demurely dressed for church on a sunny Sunday morning. Alexander Kennedy, a lumber and liquor entrepreneur from Canada, made use of the new machine-built gingerbread when he enhanced his home with Ionic columns and a porch railing with gracefully turned balusters. But the highlight is the unusual third-floor dormer with its bright sunburst. Gypsy rose, dark burgundy, dark rose beige, white, pale pink, and pale burgundy illuminate the architecture.

Jaime Becker bought the house in 1976, when she was going to college. The house had been cut into five apartments, and the neighborhood was a ghetto in the making. As time went by, she restored the house bit by bit, founded a business, married, had a child, and the neighborhood developed. Young marrieds moved in and pitched in. Heritage Hill became a federal target area for restoration grants and no- or low-interest loans. Instead of being a target area, Heritage Hill is now a historical district that is a prestigious place to live.

356 Cherry Southeast. This startling Queen Anne, with its double-take sixties trim colors, has witnessed its share of Grand Rapids history. Charles Coit, the first mortgage broker in town, built it in 1885 as a wedding gift for his daughter. She retained her maiden name and founded the Grand Rapids Art Museum and the St. Cecilia Music Society. When she died in 1900, the house was bought by A. P. Johnson Swede, owner of the first newspaper in town, who turned it into a gathering place for movers and shakers until his death in 1960. Twenty years later it was VOV—Vacant, Open, and Vandalized.

The Heritage Hills Foundation, a neighborhood architectural organization, bought the place for $1,000 to stop the house's demolition. They sold it to a couple who did some restoration, as did the next owners. Timothy Dupont-Steindurf painted the striking exterior trim in 1988, and the Buffhams moved in in 1990. Charles Buffham is a music professor, and he presents recitals of chamber music in the famed "Michigan Room," the restored 19-foot by 35-foot living room of cherry woodwork hand-carved with leaves of Michigan trees.

515 Madison Avenue Southeast. Lumber baron A. E. Stockwell built this house in 1882 and then sold it to the Martin family in 1890. They kept it until the 1950s, when the Heritage Hill area fell into the doldrums. The present owners, architect Kim DeStiger and Patricia Gardner, have done extensive work on every surface of the house. One is a fanatic about red and wanted the color scheme to be anchored by a deep, rich, royal red, which was very difficult since most reds on the market are muted or rusty. The inspiration for the exterior colors on this handsome 1882 towered Eastlake shine out from the stained-glass windows in the squared tower. The stained glass saved the day, and new colors and tones were added as the painting progressed.

Kim and Pat didn't know how long and hard the restoration would be, but they're glad they did it. To them, "It's difficult to feel true ownership of a house with such a history of families who lived here. It's more like being the curator of a treasure that you take care of and enjoy till the next person comes to bring the treasure into the future."

The Heritage Hill Historic District, which is on the National Register of Historic Places, is home to more than sixty architectural styles. The Meyer May House, a 1908 Frank Lloyd Wright gem diagonally across the street, was restored at a reputed cost of $6 million.

(Above) 35 Lafayette Northeast. Don and Dan Steenwyk, a father-and-son team of architects, dressed this Mediterranean-style 1890 Italianate with warm Riviera colors. Frederick Immen built his chateau on Lafayette Hill overlooking the city in 1888. The family of actress Elizabeth Wilson lived here from 1910 to 1940, when it was bought for use as a radio station. Wilson is known for playing Dustin Hoffman's mother in *The Graduate*, among numerous other movie, stage, and television roles. She remembers play-acting on the stage in the grand ballroom on the third floor.

The Steenwyks saved the place from being torn down for surface parking in 1971 and have rehabilitated it, so the first floor serves as the architectural office, the second floor as an apartment. See it while you can; the Steenwyks change the color scheme every six years.

131

The Stick Chickering House. 505 Madison Avenue Southeast. The Van Allsburgs, previous owners of the 1882 Stick Chickering House, worked fifteen years on its restoration. They had to remove the chicken wire from the windows, the asbestos shingles from the siding, and the rotted cars from the front yard, as well as the paint from the interior woodwork before they could think of the final exterior dress. Then they chose putty gray for the main body of the house with white to add sparkle. Blue, pink, and green were used to accent the decorative trim, which includes a shield-and-cornucopia frieze on the portico gables.

Liz and Ray Bracken, the present owners, rejoice in their home, which is lined with blond mahogany on the ground floor and still has the original hand-cast-brass window and door hardware.

COLDWATER

Wing Museum, 27 South Jefferson Street. This treasure-filled 1875 Second Empire mansion is a monument to a High Victorian way of life. Jay Chandler built it for his bride to be, Frances Campbell, who was nervous about leaving New York for "the wilderness." The mansion is similar to her home in New York State.

Mrs. Chandler returned east in 1882, and Chandler sold the house to Lucius M. Wing, who gave the place an 1880s flair. It remained in the Wing family until 1974, when the Branch County Historical Society bought it to save it from demolition. Society members have worked to pay for electrical wiring, plumbing, painting, papering, and general restoration of the woodwork, furnishings, and exterior. The showy paint scheme of two greens, dark red, and gold trim is close to the original. Note the solid stone foundation painted to look like separate stones.

The fireplace, a rarity with a warming shelf in the tile surround, welcomes visitors in the front parlor. An 1875 silver bonbon dish, an 1875 silver cofffee pot, and a hand-crocheted doily in pineapple pattern are displayed on the mahogany table. An 1875 French clock, gilded and with beveled glass, rests on the mantel, along with a silver cigar chest. Mr. Wing was proud of the moosehead; the women preferred the Grecian statue standing guard at the foot of the fireplace. The exquisite Regina Style 50 music box, or polyphon, next to the fireplace was purchased by David T. Kiess in 1897. It was originally in a flat square box, but Mr. Kiess had the William Meyers wood-turning cabinet shop of Eden, Ohio, make the golden oak cabinet. This is one of the many objects donated to the museum, although about 80 percent of the furnishings are from the Wing family.

Looking beyond the front parlor into the dining room, you can see some of Lucius Wing's additions: the inch-thick black walnut paneling and a fireplace set in the bay window with two signed Tiffany windows above the fireplace. He bought the 1893 World's Columbian Exposition rug at Marshall Field & Co. A set of Limoges fish plates shares the mantel with a stuffed owl and an English Blue Willow soup tureen.

The ladies' parlor is more informal than the overstuffed gentleman's parlor. The wonderful carved rocker, the folding chair, and the globe are notable. The marble statue is booty from a European jaunt.

Elizabeth Jewell and Thomas Oxenham, members of the Branch County Historical Society, have partially restored the original lower-level kitchen. The lady of the house never went into this real working kitchen. Wooden washtubs and a wringer are built in, with a zinc sink and cistern in the far right corner. The stove is an 1884 Sears & Roebuck cook stove, and the sewing machine is right there so the maid could sew and be warm. The hanging herbs were grown in the garden behind the museum.

The Chinese black-lacquered Eastlake 1875 bedroom suite is the only original Chandler possession left in the house. Mrs. Wing's mink muff, silk parasol with carved-ivory handle, and black silk fan are on the handmade Dresden Plate quilt. The dressing table holds family pictures, hat pins, and mementos. An Egyptian-style rocking chair with a bisque-head doll sits in the corner. The mannequin on the 1875 red velvet Grecian-style chair wears an elegant 1877 French satin party dress. Mr. Wing's gold-tipped cane and beaver hat are on the gentlemen's chest.

208 West Chicago. Fifteen years ago, this glorious 1870s eclectic Italianate was a drab yellow. The builder, Lorenzo Halstead, was a New Yorker who set up a sewing business and also built homes for sale. William Gamble and William Olejniczak are antiques dealers who are restoring the place, while trying not to disturb the friendly ghosts of two children sitting at the top of the maid's stairway.

When the owners visited San Francisco, they saw the cover of *Painted Ladies* and knew exactly what they wanted: bright clear yellow, gleaming white, and brilliant San Francisco winter-sky blue. They didn't know it would take eight months and $8,000 to paint their house, but they restored the cupola and painted in 1988. The result was so striking that the house is the cover girl for the 1993 *Painted Ladies Calendar*.

INDIANA
FORT WAYNE

Stoner's Magic Shop, 207 West Main Street. Balance, harmony, an outstanding use of color, and attention to detail on the 1884 Freistroffer Block show how even a commercial brick building can be an exciting Painted Lady.

FRANKLIN

365 West Jefferson. This rambling 1890 Queen Anne was a surprise Christmas present from Bob to Pam Gibson in 1984. Although the children got chickenpox, the family moved in within the week. They found a damp, empty house, with five big bedrooms and two staircases and hand-carved oak everywhere. The Gibsons are only the third family to live here. The first owner, John VanDiver, was a pipemaker, and his hand-carved pipes are in the town museum. His son was mayor and built the house next door.

In 1985, Pam received a sketch of the house for Christmas. The next year, there was a sketch of the house silk-screened on a T-shirt. The year after, a painting of the house with all of the family in it. Cards and stationery came next.

After arguing over colors for a year and a half, and prepping for a year, the Gibsons painted the house in 1991. They had finger-painted in the paint store for weeks, testing the colors, and finally agreed on mixed-to-order deep rose, teal green, and cream "as long as you never call it a pink house." Since they can't call it pink, the children call it "The Watermelon House."

WABASH

238 North Miami. John L. Tripi, who signs his letters "Yours for Remaining Color Conscious" and bills himself as "The Final Touch" wrote that because of the Painted Ladies, "I have developed a stronger philosophy and sophistication in my work. Colors are meant for human consumption. Let's all collaborate to save American homes from color anemia and destruction."

The colors he prescribed for this 1900 Queen Anne—barn red, drab green, and drab maize— are historically authentic but they spark a strong contrast, and the judicious choice of placement illuminates the sunburst in the tower. Coloradans would understand the desire for striping on the shingles, which highlights their rippled edges. Wabash, on the Wabash River and home of the Cannonball 8 Express, was the first electrically lighted city in the world. The historical district is once again painting and primping.

ILLINOIS
CHAMPAIGN

R.R. 1, Box 233A. Nancy Krueger sent us pictures, inspired others to gussy up, and showed us around Urbana and Champaign. She and her friend, songsmith Tommy Garza, won a Residential Heritage Award for their own home but were still finishing the details when we visited.

"People don't realize this is a hundred-year-old idea," Nancy noted. "This is the way they used to be painted. And believe me, when you're stripping paint and you run across all those colors, you know that you weren't the first one to do it. The Victorian era *is* detail. The people paid so much attention to the details, and they wanted their house to be different from everybody else's."

Since 1976, Nancy's friend Wanda Bengoechea has been saving old houses, moving them to her own lots if she has to, and doing most of the restoration work herself. She fell in love with a 1903 Queen Anne twenty-seven miles away at a garage sale. It was owned by the University of Illinois, but they didn't want to restore it or be landlords. At the last hour, they called her to say they were taking bids for it, but it had to be moved. She bid one dollar on what is called the Hunter-Thurman House and moved it to her ten acres, where there are now eight homes, with perhaps more to come.

Michael Straka, Sr., a banker in tune with preservation, bought the Hunter-Thurman House from Wendy, and he and his wife, Karen, a part-time antiques dealer, turned it into an authentically garbed Victorian princess. They also helped move and restore several of the homes in this enclave. On their trek to forty-seven states, Michael and Doug drove by what looked like enough corn to feed the world, but with the exception of some of the jokes, this is the only corn in the book.

URBANA

602 West Main Street. This house is an example of how ephemeral home ownership can be. Stuart Muir and Julie Kosarin stripped their 1886 Queen Anne of white siding and won a Residential Heritage Award for their five-year interior and exterior restoration—then had to move to Chicago so Stuart could study for an M.B.A. They used white, yellow, crimson, and eight shades of blue to paint the original clapboards and to brighten the sunflowers found on the outside of the house. The hand-painted detail under the stained-glass window next to the porch shows how creative Stuart and Julie were.

R.R. 1, Box 233B. Michael Straka, Jr., moved this classic 1875 Italianate next door when Wendy was in the middle of fixing one house and had two others scheduled—and the previous owner called and said it was now or never. With advice from his mother, Karen Straka, and Wendy, Michael restored the home. Then he painted it in creamy white, pale green, pale blue, and two roses to echo the colors of his favorite tree, a crabapple in bloom.

ALTON

703 Langdon Street. Joe Adamo, the man responsible for putting a beautiful new face on the Lafayette Square neighborhood in St. Louis, helped restore and paint this sweetly colored 1890 Queen Anne. Built by J. Wesley Beall, and lived in by a glassblower named Carhart, the house is now part of the Middletown Historic District, although a historical preservation ordinance was defeated in 1990. Greg Strobile, a commercial photographer, worked with Joe on perfecting the nine colors, which include mauve, raspberry, lavender, cream, two grays, and early mountain blue.

630 Langdon Street. Diagonally across the street from 703, Sharon Krivi and Matt Gill couldn't resist putting makeup on their 1890 Queen Anne. They stripped off the asbestos shingles and then got help from Joe Adamo on the colors. They had four they wanted, and Joe showed them how three more trim colors would bring them all together. Green, dark green, sand, olive, blue, and yellow in historical tones are well balanced.

In 1989, the Gills received a Certificate for Historic Preservation from the mayor and the Historic Preservation Board. But the biggest reward from the house was that it brought them together. A few summers ago, Sharon Krivi and Matt Gill were both in the process of restoring nineteenth-century homes, each slaving away at opposite ends of the same block. They ended up renting Matt's 1853 Italianate and moving into Sharon's Queen Anne—after a romantic Victorian wedding in the garden.

GALENA

The Queen Anne Guest House B&B, 200 Park Avenue. Thousands of years ago, Ice Age glaciers detoured around the northwest corner of Illinois, leaving in their wake an island of rugged hills rising up out of the surrounding prairies. The Indians called this land Sacred Ground. Today, the county is known as the New England of the Midwest, and Galena is known as the "Town That Time Forgot." The old mining boomtown (*galena* is the Latin for lead sulfide) boasts one of the largest collections of Victorians in all styles in the country, many of them on the National Register.

The Queen Anne Guest House was built in 1891 by W. A. Telford for William Ridd, a window-sash and door merchant who loaded his house with fretwork, all of which has been restored. Both innkeepers, Kathleen Martin and Cary Mandelka, fell through the rotted porches during the back-breaking process. Lamenting the loss of the witch's hat, or conical towertop, Kathleen quipped, "If it leaked, they took it off." They plan to put it back. The new fence was finished after this photo was taken.

Kathleen used the color scheme from page 29 of *Daughters of Painted Ladies*, the house in Hudson, Massachusetts. The olive green, harvest gold, terra-cotta, and brick red are subtle, but at first people objected. One woman said, "This is a terrible atrocity. I suppose it's historical." Neighbors protested, but then Kathleen showed the historical committee *Daughters*. Now the book is at city hall, where homeowners can look at it as a reference book.

Kathleen explains that "You feel as if the house needs you, and if you don't do it, it's going to fall down." She also reported that a man down the block wanted to paint his Victorian white—and the neighbors were up in arms!

OAK PARK

537 North Euclid. It could be said that Frank Lloyd Wright owes his fame to Victorians. He was working for a Chicago firm that frowned on outside commissions, and he designed several small "bootleg" Victorians near his home. He was caught and fired. So he opened his own practice, and that's when his Prairie style began to evolve. Oak Park is home to the Frank Lloyd Wright Historic District, surrounding the Wright home and Studio Foundation. The Victorians there are enjoying a renaissance. During the 1970s, about thirty "rehabbers" were the recipients of federal assistance through the Preservation Grant in Aid Program, in which the government matched dollar for dollar the money homeowners spent for restoration.

Ebon E. Roberts designed this "suburban" Queen Anne in 1896 as well as the "sister" house three doors down. They were built for sisters at the same time with

similar designs. *The Guide to the Frank Lloyd Wright and Prairie School Architecture in Oak Park* describes this house as the "beginning" of Prairie architecture. The present owners have restored a badly deteriorated home. They chose the colors

with deliberation, studying reference books including *How to Create Your Own Painted Lady*. The neighbors love the color scheme and think the gable ornamentation is a tremendous enhancement of a once-hidden feature.

CHICAGO

2142 North Sedgwick Street. "The Gingerbread House" is said to have been built by a Mr. Schmidt in 1884, thirteen years after the great Chicago fire destroyed the neighborhood. The house had been split up into two, then into six apartments and was finally restored to its original configuration in 1973 by the prior owner, who also brought in wood paneling and museum-quality stained-glass windows from the southside Chicago houses destroyed during construction of the Dan Ryan Freeway.

In 1978, Dr. Marshall Bruce Segal purchased the house and—before moving in—began a five-year renovation of the interior and construction of a fourth-floor conservatory, hidden from street level, which provides a view from downtown to the lake. A few years later, aided by four-story-high scaffolding and three painters, he completed the exterior painting. At the same time, Wagner & Sons repaired the tin superstructure and the mansard slate roof.

Anyone can paint a bracket or a spindle, but Marshall made each bracket a three-dimensional work of art in varying colors. Notice, too, the five to eight colors on the spindles and the colors on the dentils and cornices above.

A visionary who pays scrupulous attention to details, Marshall took two years to create the amazing color design with colorist Debbie Cole, spending part of the time sitting on the steps across the street inspecting his home through binoculars. Two dormers were painted on the second story—one with blue dominant, the other with green—and were left that way for the winter, so that the colors could be lived with. The following summer, a combination of the two was chosen, and the painting began. The house is basically brick and stone, and the restoration included color work on the porch, the bandboards and window frames, and even the fence in front. Except for the wooden porch, the rest of the exterior painted surfaces are tin.

Twenty-four exterior colors were used, and many of them had three different values. Painting contractor Tripp Sargis executed the job over a nine-month period, with on-site revisions to achieve visual balance. Notice the attention to detail on the friezes, gables, window pilasters, and roofline, as well as the careful work on the tower.

The holes on the bottom of the planter simply resulted in a novel way to apply color. Since the air conditioner is underneath the stairs, openings were cut in the risers and then covered with open iron grilles painted like little tapestries.

Color enhances design on this magical gate.

Marshall describes the central theme of his house as "eclectic whimsy," and that's what greets visitors in the hallway. A chrome car-bumper sculpture of a goat by the noted sculptor John Kearney guards the quarter-sawed oak wainscot paneling from the demolished Crane Mansion and original floor tile. The lion painting is by Jane Moore DeGraff of Chicago; on top of the newel post, the French bronze of a boy carrying a vase, inscribed in French, "The Ancestor", is by Gold Medal Winner August Moreau, and dated 1885.

Modern art and furniture with an Oriental flair feel right at home in the south parlor. The lucite block seen in the foreground was presented to Marshall for First Place in the 1989 Chicago Painted Ladies Contest. Two Victorian tree-arm gas sconces on either side of the black and ivory fireplace have been restored with new gas lines and are original to the house. An antique Chinese rug rests on the rare quarter-sawed hardwood parquet floor, which has many different-colored woods creating an intricate pattern.

The ravishing oval hand-carved, winding, floating walnut stairway with its cherry bannister is crowned by a stained-glass window that probably had the original function of cooling the house. Houses in Savannah, Georgia, with similar openings above the central stairwell have encircling natural gas lines. When gas was burned in the summer, it created an updraft that air-conditioned the house.

These sketches of possible dormer-window color combinations and plans for the newel posts give some idea of how the colors evolved.

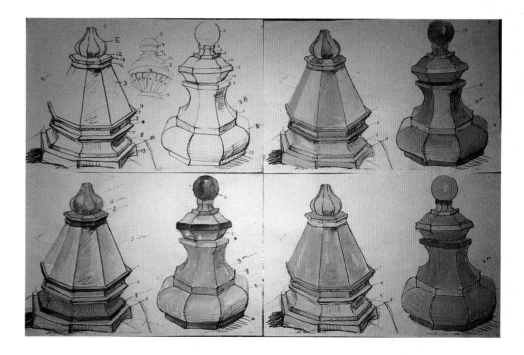

(*Opposite*) The Palladian arches and niches on this astonishing eleven-foot-tall bird's-eye maple chimney breast salvaged from the Crane Mansion hold some of the Segals' favorite pieces. The left vertical panel of the rose marble fireplace was broken, so Marshall researched American marbles and tracked down the Vermont quarry from which the original marble came a century ago to make a perfect match. Note the Lincrusta wallcovering above and the storybook made-to-order stained glass.

A Venetian *millefiori* chandelier, sunny stained glass, and an evocative wall mural make this kitchen an exceedingly cheerful place to start the day. Manuel Valesquez painted the oil-on-canvas Adam and Eve mural over a period of three years, inspired by *The Garden of Eden*, an 1865 painting by Erastus Salisbury Field. The ceramic objects on the kitchen counter are artwork by the Segals' daughters, Mia, Kendra, and Garron.

The formal dining room is lit by a flowery Florentine chandelier and three antique, hand-painted, jeweled stained-glass windows. The oak wainscoting is original to the house, but the bordered parquet floors and the coved ceiling are renovations. The marble dining-room table is set with Faenza Carnation, or Garafino, the oldest pottery pattern in Italy, made from a Chinese design chosen by an Italian princess in the Middle Ages.

WILMETTE

1134 Elmwood. When Eliot and Christine Dugan-Schiff, the owners of this extraordinary 1873 Italianate towered villa, decided to make their home a Painted Lady, they called on a friend of a friend, James Jereb, the leading color designer from Chicago who now lives in Santa Fe. Jereb's work appeared in *Daughters of Painted Ladies*. A dedicated artist who looks at a house as a canvas, James insists on doing a major part of the hands-on painting himself and then, like any artist, signs his work.

The house was built by Horace and Edwin Drury for the Asahel Gage family. The Gage Addition to Wilmette became a popular suburb of Chicago right after the Great Fire, when country living seemed safer.

The multiple shades of turquoise, cream, and crimson on the exterior were inspired by the owner's pride and joy, a dazzling 1920s Deco Chinese rug in the front parlor. Christine Dugan-Schiff is a ceramic artist. Her goal for the front parlor was to create a warm, romantic, modern interpretation of an eclectic Victorian home. She groups her collections of art pottery from 1900 to 1930 as her Victorian grandmother would have grouped family pictures.

A contemporary Australian pot and a freestyle vase created by a friend stand on the early nineteenth-century Japanese lacquered table with mother-of-pearl inlays. Raku vessels, Native American vessels, and contemporary pieces line the marble fireplace mantel. Some of her art pottery collection by Roseville, Van Briggle, and Rookwood is on the server at the right. The pedestal lights are modern, yet have a classical feeling.

ALGONQUIN

302 South Main. Larry and Shirley Ruschke, owners of a clock shop, are familiar with watching the passing of the sands of time, but the couple was honored for recapturing time with the revitalization of their Victorian home.

The three-year project began when a leak in the roof caused damage to an outside wall. As Larry dug down through a hundred years of paint, he discovered the original blue-green, which inspired him to take up the brush. As a certified master clockmaker, he had developed the workmanship necessary to master the process, from duplicating missing spindles to rebuilding the porches.

The Ruschkes bought their home on the 150th anniversary of Algonquin. They believe that it is important to retain some of the town's heritage and keep "Old Town Algonquin" alive. They also observed that "Restoration of a Victorian home is a way of life. It is continuing and never boring. One must think in terms of those who built before us and carefully plan, study, and

implement. There's an old saying: 'A good man always makes a hard job look easy.'"

The Ruschkes won Chicago's Painted Ladies Contest for their area in 1989. Chicago is the only city in the country that has a Painted Ladies Contest, which is

sponsored by the local branch of the National Paint & Coatings Association. (Is there a preservation group or paint store that would sponsor a Painted Ladies Contest in your town? We'd be happy to help judge it.)

216–220 South Main Street. Thom McNamee, a restoration carpenter, was still working on his 1895 commercial German Victorian, cream-brick storefront when we captured these bays. The building was built by L. W. Wenholz, who ran a general store there for many years. The squared bay once had a witch's hat, but it was pulled down after an electrical storm. Replacing it was on a list of to-do projects. McNamee painted in deep lavender, aqua turquoise, and pink. He calls it a candy-cane–gingerbread look for a downtown street.

WISCONSIN
DELAVAN

The Allyn Mansion Inn, 511 East Walworth Avenue. Edward Townsend Mix, Milwaukee's most prominent nineteenth-century architect, designed this Queen Anne/Eastlake house for Yankee settler Alexander Hamilton Allyn in 1885. Schoolteachers-turned-innkeepers Joe Johnson and Ron Markwell brought it back to life with an exhaustive restoration. The creamy brick house was originally, and is now, painted peachy beige and trimmed with forest and light green and cranberry and light red.

The twenty-three-room, National Register home is adorned with the original rich walnut floors and woodwork, stained glass, and nine Italian marble fireplaces. When Ron and Joe moved in, it was an abandoned furniture store. The original architect's plans were found, so the porte cochere on the west side was replaced and the entire front porch was rebuilt. The missing tower over the front entrance is to be their next project.

153

The John Rogers Civil War–era sculpture *My First Love* on the 1891 Sohmer grand piano imbues the main parlor with an air of serenity. The marvelous weblike ceiling design in this room had been painted over. The walnut overmantel Eastlake mirror, original to the house, reflects the eight-foot grandfather's clock. The fireplace is of onyx and Italian marble. The black marble clock on the mantel with an Egyptian motif is flanked by matching black marble garniture and Staffordshire dogs.

The Victorian étagère in the left corner contains part of an extensive collection of Wavecrest boxes. The framed print to the left of the étagère was among the original furnishings of the house. The Gone with the Wind lamp in the bay sits on an elaborately carved marble-top walnut table, and the piano lamp has a rare celluloid-encased feather shade. Broken Arch shades grace the six-arm brass gasolier. The sheet music for "I'll Take You Home Again Kathleen," composed by Thomas Westendorf, a Delavan native, awaits nimble fingers.

A glance at these fabulous rooms makes it quickly apparent why the Wisconsin State Historical Society deems The Allyn Mansion the finest Eastlake interior in the state. The original gasoliers in the reception and morning rooms have rare crown shades made by the Sandwich Glass Company. Except for the Eastlake side chair to the left of the archway, the furniture here is of Civil War vintage. The carpets are antique Chinese orientals, and the wallpaper is from the Metropolitan Museum Collection.

The Italian marble fireplaces in both rooms are incised with intaglio designs of mythological characters and Eastlake carvings applied with gold leaf. The large painting to the right of the morning-room fireplace in the rear is of Esther Allyn Kellogg, the original owner's eldest daughter. Gracing the marble-top Renaissance Revival table behind the Rococo Revival sofa are a lovely fluted cranberry vase, an antique clown bank, a photo album, and a little conceit of which Victorians were quite fond, a cow's hoof inkwell. The coving of the hand-painted ceiling was being restored when we took the photograph.

(*Overleaf, and left and right*) 211 South Third Street. Carol and Keith Tiffany decided to turn their 1900 Queen Anne into a Painted Lady after attending one of the fund-raising slide shows we presented in Wisconsin. They scraped and primed in the summer of 1988 and then saved for two years until they could afford the paint job. By that time, they had changed their minds several times on the color combinations.

Carol worked closely with their patient painter, Merlyn Dahl. The first rose color that she had chosen turned out to be too bright. They toned it down and started again. She came home every day at lunch to check the colors and see how they were harmonizing. Sometimes the contrast wasn't strong enough; sometimes it was too much. She painted eleven spindles on the front porch in different color combinations before she found the one she wanted: three shades of rose, burgundy, gray, and slate blue. Now people stop by just to look and say hello. A summer sunset softly illuminates the striping on the shaped shingles and the details on the porch.

MILWAUKEE

1731 North 32nd Street. Asbestos siding challenged Stewart Dempsey and Gerry Coon when they bought Koenig Schloss at Walnut Hill in 1988. After twenty-five years of deferred maintenance, the roof had leaked so much the gutters were rotted through to the soffits. They repaired the original trim and siding and added subtle new finery in five traditional colors with "inspirational help" from the Painted Ladies books. Stewart and Gerry did all the work themselves and feel that the colors enhance the details that the architect, F. W. Andree, created.

Frederick Koenig's spectacular "farmhouse" was built in 1881. Then it was turned around on its lot in 1887, when the city planned to run a street through the house, and remodeled in 1888. What was originally a late Victorian eclectic design in clapboard and gingerbread was turned into a "modern" mansion with Classical Revival details. Rather than replace the small tower, the architect built a larger frame around the old one. The house is a splendid example of a house-by-catalog, showing the wonders that could be wrought by simply picking decorative and structural elements out of a design book.

FOND DU LAC

The Pink House, 199 East Division Street. This house impelled three different people to send us photographs. The Pink House—in four pinks, green, and white—is a fairy-tale classic framed by summer foliage that brings out the bright green accent color. Rudolph Ebert, a banker and owner of a lumber mill, built his simple Queen Anne in 1892, finishing the still pristine interior in seven kinds of wood.

One of the Dorns' mothers had purchased *Daughters of Painted Ladies* during our visit to Cedarburg and gave it to them as a Christmas present. Franklin and Debbie Dorn had been tearing into the house for twelve and a half years, stripping and repolishing the sumptuous woods and Lincrusta on the inside, stripping the aluminum siding on the outside—even the gorgeous oak door and entrance had been painted white—and decided that color would be the perfect finishing touch. During three months of painting, people would scream, "Stop, it's ugly, stop." But after the Dorns finished the house, it was on the front page of both town papers—and now it's the pride of the town. Debbie recommends patience, endurance, time, and dedication—then you get to live in history.

WAUPACA

315 East Lake Street. San Francisco's Westerfeld Mansion on Alamo Square (we called it the Russian Embassy in *Painted Ladies*) inspired the color scheme of red, black, gray and white with gold leaf on this royal beauty. Cable Shearer, owner of a sawmill, kept his crew working through the depression of 1892 by building his Queen Anne home. He sold it to the Christies in 1907 for $7,000.

When Jennifer Julin's brother gave her *Painted Ladies* as a Christmas gift, she and her husband, Don, had a house in Los Angeles in two shades of blue and white, but they loved the Westerfeld scheme and promised themselves that they would use it one day. Jennifer always dreamed of living in a big Victorian with lots of oddly shaped rooms, "the result of reading Louisa May Alcott and watching movies like *Life With Father*."

They found the house in a *Historic Preservation Newsletter*, an excellent source for Victorian bargains. It was on the National Register; the interior was intact, with all the original woodwork, including the 5,000-square-foot ballroom on the third floor; and the price was $86,000. The original stained-glass window set over the fireplace with the flues running around it was still intact.

They started painting the house themselves in 1987, after mapping out the colors, following photographs of the house from 1900 they had found in the local library for shading. The neighbors saw red. At one point, Don's parents from California made a video of people making videos of their house.

The work took on a life of its own as the Julins painted. Much less red was planned, but the house "asked" for it. When we arrived in 1991, ladders were still up, keeping company with the ladders of neighbors up and down the block who were also painting.

MINNESOTA
ST. PAUL

The James W. Krapfel House, 715 Dayton Avenue. St. Paul's color laureate Neil Heidemann used his artistry so that the five colors on this 1892 Queen Anne would pick out the intriguing patterns in the spindles, the shingles, and the sunburst on the pediment.

The mailman said of the darkest color, which is a shiny, gleaming dark brown, that it reminded him of "a fish just coming out of the water and shining in the sunlight."

The James W. Krapfel house is a catalog house built for $5,000. During the 1960s and 1970s, the neighborhood was so dangerous it was called Blood Alley. A brave decorator bought the house in 1979 and did major restoration and design work. Carolyn McCann and Douglas Fifield purchased the house in 1989 and are continuing the restoration.

Douglas Fifield creates original, one-of-a-kind stained-glass pieces and made new stained-glass windows for the front door to match the exterior colors. More are in the works.

700 East 3rd Street. "I've always liked old houses, but I never imagined that I would live in one," Steve Garetz wrote for a home-tour booklet. "I saw this house and fell in love with it. I registered for the 'house raffle,' and much to my amazement, I won.

"Now the fun began with my contractor. I started dreaming about bathroom tile, obsessing about doorknob choices, agonizing over trim colors. But I was having fun. It was torture, but it was sweet torture. I had a vision of how my house should look, and it was that vision that sustained me through all the difficulties along the way. After all, if the house looks good, it was worth it."

A pattern-book Queen Anne built for $2,500 in 1883, "the Frederick Reinecker House No. 2" was raffled for one dollar as part of a revitalization program targeted at the once-blighted Dayton's Bluff area. Neil Heidemann helped Steve with his choice of blues and grays and highlighted the friezes on the bay window and the bandboard. But this exquisite bracket steals the show, a pendant dangling from the neck of a Painted Lady.

770 East 6th Street. Another home in Dayton's Bluff, which was an Indian area across the river from Minneapolis, is the Michael and Rose Walter House, an Italianate built in 1877 for $2,000. The Walters' daughter lived in the house until the 1960s, when it passed to her niece, who sold it, boarded up and ready for demolition, to Donavan and Amy Hanford Cummings in 1988. They made videos of the home before and after, an excellent supplement to photographs, to show their progress, and they frequently exchanged ideas with neighbors who were doing the same thing. Their advice: "If you love your house, heal it. Just watch out for rusty nails in your feet."

The Cummingses' goal is to make this little jewel box of a house a place the original owners would have liked to live in. Amy Cummings is an artist and she chose six colors for the exterior. She and Donavan discovered during the prep work that three of them—off-white, charcoal, and gray—were the three original colors on the house. The fan and the disks on the pillars are aluminum paint. This is the only porch we've seen with a starry sky.

635 Bates Avenue. In 1886, John Allenson built five Eastlake homes on the block. He wasn't a builder; he kept building houses because he wanted to please his wife. This was the biggest one, but Allenson ended up moving to another part of the city after giving it to his son. Allenson's daughter-in-law Minnie lived there by herself until 1981, when she sold the house to Cliff Carey. By then it had been condemned. In the 1930s, it had been remodeled, and every Victorian detail had been erased. Cliff liked the lot and the second-story porch, but he's a carpenter with, as he admitted, "an overactive imagination."

He wasn't married and found himself helping to salvage other Victorians being torn down so he could restore his home. The pocket doors, moldings, trim, ceilings, everything, had to be put back. A maple veneer had been put over the six-inch fir tongue-and-groove flooring which had to be removed. Cliff plans to grain and stencil so the fir can be seen. As he went through the house he found letters, pen-and-ink drawings, and children's poems and puzzles.

He was married with two and a half children (at this writing), and he was still having fun with the "grunt labor" it takes to do the job right. To Cliff, the most important thing is to be serious and realistic enough to know it's either work or money. He has worked with Neil Heidemann on many projects and with Neil's advice, he picked out all the details on the gables, dentils, brackets, and columns in ravishing color. We couldn't resist these polychrome rings on the finger of a Painted Lady.

IOWA
DUBUQUE

Stone Cliff Manor B&B, 195 17th Street. Located along the bluffs of the Mississippi River, just seventeen miles west of Galena, Illinois, Dubuque is Iowa's oldest city. Once a prosperous lead-mining town and busy port of call during the steamboat era, Dubuque is now discovering a future in its past.

The Stone Cliff Manor B&B, an eclectic Queen Anne built in 1863 by Samuel Root, was bought and "modernized" in 1889 by department-store owner Charles Stampfer. Alice Ersepke restored the home so she could share her love of Victorian country primitives, and her antique doll and toy collections.

The grounds are landscaped in the English style, and the interior of the house also has English detailing in the beams, original lighting fixtures, and massive structural details.

The oak library was used by the gentlemen for socializing and business meetings, so there are old tobacco tins and pipes in evidence. The bookcase and the first-edition memoirs of Ulysses S. Grant came with the house. Alice fell in love with the armor in an antique shop in Galena and traded an old parlor stove for it.

Through the Palladian entryway at the back is the front parlor, where the ladies would sit doing crewelwork near the fireplace, checking through the glass doors on courting couples in the formal parlor. The display table holds hair jewelry and old valentines. The French grape lamp is titled "The Fertility of Man."

163

With a pump organ for duets, the formal parlor is closed except for special occasions, as it would have been a century ago. There's a little plate on the wall that says, "I will honor Christmas and hold it in my heart all year long," so the Christmas tableau is up all year round. The feather tree belonged to Alice's grandmother.

The dining room is constructed with rare African rosewood and boasts a sideboard carved with an English woodcock and has a marble top as well as silver accessories. Note the antique hand-crocheted tablecloth. The 1880 Seth Thomas gongs authoritatively on the hour and the half hour, but the Art Nouveau French bronze clock with enamel face just rings sweetly. Alice's grandmother's best cotton-batting Christmas ornaments hang from the top shelf in the china closet.

The ever-vigilant duck protects the Amish and Mennonite collectibles displayed with old and new cooking utensils, advertising memorabilia, a 1780s grocery cart, a wood cooking stove, and dried herbs, making this summer kitchen a cheery place for breakfast.

890 West Third Street. In 1879, Jacob Rich, editor of a local newspaper and a friend of Abraham Lincoln, built the first house in an area that now consists of several large Victorians. The property was purchased by Rich from the Charles Poor family. The Henkels, the current owners, tell their friends, "The house went from Poor to Rich and with us owning it and having restored it, it has taken us back to Poor."

Ellen Henkel chose the greens, bieges, and burgundy on this handsome Italianate in 1990. The house had been painted in two blues and beige, but the architectural detail hadn't been brought out, so when it came time to repaint, the Henkels decided to celebrate the two hundred ornate brackets with light colors, making them quotation marks that frame the house. "The house was ugly and people thought we were crazy to buy it. Now they see its beauty. In fact, people have asked for the colors so they can use them on their homes and dollhouses." The unity and strength of the brackets supporting the bay window make us want to call them The Three Houseketeers.

OSCEOLA

The Banta House, 222 West McClane. This splendid Queen Anne was the cover illustration on the January 1895 issue of *American Homes, A Journal Devoted to Planning, Building, and Beautifying the Home* (Volume 1, Number 1), the premier issue of George Barber's magazine. It was built by J. V. Banta in 1897, and Joel and Mary Erickson bought it from Banta's daughter in 1983. They've been restoring their National Register home ever since. The Banta House is a mirror image of Barber's floor plan; houses in Johnston and Cortland, New York, and in Mobile, Alabama, followed Barber's floor plan. The gingerbread for the house was shipped in by rail from Knoxville, Tennessee, and W. B. Ballew, a local carpenter, helped build the house and cut and fit the gingerbread. He also signed every piece.

Photographs taken in 1904 suggest the original four-color scheme that Joel, who is a painting contractor, found by scraping: charcoal, medium gray, light gray, and yellow. Mary, a color consultant, chose instead to paint in taupe, dark blue-green, cream, and brick red.

RED OAK

810 Broad Street. This 1890 Queen Anne was built with its own fire extinguishing system hooked up into its cistern. Ann Iverson's grandparents bought the place on January 18, 1919. Hers is the third generation to live here, and it is now in the Heritage Hill Historic District. The paint scheme of cream with rose and blue, applied in 1987, was chosen to match the best stained-glass window in the house. The Iversons painted one side of the house and lived with it almost a year before finishing painting. Some of Ann's daughters' friends call it "The Barbie Doll House." Note the authentic use of awnings during the summer.

610 8th Street. Rich, jewel-like colors make this impressive 1880s Queen Anne, built by druggist A. C. Hinchman, picture-perfect. The previous owners had painted what once looked like a snowball in the colors shown here, said to be the original ones. In a 1909 photograph, the house looks exactly as it does today. The Kramers, the present owners, have discovered four of the original wallpapers in the house. They plan to add a bit more of the terra-cotta to highlight the exterior details. They advise restorers, "Everything takes twice as long and costs twice as much. A sense of humor keeps things in perspective."

528 Oakland Avenue. Council Bluffs is across the Missouri from Omaha. The Plains Indians used to gather here for their annual councils or meetings. At the end of Oakland Avenue is the Lincoln Monument, where Abraham Lincoln stood looking over the river to decide that Council Bluffs would be the eastern terminus of the Union Pacific Railroad.

James and Kayla Duysen chose the two blues, creamy white, and the judicious use of carriage-door red for their 1880s fairy-tale cottage. Then Ray Dewhaele and Jim Yoachem of Picky Painters picked out the details with a watchmaker's eye for precision. The Duysens bought the house in January 1987 and spent the year bringing the house back to the nineteenth century and having their first son. When it came time to paint, they knew they wanted to bring out all the flowers and gingerbread on the house, and they and their neighbors in historical Nob Hill are very pleased with the result.

MISSOURI
ST. LOUIS

1826–1834 Lafayette Street. In 1988, 103 years after this row of Second Empire homes was built, the five families who owned them banded together to restore and paint the exterior. J. H. Keser paid $18,000 to build all five units in 1885. There is only one other set of Victorian row houses in St. Louis today.

The color scheme was the most debated phase of the project. To get ten people to agree was a challenge. They hired Joe Adamo, St. Louis's color laureate, who spent four years on the job. Together, they selected Wedgwood blue, mauve, tulip purple, light gray, gold, and dark gray. The body was painted limestone gray, so it would look like stone, not paint. The color changes from blue to gold, depending on the light.

Adamo's crew fixed and replaced gutters, stucco, and wood ornamentation. They stripped, oiled, and restored the doors. On the roof, Supre Slate was used to replace the broken Vermont slate shingles and was then painted to make a pattern. The façade restoration, roof patchwork, and painting totaled $45,000. The ultimate compliment? A new row of homes has been built near Lafayette Square to look like this row.

The close-up of 1830 Lafayette shows the attention Adamo paid to highlighting the friezes, the bandboard decorations, and the window frames in a subtle but exquisite color scheme that enhances as it unifies.

2344 Whittemore Place. Lafayette Square, thirty acres of homes and buildings clustered around the oldest square west of the Mississippi, was the city's most desirable location in the 1870s. The tornado of 1896 and the opening of two new neighborhoods further out of town led to a rapid decline that lasted until the late 1960s, when houses could be purchased for $15,000. In 1969, the Lafayette Square Restoration Committee sparked an urban renaissance of the enterprising spirit that had flourished when the square was young.

Brown and pink (even if you call it rose) are an unlikely combination of colors. But together with two blues and white, they bring together the lovely, typical St. Louis double doors. The house, the oldest on Whittemore Place, was built for $4,500 in 1875 as a wedding gift from John F. Meyer to his daughter, Mrs. Moses Godlove (even her great-great-granddaughter has no record of her first name). When Nancy Garland, the present and twenty-sixth owner, moved in in 1984, she could see between the bricks in the basement and through the walls on the third floor.

HANNIBAL

(*Above and opposite*) Garth Woodside Mansion Bed and Breakfast Country Inn. These two exterior photographs, taken over a century apart, show how closely the past can be maintained. The exterior, painted in its four original colors, looks remarkably the same. The first shows the magnificent Garth Second Empire mansion shortly after it was built in 1871. Mr. Austin, the Garths' driver, awaits the next jaunt. The children's nanny is on the balcony.

Mark Twain, a longtime friend of the Garths, was a frequent guest when he visited his hometown. John Garth was a playmate remembered lovingly by Twain in his autobiography. The Garth family was in the tobacco business, and Twain learned about cigars with John.

The ten-and-a-half-foot-high Renaissance Revival bed in the John Garth room is fashioned in black walnut and walnut burl. At its foot is a tufted-leather fainting couch. Mark Twain slept in another room in a simpler four-poster button bed with a blanket roll built into one end.

The regal dining room has an eight-leaf black walnut Eastlake dining table with twelve matching chairs. The lighting fixture is a French gasolier. You can see the front parlor through the pocket doors. A seven-piece Eastlake suite in walnut is set off by painted terra-cotta walls with gilt stenciling and a Bradbury & Bradbury frieze. The Italian marble fireplace has a lion's head medallion.

The Garths' furnishings and memorabilia have remained virtually undisturbed, except for some reupholstering, since the mansion was built as a summer home. Many treasures from the days when the mansion was a museum are still on display for guests to enjoy. The doll in her stroller in the family parlor was once played with by a Garth child. The red velvet lounger shows just how comfortable Victorian living can be. Even the antimacassars are original to the house. One of the greatest joys innkeepers Irv and Diane Feinberg find in living here is that they can add to one of the greatest private collections of Victoriana in the Midwest.

GALLATIN

212 West Van Buren. Wealthy teachers, Mr. and Mrs. A. Taylor Ray built this fabulous Queen Anne in 1896 with a family member, George Tuggle, as architect. After the Rays died in 1950, the Tuggle family acquired it. Jane and Billy Due, the third owners, did a great deal of interior and exterior restoration and worked to place the house on the National Register of Historic Places. A 1904 news clipping noted that "Ray and wife are among the best and most hospitable citizens of Gallatin and their palatial home is the scene of many happy gatherings of their friends."

Jane and Billy painted this extraordinary home themselves after purchasing it in 1988. It took seven months and thirty-nine gallons of paint. The house was green and cream in 1988, but despite the wealth of architectural detail—the spindle, pendant, and bentwood ornamentation on the encircling veranda; the jig-sawed floral motifs in the gables; the heavy incised brackets; and the cornice-level moldings enriched with anthemion and acanthus motifs—none of it had been picked out.

Jane chose a blue palette, because blue

was the most expensive pigment at the turn of the century, and she thought that's what the Rays would have used. She reported, "The home is the pride of the community and we feel more like caretakers than owners."

Among the keenest pleasures of doing the Painted Ladies books is finding and giving recognition to hidden beauties like this house. Thanks to the Dues' love and artistry, this is one of the loveliest Ladies in the Midwest.

KANSAS CITY

521 Olive Street. Sun-baked greens and grays with dashes of black, pink, and crimson create a stylish frock for this shingle-and-brick 1888 Queen Anne in the historical Pendleton Heights section of Kansas City. The house had been classified as a dangerous building by the city when Jeff Zillner and Jim Shivers moved in. They lived in one room at a time to avoid debris during rehabilitation—something they do not advise. They think it's amazing what a do-it-yourselfer can accomplish with elbow grease and a saber saw.

NEBRASKA
OMAHA

The Zabriskie House, 3524 Hawthorne. This ravishing beauty is Omaha's pride and joy. Built in 1889 for New York Civil War veteran and Union Pacific General Agent Edgar Zabriskie, the house is one of the two best Eastlake-influenced houses in Omaha and one of the few remaining Queen Anne houses in the city, with intricate spindles and latticework, friezes in the front and east porches, and small carved-wood panels in each of the pediments. It is listed on the National Register.

Edgar, Jr., lived there until he had a stroke while rocking on the porch in 1968. Described as a gentle, lonely man who loved his home, he still treads softly through the halls, rumors say. Jim Bechtel is frequently told by guests at the dining table that there is someone on the porch, but he has doubts. Jim created a summer bouquet of the three dominant shades of pink, lilac, and orchid and added bands of gray, turquoise, and pale yellow cream.

LINCOLN

720 South 16th Street. Denver color consultant James Martin provided the soft yet intricate color design for this lavishly detailed Eastlake Queen Anne, built in 1893 and 1894. With its third-floor ballroom, the C. E. Yates home symbolized the affluence of Lincoln's high society.

At one point, the house belonged to successive sororities at the University of Nebraska. In the 1940s, W. J. Kraller divided the house into ten living units. His niece Theresa Brandt bought it in 1953 and still owns it. The exterior has been restored to its former glory. The interior is still a work in progress. Coincidentally, another Mr. Yates, William, is doing the restoration, papering, and painting.

KANSAS
LAWRENCE

1041 Tennessee between 10th and 11th. The hitching posts used by pioneer physician Frederic Daniels Morse still stand in front of the adorable Queen Anne home he built in 1888. A century later, Marcia Epstein and Kyle Thompson bought the house and decided to use color to call attention to its beauty and the importance of other Victorians in their threatened university neighborhood.

Marcia researched authentic Victorian paint colors, studying the light and dark details of the original paint scheme and what combinations of colors were appropriate with the dominant lavender chosen from the stained glass. Local color consultant Dennis Brown helped select the final fourteen shades, which include seven hues of lavender, pinks, yellows, and blues. At one point, during the tedious prepping and painting process, she rewarded the paint crew with multicolor tie-dyed T-shirts, which they joked about as being less colorful than the house.

Marcia and Kyle worked two years to get the house on the National Register, which was important to them because it helps stabilize the block and protect the neighborhood. (Being listed on the National Register means that the state and city can review and make recommendations on any plans affecting their home or the area surrounding it.)

Marcia says, "A frequent comment from viewers is that ours is their children's favorite house in Lawrence, and that it makes people smile—what a gift!"

701 Louisiana at 7th. During Quantrill's raid, in 1863, three men were shot on the corner of the lot where this imposing Queen Anne stands. Now a garden of Kansas prairie grasses and wildflowers frames the house, which was built for dry-goods merchant George Innes in 1887.

Burdett and Michel Loomis became the fourth owners in 1985. Their first job was to remove the notoriously ugly siding, then twenty coats of old paint. Working with Dennis Brown, they chose two beiges, two greens, cream, rust, and a dash of lavender and painted the carriage house in 1985, the house itself in 1986. They wanted their home to fit into the neighborhood, but they also wanted a scheme that would cause a neighbor, walking by for the 101st time, to say, "I never saw that."

The Loomises have turned their third-floor ballroom into a personal gallery for their contemporary sculpture and paintings. Their work on the house has definitely helped spur others to undertake restoration and paint more imaginatively.

FORT SCOTT

521 Wall Street. The sheet-metal façade on this main-street commercial building, the 1884 Italianate "Key Industries—The Aristocrat of Overalls" Annex, was in terrible condition when the town asked David Irvin, architect, builder, and color designer, to tackle it. Many of the major architectural elements had to be completely restored. Luckily, the W. F. Norman tin ceiling and metal company, which has been making pressed-tin ceilings for more than a century, is nearby.

David Irvin has been responsible for the restoration of most of downtown Fort Scott. The owner had suggested three colors, but somehow, the architectural elements and decorations demanded seven. On this job, David did a lot of the restoration work, working with the local sheet-metal shop, then attaching new tin with screws and pop rivets. He even painted it himself in the winter of 1991.

Fort Scott, established by the U.S. Army in 1842 as part of the "permanent Indian frontier," was one of the biggest and most important cities in Kansas until the early 1900s. Now, with the Fort Scott National Historic Site and the blossoming of its Victorian buildings, it is becoming a popular travel destination.

210 West Oklahoma. This commercial brick building opened in 1893 with a dry-goods store on the ground floor and the offices of the Territorial Secretary upstairs. It has contained a printing shop since 1926. The Historic Preservation Commission approved the colors the owner chose to use after the pressed-metal roof gables had been restored. The ball on the center finial is a bowling ball.

401 East Cleveland Avenue at Ash. On April 22, 1889, thousands of pioneers, merchants, and families in the Oklahoma Land Run joined in giving birth to a new city, the new capital of the state of Oklahoma. Overnight, tents and wagons were transformed into Victorian towers, spindles, and arches. Although the capital was moved, Guthrie, the Victorian "palace on the plains," remained. Today, the population of thirteen thousand has joined in renovating the entire town.

This unusual Queen Anne was designed in 1883 by Joseph Foucart, who designed much of downtown Guthrie. It was built by awning and tentmaker merchant P. J. Heilman, who once made a saddle for Tom Mix and went bankrupt twice in the course of building the house. He wanted the house to be tornado-proof, so the walls are eighteen inches thick. Kimberleigh and Lundon Humber bought the house in 1988 and painted it in 1990 using the Painted Ladies books and Roger Moss's *Victorian Exterior Decoration*. Originally, the trim on the house was red and black, and although they wanted the colors to be Victorian, the Humbers also wanted the house to fit in with the neighborhood. Both the neighbors and the historical society are pleased with the light and dark green and brick red.

EL RENO

The Goff House Inn, 506 South Evans at West Watts. William Goff, a land agent for Anheuser Busch, built this rare Colonial Revival/Queen Anne home for himself in 1900, then added another section in 1910 so the house could be used as a boardinghouse for railroad workers.

Historians from Guthrie did scratch tests to find the original colors, and the lovely springlike design you see—white, yellow, light blue, medium and dark green, and pumpkin—is what they found. Previous owners Ron and Betty Wiewel received an award of excellence from the state for their restoration of the house, which had been empty for eight years and is on the National Register. They explained their need to restore an old house that was both a landmark and an eyesore: "It was like the house was calling out, 'Don't leave me.' This house used to cry, 'Please come help me.'"

THE SOUTHWEST

The Southwest includes two of our favorite places: Colorado and Galveston. A trend-setting state with its share of individualists, Colorado is heaven if you like winter. The crystal-clear air, the natural beauty of the mountains, the inviting valley mining towns with their colorful histories, and the sense of spaciousness sing a siren's song. The state is well represented with houses in eight towns, including Denver with James Martin's controversial dragon house.

Galveston is the Victorian jewel of the Gulf Coast. By calling attention to its fine collection of Victorians, the "Queen City of the Gulf" is creating what we call the Cape May effect. The economically depressed city is in the slow process of transforming itself from a collection of white elephants into a fully restored Victorian town.

With the help of the Galveston Historical Foundation, the downtown Strand area has become a colorfully restored historical district that is a magnet for visitors. The four Galveston houses in the book are all distinctive. We are delighted that an honorable-mention house in *Daughters of Painted Ladies* made the final cut in this book. We hope that this will encourage honorable-mention homeowners in the books to send photos if they repaint their houses.

In Dallas, the Meadows Foundation spent $5 million on an impeccable restoration of a block of Victorians that are now wheelchair-accessible and used as offices by non-profit organizations.

In Austin, the Franklin Savings Association is turning Victorians into branch offices. We certainly hope this becomes a trend.

The Castle in Virginia City, an original vein of Victoriana, is the historical centerpiece of this silver-mining gem in Nevada.

If you don't mind extremes of weather and you like solitude, the Southwest is for you. Although it does contain major cities, it's the ultimate land of wide-open spaces. Even the parched, biblical beauty of Utah makes this part of the country well worth a visit.

TEXAS
DENISON

1200 Morton at Perry. Here's a surprising touch of Mississippi Steamboat in northern Texas. It's the doorway to a stunning Queen Anne built in 1890 by Paul Waples, founder of the Waples Platter Grocery Chain (now the White Swan), when Denison was bigger than Dallas. The wood was imported from Canada, and the Italian marble fireplaces had inlaid murals with portraits of the Waples children in the surrounds.

Walter and Nancy Capehart are in the middle of a complete restoration, which includes removing the aluminum siding. To them, "Owning and renovating this home is something we chose to do to help preserve a part of our past which, once destroyed, can never be replaced. It is our duty to our forefathers, who strived to give us this freedom and beauty. Each time we complete a project, we find great reward in saying, 'OK, we have this back the way it was, the way it should always be.'"

DALLAS

The Wilson House, 2922 Swiss Avenue. In 1889, newlyweds Henrietta and Frederick Wilson bought a large tract of land from Henrietta's aunt and built a beautiful Queen Anne mansion for themselves. Then they built six frame houses on their block to rent to their friends. Their son lived in the Swiss Avenue mansion and continued to rent the other houses on the Wilson block until 1977, when he had to sell because of his health. By then, the Wilson Block was the last vestige of the Victorian era in Dallas and was surrounded by a depressed, decaying neighborhood.

Restoration builder Dave Fox bought the block and worked with the Historic Preservation League, developer Jim Coker, and the Meadows Foundation to restore the Wilson Block as a whole. The goal of the Meadows Foundation's $5-million effort was to put together a community of nonprofit agencies working together, side by side. Together, they created a model preservation miracle.

Each building has been meticulously restored, right down to the original Victorian polychrome exteriors. The Wilson home is a golden yellow with dark green and Rookwood red accents and

black sashes. Historical photographs influenced the design of arbors, fences, and gardens. Replicas of turn-of-the-century streetlights, a gazebo, and a lecture green have been added. Behind each building is a chair lift to make the building wheelchair-accessible.

The award-winning Wilson Block is now the headquarters of the Historic Preservation League and the home of other non-profit agencies and communal amenities

in a safe setting that has inspired urban rehabilitation and economic revitalization. The Meadows Foundation has already started work on bringing faith, hope, and charity to salvaged Victorians across the street on the Beilharz Block. The Meadows Foundation quotes Mother Teresa in their brochure, "There is plenty for all of us to do...I do think that if people were to see, really see when they look, many things could happen."

COLLEYVILLE

5319 Bluebonnet Drive. A merchant named Wofford built this classic Queen Anne in Athens, Texas, in the 1860s, and his children modified it in the 1890s. By the time Donita Wiggins found it in 1987, it was in danger of destruction. She moved it 120 miles in seven stripped-down pieces to its present site next to the Bluebonnet home that appears in *Daughters of Painted Ladies*. Everything had to come off and be numbered before the move. Afterward, it was like putting together a giant puzzle, using the numbers and hundreds of photographs as a key. The roof had been destroyed, so Donita took it back to the original roof line with a widow's walk.

Donita wanted a tranquil house that would harmonize with her own yellow home next door, so she chose sky blue, dark blue, dark red, white, gray, and black for the exterior. She was the general contractor and supervised every aspect of the interior and exterior work, even doing much of the work herself. She painted the details on the gable while it was still on the ground and carved trim to patch trim that needed restoration. The job took eighteen months to complete, but she loved doing it and is deservedly proud of her efforts. Donita feels that saving homes is part of preserving America, and she's planning to move endangered houses to create a new neighborhood.

The Tips House, Franklin Savings Association, 2336 South Congress Avenue at Oltorf. After emigrating from Germany and serving in the Confederate Army, banker and merchant Walter Tips built this handsome Italianate in 1876 on West 7th Street. Presidents William McKinley and Theodore Roosevelt were guests at Tips House, which was built with heart-grain lumber. Most of the hardware and woodwork in the interior is original.

Franklin Savings saved the place from demolition, moving it and restoring it as their South Congress Office. The dark gray with light gray and red trim reflects the original exterior. The painstaking restoration has resulted in the house's designation as a Texas Historical Landmark.

GALVESTON

Jacob Sonnentheil Home, 1826 Sealy. This astonishingly elaborate Carpenter Gothic mansion was built in 1887 for merchant Jacob Sonnentheil after the Sonnentheils' home a block away and the home on this lot burned down in a disastrous fire. Mr. Sonnentheil's fortunes continued to go up and down, and after he died, Theodore Stubbs was able to purchase the house for a silver dollar.

Evidence suggests that the architect-builder was Nicholas Clayton, who is known for building Galveston's famed Bishop's Palace. The two-story galleries are the most noticeable of the exterior features, a striking demonstration of Victorian craftsmanship. The carved heads on the pilasters represent different European nationalities. The Ionic capitals were carved in Italy and shipped over for the builder.

The floor-length windows that open onto the galleries combine with the open-pattern lattices to draw in and circulate cool air through the house, a necessity in Galveston.

The Frederick W. Beissner Home, 1702 Ball. Frederick W. Beissner, a clerk at a cotton brokerage, and his wife, Mary, built their lavishly lacy Queen Anne bouquet in 1887, a year after a fire had destroyed forty blocks on Galveston Island. Builder William H. Roystone, an architectural superintendent and manufacturer of carbon graphic wood tiles (which have a design burnt into them) had worked for Nicholas Clayton. The lavish gingerbread and floral decorations have been brought to life with a deft use of color.

Sunflowers, which also enliven the house in Providence, Rhode Island (see page 29), were extremely popular during the late Victorian era. Oscar Wilde even wore them in his lapel and visited Castle Sunflower on Beacon Hill in Boston, shown in *Daughters of Painted Ladies*. This 1988 paint scheme persuaded the present owner, James Godfrey, to buy this Texas and National Register treasure.

Sweeney-Royston Home, 2402 L Street. James M. Brown, whose home, Ashton Villa, is one of Galveston's most important house museums, built this delightful Queen Anne cottage as a wedding present for his daughter Matilda and businessman Thomas Sweeney in 1885. Matilda's wedding gown is still on view at Ashton Villa. All of the fanciful decorative woodwork on the front porch, purported to have been designed by Nicholas Clayton, was stripped in the hurricane of 1915. But the carved-cypress storm doors still open to reveal equally impressive inner doors, as well as woodwork and wainscoting of walnut, mahogany, long leaf and curly pine.

We photographed the house in different colors for *Daughters of Painted Ladies* (see below), but it ended up as an honorable mention. The owners repainted the house in its original colors. We thought you would like to compare the schemes for yourself.

Reymershoffer Home, 1302 Postoffice Street at 13th. German immigrant Gustav Reymershoffer, whose name is still on the gate, built this Queen Anne in 1886-1887. He and his brother John, who lived next door in a notable Victorian torn down in 1965, ran the Texas Star Flour Mill. One of Gustav's three daughters, Elsa, lived in the house until Mary and LeRoy LeFlore bought it in 1985.

The LeFlores did the five-color scheme in mauve, light blue, teal blue, light green, and white. Mary says she was tired of looking at color schemes that were "chicken." They wanted to capture the architectural details in colors that were bold, but not garish, and they're very pleased with their decision. The LeFlores are members of the Galveston Historical Foundation, which is working to restore the island once called the Wall Street of the Southwest.

COLORADO
DENVER

1542 Williams Street between Colfax and 16th. Lee Reedy bought this outstanding brick Queen Anne in 1984 as the office for his award-winning advertising and graphics firm. He collaborated with his next-door neighbor James Martin of The Color People to create this superb five-color, high-contrast design, the only one like it in Denver. Then Lee and Heather Bartlett painted the lime green, neon purple, and red dragon, which came from China.

James feels that the dragon overwhelms both the architecture and his color scheme. Lee wanted the house to be a reflection of his firm's creativity and attention to detail. When clients visit, they love the charm and craftsmanship of the house and its contrast to their stark modern offices.

This whimsical dragon is in keeping with the Victorian spirit of play and passersby may be drawn to look at the house, which they might not have noticed if the dragon weren't there.

NEW MEXICO
LAS VEGAS

(*Opposite*) 1201 8th Street. Las Vegas sits at the meeting of the Great Plains to the east and the Sangre de Cristo Mountains to the west. The name means "the large meadows." It was on the plaza in Las Vegas that General Stephen W. Kearney claimed the territory for the United States and sparked the Mexican War of 1846-1848. When the Atchison, Topeka, and Santa Fe Railroad hit town in 1879, a Victorian enclave grew up next to Railroad Avenue, not far from the original adobe village.

This 1907 dwelling added Classic Revival columns to a semi–Queen Anne structure. Patty Nelson painted her all-white house six colors in 1990, choosing a warm southwestern look in antelope peach, rust, sea green, white, and gray with black sashes after reading *How to Create Your Own Painted Lady*. She reports that people either love or hate it—but *she's* very happy.

COLORADO
DENVER

The New Terrace, 900-914 East 20th Avenue at Emerson. The New Terrace was originally built as rental units in 1889, when terraces, and the concept of apartment living, were new to Denver. By the 1930s, the dome on this Queen Anne was painted gold. Times changed again and the house was in a transitional neighborhood, and now it's townhouses, but it remains the most eclectic surviving terrace structure in Denver and the most important structure in the San Rafael Historic District.

Architect Chris Craven and artist Ginny Swem did the six-color design and faux finishes on this National Register building in 1989 as a 100th birthday present to the house. Their goal was to give gentle emphasis to the remarkable architectural embellishments on the façade, and yet to tie in elements that could distract from the effect of the whole. The painter, Errol Cerovki, was so pleased with the result that he decided to move in.

The Gebhardt Mansion, 2253 Downing Street. Also in the San Rafael Historic District, the Gebhardt Mansion is one of the finest examples of the Italianate/Second Empire style in Denver. It is said to have been designed by the owner, businessman Henry Gebhardt. Dr. Charles and Kathy Brantigan, the third owners of this brick home, bought it in 1987 and use it as an office. It is also home to the twelve-member Denver Brass (Kathy plays tuba), which practices on the third floor.

When the Brantigans bought the house, the building had been vacant for three years and headed the endangered-species list of the Denver Landmark Commission. They planned a museum-quality restoration, and the red tape and battles with city bureaucrats continue, one city agency arguing with another over which has more authority.

Kathy created the historical color scheme of light green, yellow, and terra-cotta, matching the original colors, and painter David Wallace applied the design after a chemical cleaning of the bricks.

The original light fixtures and shutters remained, and samples of the original wallpapers helped the Brantigans select documented reproductions. They still retain a life-saving sense of humor and see themselves as caretakers, preserving a designated landmark for the next century.

1325 Race Street between 13th and 14th Avenues. Built just before the silver panic of 1893, this imposing 1891 Queen Anne has managed to survive as a single-family dwelling. The house, which cost $10,000 to build on land that cost $3,800, was built in "Wyman's Addition" to Denver, a large tract of farm land. Wyman's Addition is in the process of being designated a historic district. Mr. Hugh Hastings paid $26,500 for it in 1893 and he lived there until 1907, when his fortunes fled. It was sold for ten dollars in 1909. Evan Evans, son of the first governor of Colorado and a member of the family that built the house, lived here from 1914 to 1951.

James Martin of The Color People worked with owners William Kent and Warren Bellows on their choice of seven colors: purple, light and deep turquoise, deep red, sand, beige, and two gold leafs. The owners wanted a "San Francisco–style" home, and James wanted to give it to them while keeping the house from looking like a circus on their conservative street. He used the colors to give the house the grace and balance the architecture lacks. Because of the gilded ornaments, James and the owners call the scheme "Southwest Victorian Egyptian."

(*Opposite*) Original light fixtures and gleaming wood floors and walls illuminate this welcoming hallway with the dining room beyond. A stained-glass mountain and forest scene with a lake and a small waterfall was being designed by San Francisco's Roy Little and James Raidl for the stairway window when this picture was taken.

The 1895 newel-post lamps by August Moreau were installed when electricity arrived. These enlightened ladies from Paris, *Reine de Flots* ("Queen of the Waves") and *Reveil de Mai* ("Spring Awakening"), are still in place. William and Warren feel they are the nurturing guardian spirits of the house.

PIC Technology, 1750 Gilpin Street. James Martin of The Color People used yellow and persimmon as punch colors in a basically gray-green color scheme for this relatively simply designed trim, and the colors sing.

James describes his job as making things work: "It's essential when doing a brick house to use the colors to weave a web that holds the building together. Here we used colors whose values blend with the values of the brick and picked up a touch of the brick with one of the peach colors. The house was all brown when we started. It had always been all brown and no one had ever noticed it. This house has undergone a renaissance. The colors bring it to life and show off the incredible balance and detailing the architect designed into it.

"After years of doing this, we know which white is which. We want the building to make a statement. We address and respect the architecture. We don't just go in there and slap on an inappropriate scheme, and we don't try to make a 'grand' building look cute. I tell clients that they should be outstanding without standing out."

BLACK HAWK

The Lace House Museum, 161 Main Street, off Highway 119. Dripping with trim, The Lace House is one of the purest examples of Carpenter Gothic architecture in America (unless of course, it really is a mocha layer cake in disguise). It was built in 1863 by tollgate keeper Lucien K. Smith for his bride, Mary Germain. Smith followed the dictates—and may even have followed the plans—of A. J. Downing, who said, "Architecture is delightful in itself and valuable to society in proportion to its power of exalting the soul and refining the intellect."

Gold was discovered on May 6, 1859, between Black Hawk and Central City, and the area exploded. The two towns got their patents from the federal government in 1864 and became part of Colorado in 1876, when the territory became a state. The Lace House was restored by the city as part of the state's centennial celebration. Original scrapings were color-matched for the soft cream, beige, and brown scheme. The house is now a museum of daily life in Colorado in the nineteenth century.

GEORGETOWN

The Maxwell House, 409 4th Street. In the late 1850s, a gold rush brought two Kentucky brothers, George and David Griffith, here to seek their fortune. The gold wasn't there, but silver was, and they founded a quickly flourishing town named after brother George. Local magnates and the many professional people who followed to sell their services brought Victorian architecture with them, including an opera house and deluxe hotels. The 1893 silver panic emptied the town until it was "rediscovered" by skiers and preservationists in the late 1950s. The town is now part of a National Historic Landmark District, along with the silver-mining area and the neighboring town of Silver Plume.

In 1867, Virgil and Mania Potter lived in a small cottage and ran the general store. They grubstaked two prospectors who found a rich vein of gold and silver at the Colorado Central Mine, and with their share of the fortune, they built a new front section on their home in 1890. They lost everything in the demonetization of silver in 1893 and had to sell to Frank Maxwell, a young mining engineer from Cornell University who lived in the house until 1943. The Frost family, who still work in mines and metallurgy, have lived there since 1955 and have tried to keep the home as it was in the days of Frank Maxwell.

Their towered 1890 Second Empire Queen Anne has always been painted in three pinks and chocolate brown and is one of Colorado's most famous Victorians. The snowy fretwork and filigree details resemble the icing on a ginger-bread cookie.

The Bowman-White House, 9th and Rose. John Henry Bowman, owner of the American Sisters Mining Company, built his eclectic Gothic Revival/Italianate cottage in 1892, just before the crash. His daughter Mellie married lawyer J. J. White in 1901 and lived in the house until 1968.

The Georgetown Historical Society, a private, nonprofit preservation organization, bought and saved it in 1974 and is in the process of restoring it as a house museum, the second of five in Georgetown. In 1991, the society purchased an extensive collection of original furnishings and personal items, including Mellie's wedding dress and her paintings. The exterior is painted in three historically authentic colors, but chemical analysis of the original colors, thought to be yellow with red and gold trim, was in the works when this picture was taken.

LEADVILLE

The Herald Democrat Newspaper & Museum, 717 Harrison Avenue. At 10,000 feet, Leadville is the highest town in America. The *Herald Democrat*, formed by the merger of four newspapers in 1885, boasts as past owners and publishers such famous historical characters as H. A. W. Tabor (once married to Baby Doe) and Simon Guggenheim. By 1986, the *Herald Democrat* was Colorado's last daily printed on letterpress equipment. This National Register building, which houses the paper and museum, was built in 1895 as a funeral parlor. The delightfully romantic color scheme uses historical colors in a way that would make Molly Brown—another Leadville citizen—smile.

ASPEN

232 East Bleeker Street at Monarch. Bill and Susan Parzybok call their 1882 Queen Anne cottage the "dollhouse" because it's small and cozy. Thick walls on the right side of the house attest to its origin as a miner's log cabin. The left side of the house was added in the early 1900s for Aspen's first kindergarten.

Bill and Susan got married in the little National Register community church two doors down and love the skiing, the music festival, and the area. They narrowed their color choices with swatches and a dozen quarts of paint on the back of the house to come up with two dark greens ("woodland night and green glaze"), "primitive" pink, and "plum prelude" lilac. They may sound like great names for lipstick, but the result is a carefree, happy-go-lucky combination of colors that's perfect for a vacation home.

TELLURIDE

229 North Pine. This 1890s Episcopal ministry, remodeled in 1983, was painted two blues and a white when Sally Puff-Courtney moved in. Too many people copied the scheme, so she knew that something fresh had to be done. First, she tried peach, but then she came up with vibrant green, purple, and mustard. The exuberant pansies and daisies were hand-painted by interior designer Robin Cannell Baker. The artist's acrylic paints she used for their variety have held up very well in Telluride's freezing to steaming climate. This sweet entryway is a mountain bouquet that blooms all year.

OURAY

512 Main Street between 5th and 6th. The majestic San Juan mountains of southwestern Colorado form the picture-perfect backdrop for this turn-of-the-century commercial storefront. The brick façade, with its tin cornices, has been faithfully restored and authentically painted to reflect the original Victorian splendor of the Ouray Gallery housed here. The original pressed-tin ceiling and heart-of-pine floor have been faithfully restored. Ouray was once called "The Switzerland of America," and the town thrived after it discovered that preservation is good for the pocketbook as well as the soul.

TELLURIDE

(Opposite) 465 Pacific Street. The gate above the town's main thoroughfare reads "To Hell You Ride," and some disappointed silver miners may have agreed, once they got there. On occasion, it called itself the "town without a bellyache." Good times and bad have come to Telluride, but since the early 1970s, the feeling of history that pervades the town has been no accident. Since 1973, every new structure has had to pass the scrutiny of the town's Architectural Review Commission. "Telluriders are aware of history almost to a fault," says town planner Lance McDonald. "Even outbuildings are protected." The new must blend in with the old.

This simple Stick structure, built in the 1880s, is one of Telluride's oldest buildings. In the 1960s, it was called the "Freak House" because it was a hangout for visiting ski bums. It was restored, with an addition, in 1986. The owner asked Lynn Robinson of Design Forum in Denver to coordinate the project with local architect Bill Kees and the historical review board, which specified all materials used inside and out. Robinson created the taupe, mustardy cream, rust, orange, raspberry, grape, and blueberry color scheme. The rainbow effect in the gable shingles is a Colorado signature.

Natalia's 1912 Restaurant, 1161 Blair Street at 12th. This 1901 building is an addition to the building next to it, which was built in 1883. It says 1912 on the façade because that was the year in which Bob Rezka's father came to Canada from the Ukraine, and Bob figures he wouldn't be here if his father hadn't come to Canada.

Bob and Natalia saw an ad in the *Arizona Republic* for a restaurant lease and came to Silverton in 1984 to start the restaurant. Now they work from May to October and return to Arizona for the winter.

The three colors of cream, rust, and black are used in a fantasy of lace and jigsaw patterns. The Durango–Silverton narrow-gauge railroad, which carries two thousand people a day and was used for the movie *Butch Cassidy and the Sundance Kid*, stops sixty feet from the restaurant's front door—where passengers immediately head for a picture. The building was built as one of the first dens of iniquity on Blair Street, and there are plans to turn the upstairs rooms into a museum or a B&B.

Indian Trading Post, 1228 Greene Street. Built in 1896 by photographer and saloon owner John V. Lorenzo and his partner, Joe Grivetto, this picturesque building was the Chicago Saloon, a port in the storm to countless Italian immigrant miners through the years. It was thought to be more respectable than the Blair Street taverns but still made its own liquor during Prohibition, as did a majority of Silverton saloons. Max Ortega's Indian Trading Post uses vibrant native American colors on this Italianate storefront.

OURAY

(Opposite) 310 Main Street. Brilliant native American red, yellow, and glossy black shine in the Colorado summer sunshine on this 1890 Queen Anne cottage. Steve and Terri Holliday were surprised when some historical purists complained about their color choices, but Steve felt that red is close to being historical—and he liked it. The house was barn red, and the other colors seemed to fall into place. Steve picked the colors, and Terri decided where to put them.

Terri is a seamstress, and the house is a perfect "gallery" to display her Victorian-style craft goods and draperies. It had been remodeled to death in the 1960s and is closer, now, to what it should be.

Steve noted, "The house has been called the Piñata House, the Circus House, the Christmas House, and other names. We were the first to be so bold in Ouray, and I'm proud to say we started a trend. People started taking photos before we were finished and haven't stopped. We have friends in the photo-finishing business across the country who have seen our house in photos by people we don't even know. The best thing about pouring heart and soul and dollar after dollar into a house like this is to see a cold, lonesome building turn into a home that becomes grander every year."

WYOMING
CHEYENNE

1811 Evans Avenue. This cheerful Queen Anne cottage, built in 1892, is in the Rainsford Historic District of a town located on the Oregon Trail. In 1987, Jonna Hilzer-Dickie bought what she calls "a poor man's Victorian," once owned by the Union Pacific Railroad. It was badly in need of a face-lift. Jonna received a Certificate of Special Recognition for Historical Preservation from the city for her restoration, which culminated in this four-color scheme. The house is on the National Register. Note the turned posts with scroll brackets, fretwork, and solid cutout quarter-fan supports.

(Above, below left, and opposite) The Whipple House, 300 East 17th Street. Banker Ithamar C. Whipple and his wife, Virilla, built a home to reflect the status of a wealthy Cheyenne businessman. Constructed in 1883 along Cattle Baron's Row, The Whipple House is an eclectic blend of Italianate and Gothic Revival.

The Whipples sold it to John W. Lacey, an attorney for the Union Pacific Railroad as well as for notorious cattle thieves. He also defended oil magnate Harry Sinclair in the Teapot Dome scandal. The National Park Service describes The Whipple House, now on the National Register, as a "superb example of the successful use of a historic building." It's an office complex that also serves as a photo gallery of Wyoming and Whipple House figures.

In 1982, two weeks before the vacant, derelict house was to be demolished for an office building, Betty Anne and Lenny Beirele purchased the place because they couldn't stand the thought of Cheyenne's losing this legacy. "It was not a rational decision. It was a passionate one," says Betty Anne.

The price was only $85,000, but making the house usable cost almost ten times that. First, it was to be a restaurant, because the Beireles truly wanted to open the place to people. Mr. Beirele is a dentist, so Betty Anne became the restaurateur. Even Mr. Whipple's bank rejected their requests for loans, but national and state funds helped, and the city managed to bend a few rules.

Leonard remembers that "City officials came around pretty quickly once we pointed out that meeting the parking requirement would mean tearing the building down to put in the parking lot." The fact that the restaurant provided thirty jobs and paid property taxes of almost $5,000 a year, rather than the $370 paid before rehabilitation, proved the profit in preservation.

Betty Anne chose slate blue, pinky beige, and ivory—"a Wyoming sunset"—for the color scheme.

The superb floor-to-ceiling walnut chimney breast in the parlor is original, as are the Italian hand-painted tiles and the brass firebox. So is the stained-glass window, with thirty-five faceted jewels that adorn the split-flue chimney flanked by beveled-glass mirrors.

In talking about the change from restaurant to office building, Betty Anne, who is on the board of the National Trust, genuinely feels that the house has its own agenda: "Our role was to bring it back from disappearance, and now it wants to do something else—and it will decide what and how."

UTAH
SALT LAKE CITY

83 North N Street between 1st and 2nd Avenues. Bryan and Janet Sirstins bought their 1899 Eastlake-inspired Queen Anne cottage in 1983, the year before they were married. The house, built for a carpenter named Henry A. Ferguson, had been condemned. The neighbors had petitioned to have it torn down, but because it was within the Avenues Historic District, the request was denied.

Bryan is also a carpenter, and he did most of the remodeling and restoration himself. Since the gingerbread had been stripped away, Bryan made some out of 1940s pine kitchen cabinets found in the house. He doubled the square footage of the house by adding three bedrooms and a bathroom under the roofline. The final touch was a five-color scheme of browns, tantalizing green accents, and white that makes this cozy cottage blend in with the greenery around it. The Sirstinses' home now blossoms on property that was once part of Brigham Young's fruit orchard, and local homeowners now ask their advice on colors.

(*Opposite*) The National Historic Bed and Breakfast, 936 East 1700 South. The Metropolitan Investment Group in 1891 paid an architect named Perkins (notable because he was not a Mormon) to build a block of homes in a newly developed suburb of Salt Lake City, for trolley lines had made suburbs feasible. The National Historic B&B is one of seven buildings still left in the Sugar House area from that group.

After several rentals, the first owner, Byron Cummings, the first Dean of Arts and Sciences at the University of Utah, paid $2,531 for the house. In 1947, it was divided into four apartments. Mike and Katie Bartholeme restored the house in 1983, turned it into a bed and breakfast in 1985, then painted the "San Francisco–style" color scheme in 1987.

OGDEN

726 25th Street. In 1889, when gentiles in the Liberal Party won every seat in the Ogden City Council, beating the Mormon-supported People's Party, a real-estate boom was sweeping the country. At the same time, the Transcontinental, the Central, the Pacific, and the Union Pacific railroads, all used Ogden as a transfer point, and two new railroads, one serving Salt Lake City and the other Idaho and Montana, used Ogden as a connecting point to the main lines.

Andrew J. Warner's 1895 Victorian home was built at the height of Ogden's stature as an intermountain rail center. Warner was a real estate agent who moved to Los Angeles in 1906. This house was the twenty-fourth structure in Odgen to receive a water permit. The bargeboard flanks a pigeon-hole design which has for its base nine turned knobs, all set in geometric patterns. With the mosquelike, onion-shaped dome over the Queen Anne stair tower, the house is an excellent example of an eclectic Queen Anne. The sun-baked colors on the exterior are original to the house, which was still in the process of being restored when we photographed it.

(Above and opposite) 678 East South Temple. Emanuel Kahn and his brother, Samuel, merchants who started a chain of grocery stores, brought architect Henry Monheim from Denver to design this mansion. Monheim, whose crowning achievement was the City and County Building, liked Utah so much he stayed. The Kahn House is on the National Register, and it is notable for the twelve gables; the highly ornamental exterior moldings, grills, railings, cornices, and finials; and the fan-shaped gingerbread.

Restoration architect Steven T. Baird acquired the house in 1979 and turned the 1889 Queen Anne home into his offices, a noteworthy example of adaptive reuse. The interior was stenciled by San Francisco stencil artist Larry Boyce, who used some of the original stencils found underneath the wallpaper, Baird used gray, black, and orange, historically accurate colors, to decorate the newly freshened brick.

The Castle, 70 South B Street. Virginia City's famous Castle was one of the finest mansions in the West when it was built in 1868 by Robert K. Graves, a mine superintendent and stockholder of the Empire Mine. Inspired by a castle in Normandy, it remains precisely as it was built on millionaires' row during the Virginia City boom. The stone wall creates an imposing approach to this towered Italianate villa, once called "the House of Silver Door Knobs."

All of the fireplaces in The Castle were closed because of the Virginia City downdrafts, and stoves were installed when needed. Large French gold-leaf mirrors hang over the mantels throughout the house. The chandelier in this room has hand-cut Bohemian etched-glass globes, and prisms made of hand-cut Czechoslovakian rock-crystal pendants. The windows have counterweighted olivewood shutters that are also louvered, so they can go up and down and also regulate the light. The lace curtains in hollyhock and morning-glory patterns were made by Belgian nuns.

In this room also, the English walnut table expands to fourteen feet, seating twenty-six. The sideboard is of German and Circassian walnut, with carvings of fruit and game birds on the doors. Hand-colored Italian lithographs of hunting scenes hang on the walls. The fireplace is made from Carrara marble. The ebony "Goddess of Progress" clock on the mantel is French.

In the bedrooms, French bronze light fixtures hang from hand-painted medallions, and the walls are painted a light polychrome in the French style. Some of the original white paint still exists, since it was supposedly made with arsenic for whiteness and lead for longevity. The bed, dresser, and commode are of carved rosewood. An uncle is said to have bought the trio at Versailles. A seven-piece English Laughlan hand-painted commode-set on the bureau is a family treasure.

The Castle has been owned by four generations of the McGurk family, who have lived there, maintained it, and now share it with the public.

Most of the furnishings were shipped by boat around Cape Horn to San Francisco, and then by mule and ox teams over the Sierras. Workmen and artisans were also imported from Europe. The "Goddess of Light" bronze newel-post statue in the hall is from France. Silver European stair rods hold the carpet in place on the Italian hanging stairs. The balustrade on the stairs is black walnut imported from Germany. The hand-blocked wallpaper is French.

THE NORTHWEST

The Northwest runs the gamut from the gray, green, gorgeous pine forests in the north and along the coast with its "liquid sunshine" to the hot, dry, mountainous country inland.

As it was in *Daughters of Painted Ladies*, the star of the Northwest is the Cape May of the Pacific, Port Townsend, Washington. Its well-tended Victorians and its lovely setting on Puget Sound make Port Townsend a popular getaway spot.

Just one look at the four-story Ann Starrett Mansion in Port Townsend will show anyone why it's a National Historic Landmark. The spectacular staircase ascending to an eight-sided solar calendar is literally and figuratively one of the high points of this book.

MONTANA
BUTTE

845 West Broadway. Gold and silver mining increased the city's population of forty men and five women in 1866 to fourteen thousand in 1885. However, it was Butte's copper, critical to the electrification of America, which gave Butte a 41 percent share of the world copper market and a population of almost 100,000 in 1910.

With the help of colorist Kitty Wargny of Lavender Brush, homeowners in Butte are going for broke, highlighting the ruffles and flourishes of their Victorians with both authentic and modern colors. This adorable twin-towered 1890 Queen Anne, built by a lawyer named Thompson Campbell, was decked in gray, plum, rose, bone, and navy blue a century later because Kathy Cox liked the way they played together on a dress. Now she thinks that the house looks like a big wedding cake.

IDAHO
BOISE

1601 North 7th Street. A burst of color radiates from this 1901 Stick/Eastlake cottage. Anton Guretsky, who owned the Boise Sash & Door Company, used whatever millwork was handy on his home. Robert Payne, then a restoration-design consultant, purchased the house in 1981 from a Japanese family that had been interned during World War II, and he polished all the worn spots so he could rent it. He picked a color design out of *Painted Ladies*. It was the boldest statement he had ever put on a house, but the house was also the boldest statement as far as millwork and gingerbread went, and the Boise Historic Preservation Society gave him an award for his efforts.

WASHINGTON
BELLINGHAM

The Shields House, 2215 Utter. The "before" picture of this winsome Stick/Eastlake home is on page 100 of *Daughters of Painted Ladies*. Lumberman Robert Shields built his home in 1895 and trimmed it inside and out with lavish woodwork. Bird's-eye maple and burlwood maple line the living room and stairs. Penny and Jeff Hinkel bought the house in 1987, and Jeff painted it himself with student painters in 1990.

Penny chose eight colors to create the feeling of an old quilt. After they were on, Penny realized that the shingle pattern in the gables resembles a quilt pattern called Grandmother's Flower Garden, and of course, the underlying goal of the restoration was to make it look like a house a grandmother would feel right at home in. The embossed panels on the front and the north side of the house are painted with copper paint.

The house, now on the National Register of Historic Places, is in the Eldridge Avenue Historic District. "Our home is a never-ending project," remarked Jeff, who was painting murals inside the house.

COUPEVILLE

The Victorian Bed and Breakfast, 602 North Street. Located on Whidbey Island off the coast of Washington, Coupeville is called the City of Sea Captains because of its many seafaring settlers. The Victorian homes have been preserved by protective neglect, and they are now coming alive with the encouragement of the growing number of visitors.

Sawmill-owner H. L. Lovejoy built this Italianate in 1899 for Jacob Jenne, a hotel owner and saloon keeper who furnished it in the eclectic style of the day. Jenne put in closets and a hot-water heating system still used today. The kitchen had the first running water on Whidbey Island. A few pieces of furniture belonging to Jenne, including a long sideboard in the Jenne Room, are still being used by guests.

Dolores Fresh bought the house in 1988; brought her own family keepsakes, furnishings, and flair; and gave the house a new life as a B&B. She chose a dignified yet perky color scheme of Delft blue, white, and burgundy. According to Dolores, "To preserve our heritage is a thrill and delight."

PORT TOWNSEND

Heritage House, 305 Pierce Street. Once the second busiest port of entry in the United States after New York, Port Townsend, built on the tip of a tiny peninsula jutting out from a larger peninsula, is still best reached by boat. In the 1890s, the Union Pacific Railroad planned to make Port Townsend its terminus, and scores of breathtaking Victorians lined the streets. The trains never arrived. The town's fortunes tumbled, but the Victorians remained, frozen in time. Today, Port Townsend is the Cape May of the West, a bustling tourist town, and many of the Victorians are B&Bs and commercial buildings.

Built in 1878 by John Fuge, an English shipbuilder, who also built many of the surrounding homes, Heritage House sits on a bluff with a commanding view of the bay and snow-capped Olympic Mountains beyond. Captain Plum, a retired seaman, bought the house in 1890, and pictures of the family still hang in the dining room.

In 1984, the Broughton and Ellis families bought the Italianate home, by then in sorry condition. Their hard work earned them the Jefferson County Historic Society's coveted Mary P. Johnson Preservation Award for "exemplary restoration and continued maintenance of historic structures," and the house is now on the National Register. The springtime yellow, green, and white exterior looks almost as it did in 1880, when Captain Plum and his family gathered on the front porch.

Ann Starrett Mansion, Victorian Inn, 744 Clay Street. The Starrett mansion, situated on the bluff overlooking the mountains and sound, epitomizes the heart and soul of Port Townsend, for it is a four-story architectural extravaganza symbolizing the beauty of the past. Built by wealthy contractor George Starrett in 1889 as a wedding present for his wife, Ann, this magnificent Stick-style Renaissance villa is a National Historic Landmark.

Each gable of this cream, teal, and green exterior has its special adornment. Starrett, who employed ships' carpenters for the exacting work, is responsible for the construction of 350 buildings here, including a sawmill, a dry dock, and a mortuary.

217

(*Opposite*) The construction techinque used to build the free-hung, three-tiered spiral staircase is still a mystery. Crowning the house is one of the most unusual domed ceilings in America. The eight-sided dome is a solar calendar with frescoes that depict the Four Seasons and Four Virtues (four graces and four nymphs) in eight panels. Small dormer windows are situated on the roof of the tower, so that on the first days of each new season, the sun shines on a ruby-red glass, causing a red beam to point toward the season.

In 1962, George and Lorraine Nichols bought the house for a song. The outside was mustard yellow. The inside had been trashed, with fallen plaster, peeling paper, and water-stained ceilings. The panels at the top of the staircase had been covered up. The Nicholses and their children learned restoration as they did it.

Bob and Edel Sokol have now taken up the lance, and their advice for those who seek to preserve our heritage is "Always choose a historical landmark for your lodging when you travel. By your patronage, you are helping with the restoration and upkeep of these properties—you are helping to preserve American history by sleeping in a bit of it."

The elaborate polychrome details and moldings on these two pages and on the previous page feature carved lions, doves, ferns, and flowers and have been restored to re-create the Victorian decor. The stenciling for what has been called "the grand bonbon of them all" was created by San Francisco's Larry Boyce, who bicycled 240,000 miles around the country for eighteen years, supporting his travels with his artistry.

TACOMA

912 North I Street. Henry O. Geiger built this embellished Stick-style home with Queen Anne elements in 1889 at a cost of $4,500. After surviving thirty years as a boardinghouse, then the threat of demolition, the house has been blessed with owners who love it. Skip and Jane Easley are restoring it inside and out. The three Easley teenagers have also pitched in.

The Easleys presented their home with a perennially springy eight-color scheme, which highlights the chamfered windows and latticework. Sunshine yellow lights up the twenty sunbursts.

Skip reported, "We're just glad to have the opportunity to do it. We don't see ownership of this house as ownership, but as the opportunity to preserve it. In a way, it's a gift to the first owner, Henry Geiger. If we hadn't done this, the place would have been demolished and would now match the forty-condo complex across the street."

Jane explained, "Our house is like a canvas. You can use all your creativity and ideas that you could never do in a modern home. If you want a lattice and sky in one room, you can do that. If you want a castle painted in the staircase, you can do that. If you want to grain and use 'paint magic' on your wood, you can do that. If you want bird cages and fruit panels on your ceilings, you can do that. The list is endless.

"Restoring a Victorian house is a little like having a baby. When in labor, you are miserable, but after it is over, you can sit back and love and admire the results. And you wouldn't have it any other way."

CORVALLIS

340 Southwest 5th Street. To celebrate the centennial of the James O. Wilson House, an 1892 Queen Anne, Pat and Jay Mackie installed new balconies, a new ridge crest, and a front porch on their pattern-book "Elizabethan cottage." The house was still a work in progress when Doug took this photograph. Like the Wallers, the Mackies appreciate the aesthetic rewards of living in nineteenth-century surroundings. They feel they are investing in their heritage: "Our Victorian home endures, endears itself, and enfolds us like a cozy grandmother. Its cheerful spirit brings a smile to the faces of all who enter or pass by. But we are the lucky ones who can call it 'home.'"

ALBANY

The Skipton House, 416 4th Avenue S.E. George Barber would applaud the delicate mauve and taupe colors that have been used to highlight the unusual board-and-batten stripwork, the curved shingles, the ripple work, the tiara on the gable, and the wonderful spoolwork on the porch of his fairy-tale-pretty, pattern-book house.

The Skipton House, a Stick-style residence with Eastlake details, is located in the Hackleman District of Historic Albany. The owner of an Albany livery stable built it in 1885, using Barber's Design No. 11 for "a tasty, inexpensive house."

Albany was founded by two New York farming brothers during the 1840s, when the Donation Land Claim Act granted each white male citizen over eighteen 320 acres of land if he was single and 640 acres if he was married. It quickly became the county seat, with a school, a newspaper, a courthouse, and enough commerce to make it a shipping center. When the main highway bypassed the town, and post–World War II housing developed outside the city, the old downtown and residential neighborhoods were left intact. Today, homeowners enjoy restoring, preserving, and cherishing their past in this "house-proud" town.

CALIFORNIA

From Eureka to National City just south of San Diego, the Painted Ladies in California are mostly on or near the coast.

Alameda had a major surprise in store for us. *Daughters of Painted Ladies* has two houses in Alameda; this book has eleven, more than any other town in the country. While most East Bay communities have modern municipal buildings, Alameda lives serenely in its own time zone. Rather than summoning bulldozers, this island city in San Francisco Bay is spending vast sums to preserve and strengthen its 1902 Colonial Revival library and its 1895 Romanesque Revival city hall.

There are two thousand eight hundred Victorian homes in Alameda, one of the finest collections in the country. The Alameda Historical Museum is helping to inspire homeowners with its Benjamin Moore computer, which enables homeowners to experiment with colors.

Thanks to museum curator George Gunn's book, *Documentation of Victorian and Post Victorian Residential and Commercial Buildings, City of Alameda, 1854 to 1904*, which includes the address, style, year of construction, builder, architect, cost, original owner, and exterior alterations, Alameda has the most complete, easily accessible documentation for its Victorians of any city that we know of.

Because Alameda's in the Bay Area, its homeowners have been influenced by San Francisco's Painted Ladies, and they have access to Bay Area craftspeople as well as their own. San Francisco colorist Bob Buckter estimates that he has done color designs for about four hundred homes in Alameda. One color consultant doing four hundred homes in one place is a feat that will probably never be equaled.

Among the Bear State's other notable achievements are Preservation Park in Oakland and Oxnard's Heritage Square, which are discussed in the introduction; Bob Buckter's sweetheart of a valentine to Oakland; Dick Langdon's Victorian Annex to the Union Hotel in Los Alamos, with its remarkable fantasy suites; the lovely work of colorist Chuck Vedder in Riverside; and the extraordinary Villa Montezuma in San Diego, another tribute to art married to attention to detail.

Altogether, California presents a varied, stellar sampling of artistry in color, design, and architecture.

EUREKA

(Opposite and above) 216 Hillsdale. Eureka is best known as the home of The Carson Mansion, the "one-stop museum of drop-dead Victoriana" designed by the Newsom Brothers. A paler version of the portico of this 1893 Queen Anne cottage designed by the Newsom Brothers appeared in *Daughters of Painted Ladies*. Francis Mowry constructed the place for A. W. Torrey. Mike Walword, the present owner of this flashy little lady, went to what he calls "hotter" colors in 1989, brightening the green and rust, and adding a yellow band. He wanted to give the house, with its radiant radiating spindlework, horseshoe arches, and unusual balconettes on the upper level, rhythm, and we feel he succeeded.

FERNDALE

923 Main Street. California's best preserved Victorian Village remains a popular magnet for visitors. Once called the Cream City, Ferndale has been granted Landmark Status by the state. The "butterfat palaces" were built by rich dairy farmers and are blooming as homes, B&Bs, and other businesses.

The intricate detailing on this 1894 Stick/Italianate dwelling has been highlighted with an authentic color scheme. The first owner, Lucius Smith, put palm trees in front of his home to prove he was in California. Later, the place was a barrel factory, and more recently the lady of the house sold flowers from the hothouse that remains in the back garden. The palm trees were removed in 1971. One of them still reaches for the sky in Disneyland.

439 Berding. The seductive pink roses on this stately 1899 Stick cottage bring smiles to passersby. This is a good example of how just a few spots of color bring a whole façade to life. Clay and Elaine Chenoweth moved into a house that needed Tender Loving Care: "We bought a large funnel and poured money through it for two and a half years."

When it came time to paint the exterior, they chose cream, dill, Irish cove, and rose, after prayer, sleepless nights, and nightmares of five or six colors of rose. Clay painted the roses himself after the painter threatened his life—yet people really love the roses.

The Chenoweths' comment about their travail reminds us of how after a slide show in Redlands, a member of the audience told us how to make a small fortune: "You start with a large fortune and buy a Victorian."

HEALDSBURG

The Grape Leaf Inn, 539 Johnson. If purple makes you purr, you will love The Grape Leaf Inn. One of the Sweet family members was told, in art class, that one should never use the color purple on a house. The family took that as a challenge when they opened their 1900 Queen Anne as The Grape Leaf Inn. Lavender, grape, blue, and many shades of purple glow in, and on, the house, from this enchanting doorway to the gold-starred cornice boards on the exterior, the daisies and roses in the garden, the wall and floor coverings, the linens, and even the bubble bath.

The family literally raised the roof, adding ingenious skylights for light and transforming the attic into four bedroom suites, but it's hard to see the changes from the ground.

SANTA ROSA

The Gables, 4257 Petaluma Hill Road. Cream, rose, burgundy, and a gentle accent of green do justice to this lovely fifteen-gabled Gothic Revival B&B. Built in 1877 by gold miner and farmer William Roberts, the house is on the National Register.

Innkeepers Jim and Judy Gagne painted it in 1991, after "testing" their color combinations in their chintz-and-marble dining room. Judy worked with a patient paint salesman who hand-mixed each color, aiming for shades she had only imagined. They started with one quart of each color. The first afternoon they tried their rose base color on a back wall. It looked fine then, but the next morning it looked like medicine. It took three more tries to get the rose right. Jim and Judy love the feel of living in a home that was once neglected. She loves the sense of history, the wide moldings, the high ceilings, and the feel of a grand old lady brought back to the glory she deserves.

NAPA

The Stoddard House, 2230 First Street. Once a B&B and now an artist's residence, this adorable 1898 Queen Anne Cottage is dressed in two peaches, two blue-grays, lilac, purple, gold, and ochre to vie with the flower garden. Joan Osgood chose the colors and saw the finished house in her mind's eye from the outset. Her husband did insist on changing one trim color from "battleship gray" to a blue gray. They both relish the results.

Architect Luther Turton designed The Stoddard House for William J. Stoddard, a local grain-mill owner who paid ten dollars in gold coin for an acre lot in an area then outside the city limits. The house was a wedding present for his new bride, who lived there until her death in December 1977, two months short of her 102nd birthday. Although it is a cottage, the house has three thousand three hundred square feet of living space on two floors and is built entirely of redwood. The pocket doors and other doors still carry the original finger-grain staining to look like oak, and many of the windows still have the original wavy glass. We took this picture on a warm October day and were pleased to be greeted by a scarecrow with pumpkins.

ST. HELENA

The Richie Block, 1335 Main Street. The architectural cornerstone of Main Street in the wine country town of St. Helena is painted in green, black, terra-cotta, and white, to offset the robust brick, as they did when the block was built in 1892. This eclectic Gothic Italianate still functions as commercial property and will celebrate its centennial in 1992. The third floor has served as the St. Helena (Caymus) Lodge No. 93 for Free and Accepted Masons since 1893.

NAPA

The Blue Violet Mansion, 443 Brown Street. This many-gabled 1886 Queen Anne mansion has been painted in three blues, a white, and a tan as part of a careful restoration. Architect/contractor W. H. Corlett built the residence for Emmanuel Manasse, superintendent of the Sawyer Tannery, still one of Napa's largest enterprises. Corlett is credited with designing many historic homes in Napa. The Manasse Mansion has changed from a single-family dwelling, to duplexes, to a single-family home, to a six-apartment complex and is now, mercifully, a bed-and-breakfast inn, which will allow it to remain a lovingly maintained Victorian treasure.

The Blue Violet Mansion opened as a bed-and-breakfast inn in 1991 with a romantic gazebo in the back garden. The last owners chose the color scheme. Bob and Kathy Morris are finishing the interior restoration and planning a new, exciting multicolor scheme.

PLACERVILLE

Combellack-Blair House, 2059 Cedar Ravine. After silver made miners robber barons, the Gold Country's "Hangtown" became respectable and changed its name to Placerville. William Hill Combellack built this peppermint-sherbet Queen Anne in 1895 for $2,500 and lived in his home until 1924, when Arthur J. Blair and his family moved in for fifty years. Both families became prominent merchants and today continue to own and operate their family businesses.

For a while, the house was painted a bright green and white, but this more romantic color scheme was painted in 1989, in dusty rose, creamy white, raspberry, and brown-black. The bed-and-breakfast inn is designed to make visitors feel as if they've stepped back into 1890.

OAKLAND

(Opposite) 314 Fruitvale Avenue at Costello. Jack London played cards in this 1889 Queen Anne cottage, which is said to have been a bordello and a governor's summer home. At the turn of the century, Fruitvale was, as the name suggests, fruit orchards.

A Painted Lady is a felicitous blend of color and architecture. Rarely, however, are these elements evenly balanced. Usually, the architecture is stronger than the color. But with this design in cream, dusty rose, gray-violet, burgundy, and dark blue-gray, Bob Buckter has achieved a perfect marriage of color and architecture.

The colors may change, but it will be hard to improve on the choice, range, and balance of colors and the way Bob placed them to bring out the architectural details. Note that none of these colors is loud, and remember that this home is not the biggest or fanciest in town. Bob has just made the most of what the house has, which is all that any homeowner could wish for.

3148

ALAMEDA

940 Santa Clara Avenue. The firm of Marcuse & Remmel charged San Francisco accountant Frank L. Van Meter $2,800 for this delicious Queen Anne/Colonial Revival home in 1895. The neoclassical swag or garland was one of the details the builders used in their interpretation of Colonial Revival, and this house is said to have introduced the Colonial Revival style to Alameda. Note the high basement and ship-lath siding, also characteristic of Marcuse & Remmel.

The Bushnells, the present owners, chose a royal combination of two shades of plum, white, and gold leaf to give it that extra dazzle. They spent weeks and hundreds of dollars trying out colors on the side of the house. They wanted something no one would duplicate. Then the tulip tree in the back yard bloomed, and they decided to copy the colors of the blossoms. The painter took flowers to the paint store for color matching. Now this comfortable home looks like a plum-wonderful gift tied up neatly with white ribbon.

1558 Pacific. This 1891 Queen Anne cottage was designed and built by A. W. Pattiani for H. P. Moreal, a real estate broker, at a cost of $2,500. The previous owner did the six-color scheme of two mint greens, blue, cream, and plum, which also pleases the present owners, Ronald and Marilyn Hudson.

1631-31A Sherman. The elaborate gable treatment and cast-plaster ornamentation in this 1894 Queen Anne cottage is typical of Marcuse & Remmel. The original owner, Max Walter, paid $2,250 for his home. Marcuse & Remmel went out of business after just nine years, but they have left Alameda with dozens of homes like this. The heavy stucco masonry in the gables is a detail frequently found in Alameda.

Although the original bandboard frieze, the dentils under the windows, and the acroteria have been removed, the Bob Buckter color design of gray, white, navy, and burgundy brings out the best in this cozy study in curves.

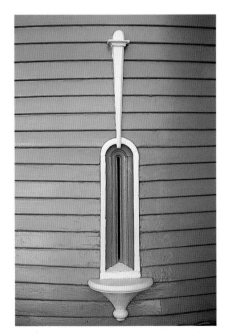

1441 Grand Street at Santa Clara. Dr. C. H. Lubbock paid architect/builder David S. Brehaut $3,043 to build a Queen Anne residence with Colonial Revival touches in 1897. He even had a side entrance for his office. Almost a century later, William and Carolyne Dondero paid almost ten times that price to purchase and restore the place, including this sculpturesque air vent. They chose Imperial White, Aries Rose, Hidden Blue, and Dust-Storm Taupe for the exterior and call their house the Queen Lady, for its design and after the "lady of the house."

2202–2202 ½ San Antonio Avenue. Builder John E. Langren built this Queen Anne residence, named Lucky Lady, for himself in 1891 at a cost of $4,000 and then subdivided his lot and built another house to sell.

Wally Wong stripped away composition siding and painstakingly restored the exterior in 1988. Bob Buckter, who has turned San Antonio Avenue into one of the most colorful streets in America, helped with ideas for the appliqué millwork that needed restoration and then did the colors. The marvelous waffle-stars pattern and waffle-fan incising on each side of the bay window are superbly picked out in a pretty shade of dark rose on dark teal to complement the pale dusty blue, dark teal, taupe, cream, peach, and gold leaf.

(Opposite) 1602 San Antonio Avenue at Paru. San Francisco attorney William Rigby paid pioneer builder C. H. Foster the comparatively major sum of $6,000 for his impressive Stick/Eastlake home in 1889. Charles H. Shener designed the building especially to fit the lot in the last year that the Stick/Eastlake style was used in Alameda.

Barbara and John Taforo have underplayed its massiveness with a four-color scheme of mauve, light mauve, and brown with a red accent.

2254 San Antonio Avenue. Thomas I. Pyne also built this amusing Queen Anne in 1892 for $3,500. Bill Galli, known as Geppeto the Carpenter, purchased this home in a sorry state of repair. He has done a glorious job restoring the exterior and the interior and has restored other Alameda residences as well.

Colorist Bob Buckter collaborated with him to pick up on the lighthouse-like tower, with its charmingly out-of-scale cresting, and caressed the façade with sea blues and white. Bill did not want loud colors and was against using the aubergine Buckter prescribed, but Bob explained that it was needed to make the rest of the scheme work. The colors used are a gray-green with a bluish cast; Peppertree, for the main body; Mishima teal for the accent; turquoise and aubergine on the frieze border and panel molding; light blue on the column caps; and gold paint. The decorative panel on the side reflects the pattern in the stained-glass windows.

2242 San Antonio Avenue. Speculator Thomas I. Pyne built a Queen Anne home for $5,000 in 1891 and then sold it the next year to wholesaler Earl A. Fargo. The art-glass window in the front entry is original. When Pat and Max Layard took over from the last owners, who had spent eighteen years restoring the place, a great deal of work still lay in wait.

Bob Buckter's unusual, richly colored design, which includes gold-leaf buttons, accents the Moorish angles on the portico and the intertwined serpents in the pediment over the front porch.

Pat had always wanted to live in a turn-of-the-century house. She feels that "A Victorian has its own personality, derived from its original architect and builder and expanded by one or more occupants over a long period of time. A Victorian has its own inherent character, evidenced by its interior and exterior ornamentation. A Victorian, therefore, becomes the 'owner,' the 'dictator,' who determines the basic character of the house. It takes control; it 'talks' to you. It almost literally says, 'Yes, that's a great color (or wallpaper, or addition, or shifting of a wall, or whatever)' or, 'What? You're going to do what? You've got to be kidding.' A Victorian could never be described as 'basically a series of four walls' regardless of ceiling height!"

2258 San Antonio Avenue. Thomas I. Pyne really went to work on this Queen Anne. In 1889, it cost $6,000, but that included all of the gingerbread on the portico and the hand-sawed shingles on the third story.

Pat Bail selected a series of grays with blue accents and a gray body in this five-color design, with suggestions from Bob Buckter on how to highlight the panels, the overscale dentil blocks, and the large brackets. The many shades of blue and white seem to suit this elegant grand dame with its gorgeous pediment.

Pat's son, artist Jon-Paul Bail, helped landscape the Victorian garden. Pat believes that "You have to love the house and be willing to make the financial commitment to restore the house to its original form. You have to compromise between what is practical and what is pleasing to the eye and perhaps spend more than you had planned for the joy and satisfaction of taking a neglected building and making it a source of pride to the community."

2153 San Jose Avenue. The Patton Brothers built this transitional Queen Anne/Colonial Revival residence in 1897 for San Francisco lumberman William Westover at a price of $4,500. Cathy and Heath Hamilton watched as many of the homes in Alameda were transformed into works of art, and they succumbed to the desire to own a Victorian. They bought the place in 1988 and removed the aluminum siding from the original ship-lath siding. One nice surprise was finding beautiful wood wainscoting under two and a half inches of reinforced mortar. They selected a historically authentic color scheme based on The Fitzgerald House in Cortland, New York (see page 51).

3256 Garfield Avenue. David S. Brehaut followed architect Charles Shaner's renderings when he built this sweet Queen Anne cottage in 1894, for $1,500, for landspeculator David Hirschfield. Hirschfield sold it in 1911 to Cornelius Townsend, and his family lived here until 1960.

George Gunn, author of *Documentation of Victorian and Post Victorian Residential and Commercial Buildings, City of Alameda, 1854 to 1904*, and *Buildings of the Edwardian Period, City of Alameda, 1905 to December 31, 1909*, has given his home an enchanting look in three shades of lavender to detail the ribbony frieze. Note the rough-dash plaster put on with a trowel in the gable, a characteristic of houses designed by Shaner.

Brehaut's contracts for buildings lasted for ninety working days, with no extensions, and he delivered. It is said that one of Hirschfield's claims to fame is that his missionary parents sent the first eucalyptus seeds to California from Australia.

SANTA CRUZ

(Opposite) 203 Highland. Carpenter-builder James Stewart McPheters built his own home, a French Second Empire mansion, in 1882. He leaned heavily on the pattern book of A. J. Bicknell & Co. for the design ideas for his "gabled-ell" suburban cottage and planted the palm tree so people would know he was in California. When George and Gail Michaelis-Ow bought the house in 1975, it was painted pink, after being white for a few years. The Ows worked with colorist Charles Prentiss and painted the house in straw, lemon, chocolate, and raisin.

In 1989, the Ows built a matching carriage house two-thirds the scale of the National Register main house, complete with trimmings. Drawings for the house in pattern books showed that the original plans did call for a carriage house, and these helped persuade the neighbors to rally for such an ornate addition. The addition inspired a new paint job with a new look, and the Ows worked with Charles Prentiss to select and place the ten colors that gild this outstanding building with a superbly detailed color scheme worthy of the architecture. The palm tree still shades what has become one of the most beautiful blends of color and architecture in the country.

411 Cedar. The delicious colors chosen by Doni Tunheim of Fresh Façades for this 1865 mini–Gothic Revival make this gable a small-scale work of art. Since the building is used for law offices, Ed Newman asked Doni for four different color schemes so the staff could vote. The unanimous decision was for green, lavender, white, and gold. The combination is different, tasteful, and a gift to the architecture. Alas, trees prevented us from shooting more of this gem.

WATSONVILLE

107 East Beach Street. Chuck Haggerty lamented to Doni Tunheim that no one noticed his real estate office, as it was dwarfed by a large commercial building. This lively color scheme was selected, and now everyone can find him. Chuck had his signs repainted to match the building. The use of black adds punch to the brown, wine, lipstick pink, and white-cream color combination on this cute 1890 Stick cottage. Doni's unexpected use of lime green in a line on the gables and under the cornice adds that special zing, as it does on The Gatehouse Inn in Pacific Grove.

128 East Beach Street. "Judge Julius Lee's cottage is reaching up into the air, and is up to date in every way and is entirely new to this section in its architectural design. W. H. Weeks is the architect and J. S. Jennings is the builder. The foundation of granite is a solid structure and far superior to wood or birch." The local paper wrote this in 1894, shortly after this Queen Anne was built on land Lee had bought from Dr. Will Rodgers for ten dollars in gold coin. Lee was the county's first district attorney.

The present owner, historian Mrs. Betty Lewis, purchased the house in 1966 from Lee descendants. A close-up of the bas-reliefs of dancing ladies flanking the front door appeared in *Daughters of Painted Ladies*. Doni Tunheim used seven shades of gold, peach, white, and orange to give the house a delightful glow. The house is on the National Register, is a landmark in Watsonville, and has been called a "Victorian Masterpiece" by the Santa Cruz Historical Trust.

265 East Beach Street. Sea green glides over the curved and patterned hand-carved rippling shingles on this 1897 transitional Queen Anne/Colonial Revival residence. Architect W. H. Weeks built this home for Steven Scurich, Sr. Yvon and Lila Atkins painted the house just before the 1989 earthquake. The green was already on the house, and they added yellow, gold, and burnt orange to brighten their home.

PACIFIC GROVE

(*Opposite*) The Gatehouse Inn, 225 Central Avenue at 2nd Street. Pacific Grove came into being as a Chautauqua-like religious retreat, where musicians and speakers mixed with ministers in entertaining families during summer. A locked gate divided Pacific Grove from the sins of Monterey, and every time people wanted to enter or leave, they had to climb down from their carriages, open the lock with a key, go through, and then relock the gate. Judge Benjamin Langford, a State Senator, summered in Pacific Grove to escape the Sacramento Valley heat, and he built this Italianate towered villa in 1884. One night, he simply chopped down the gate—and it was never put back up. Langford relatives lived in the house until the 1960s, and Pacific Grove residents always called it the Gatehouse.

The Langford house was a personal favorite of novelist John Steinbeck, whose family lived across the street. Joyce and Kent Cherry were visiting Monterey from Chicago in 1975 and fell in love on the spot with what was then a derelict disaster, a hippy commune with black-painted floors. They put fifty dollars down, went home to Chicago and liquidated everything, and moved back to Pacific Grove, to spend fifteen years living in the house, cleaning, polishing, restoring, papering, and painting, then doing it again so they could open an elegant B&B that mixes Victorian with Art Deco and modern touches.

When they painted the place in Navaho white, lime, pumpkin, and bright yellow in 1976, the townspeople were up in arms, but now everyone is thrilled. Joyce advises other Victorian owners that you "have to have a lot of courage, be very handy, or have lots of money—but most of all, you have to love your house. My dream was a Victorian on the ocean, and now I have it, and I love it."

PACIFIC GROVE

Victorian Corner Restaurant, 541 Lighthouse Avenue. Deep oily green, bright red-orange, turquoise, and ochre are crowned by a rising sun on this bright but historically accurate commercial building. This 1893 Eastlake building is one of the oldest commercial sites in town. Note the original pilasters and segmented windows, as well as the original stained-glass window over the front door. Inside, the chandeliers are from the original interior of 613 Lighthouse Avenue. The restaurant is lined with historical pictures showing the site, the small park across the street, and the town.

SAN LUIS OBISPO

Jack House, 536 Marsh Street. The Jack House, a handsome Italianate, was built between 1876 and 1880 following the architectural plans drawn up by Mrs. Robert E. Jack, née Nellie Hollister, who worked with a catalog company. Jack came West from Maine and was successful as a banker, farmer, and land developer. Nellie was part of a noted California farming family and became a book collector and garden enthusiast.

Their descendants donated the house, its well-stocked library, and the gardens for public use in 1975. By renting the gardens for weddings and parties to help raise funds, supporters raised the money to help the city restore the house. The final touch was the 1990 painting of a vivacious five-color scheme on the exterior, based on the original colors of the house. Nestled in its quiet gardens, this finely detailed exterior makes The Jack House one of the loveliest house museums in the country.

LOS ALAMOS

The Union Hotel and Victorian Annex, 362 Bell Street. The Russian immigrants who built this frosted Queen Anne in 1884 could never have dreamed of the fantasies that would be played out here a century later. In 1979, dreamer Dick Langdon bought it, totally abandoned in Nipomo, forty miles away. He cut it into five pieces and moved it to his property in Los Alamos. Then he gutted it and spent nine years, working with two hundred artists, sculptors, and craftspeople, transforming the place into six fantasy suites.

Langdon's first residence, an 1880 hotel next door, still functions as a Victorian hotel, with lace and red velvet, rooms with and without bath, a Victorian family-hotel dining room, and billiard tables upstairs and downstairs behind a splendid back bar. He bought the hotel and moved in on a whim and has been fixing it up since 1972.

For the Victorian Annex, he chose a sunny hot-weather yellow and white and was "badgered" into adding a third color, clay red, to go along with the red brick and mahogany used in the fifty-five-foot clock tower and the exterior steps and porches that had been added. When we took the photograph, Dick had not yet added the third color to the front of the house, which appears in *The Painted Ladies Guide to Victorian California*. This is the first time, since the Crayola House in Providence illustrated in *Daughters of Painted Ladies*, that we have photographed the back of a Painted Lady.

The face is one of several life portraits sculpted by one of Dick's assistants of the two dozen chief workers on the house. The mahogany "frame" was also carved to order.

The goal of many Victorian restorations is to be able to "open the door and walk into 1880." This happens in the Union Hotel. But in the Victorian Annex, you open the door and walk into a Gypsy campground, where birds warble in the trees painted on the walls, which are painted to represent the four seasons, where a waterfall gurgles into a soaking pool, and you sleep in a gypsy wagon. Or you can walk into an oasis and sleep in a sheik's tent. Those who prefer the ocean can spend the night in a pirate-captain's cabin, listening to the ocean while burrowing through a treasure chest. Each suite has theme sound effects, games, robes, music, and movies enveloping guests in another world.

You can also sleep in a Roman chariot (see opposite) while watching Rome burn from the marble hot tub. For a Parisian weekend, you can step through the door into a Bohemian garret (see p. 252), where an easel, paints, and brushes stand ready and you climb up into the attic to sleep looking out over a Parisian skyline. Or you can step back to the 1950s and sleep in a Cadillac convertible (see opposite) at a neon-lit drive-in movie. The Victorian Annex is a remarkable achievement created by a visionary whose achievements justify his belief that anything is possible.

This is the Bohemian garret at the Victorian Annex in Los Alamos.

VENTURA

The Victorian Rose Historical Wedding Chapel, 896 East Main Street. This delightful cream, pink, and lilac Gothic church was built as St. John's Methodist Episcopal Church on the outskirts of town in 1888. The architect was Selwyn Locke Shaw. It is the oldest Protestant church in Ventura, and when it was built it was thought to be "too far from town." Although no longer affiliated with any denomination, the chapel is a city landmark—now in the center of town—available for weddings. Its ninety-six-foot steeple and stained-glass windows are original.

LOS ANGELES

1320 Carroll Avenue. The color in the stained glass and pilasters of this enchanting 1887 pure Queen Anne doorway were inspired by the original green color of the house. Planaria Price used bottle green with maroon and gray, and Bob Buckter gave her "positive reinforcement." Planaria, who also owns the nearby Eastlake Inn, buys and restores derelict Victorians, then sells them so she can keep saving houses. Thanks in part to the continuing efforts of Planaria Price and her partner, Murray Burns, Carroll Avenue provides a haven for one of the finest collections of Victorians in the country.

253

1330 Carroll Avenue. Samuel and Joseph Cather Newsom built this Queen Anne home for the Sessions family in 1888. The swoops and swirls remind us of a Bach partita. When we took the photograph, the scaffolding was still up for this gleaming paint job in five authentic colors that make the house shine. The spider web on the second floor and the orange lights around the portico are the home's salute to Halloween.

Grier-Musser Museum, 403 South Bonnie Brae Avenue. Anna Krieger and her daughters, Susan Tejada and Nancy Baron, restored this 1898 Queen Anne and opened it as a museum in honor of Anna's mother, Anna Grier Musser, in 1984. The Victorian rooms inside are filled with the family's constantly changing collections of antique furnishings, curios, and memorabilia. The shades of pink and green on the exterior of this hidden treasure are original to the area. They are a sun-dried variation of the colors of two houses in *Daughters of Painted Ladies*: the Hale House and 724 East Edgeware.

PASADENA

442 Summit Avenue. This transitional 1895 Queen Anne Craftsman cottage was the second house designed by the great Craftsman architects Charles and Henry Greene. Susanna Yoakum's grandfather, Willis Eason, paid $4,000 and moved in in 1923, and she has lived there since she was nine days old. Her life's work has been restoring the house.

Every bit of the house has been stripped down to the bare wood; all the shingles were replaced, and every window was taken out and reweighted. The front porch was extended to its original size, with a new tongue-and-groove floor in which no nails were used. The original 150-pound redwood pillars were taken down, sanded, and put back. Duplicates of the rain gutters were handmade with sheet metal, and the ornate doorbell and pediment were restored. In the course of prepping the house, Bob Buckter found scars of the pediment scrollwork and replaced the plasterwork.

When it came time to paint, Susanna worked with Buckter and his brother Don, now a San Francisco painter, on a monochromatic gray-green scheme because she wanted something feminine. The five colors range from mushroom to bayleaf.

Susanna believes that it's important to treat workers well and serves them lunch and sometimes dinner. Her carpenter, Harry Legg, never takes shortcuts. In 1988, the Yoakums received Pasadena's Golden Arrow award for beautification and restoration.

On a tour of the nearby Greene and Greene masterpiece, the Gamble House, the guide tells the story that when the house was being built, someone asked a carpenter why he was lavishing so much craftsmanship on the attic, when almost nobody would see it. His reply: "The angels will see it."

RIVERSIDE

3121 Mulberry. The detailing on this sweet (1884/1890) Queen Anne makes it look like an enchanted castle. Civil War veteran and lawyer L. C. Waite moved to the new colony of Riverside in 1870, married Lillian, the only daughter of the city's pioneer doctor, and in 1884 built a frame house on the block he had purchased. In 1890, he hired contractor A. W. Boggs to add a grand new eleven-room addition, following plans drawn by architect A. C. Willard. Daughter Lillian lived there until 1942, when the house passed on to less-loving hands.

In 1960, Kathryn Maddox moved in and started roofing and restoring, a chore that has not been completed—although you couldn't tell that from the cheery new paint job of two greens, brown, cream, and terra-cotta by colorist Chuck Vedder. Note the original stained-glass window in the left front parlor and the ruffly cresting on the roof and towers. Vedder feels that he does much more than just paint houses: "We rewrap a gift that was given us so that our children and future generations can see the history in these houses."

(Opposite) 3209 Mulberry at 2nd Street. Only Hans Christian Andersen could create just the right character to live in this fanciful 1893 Queen Anne cottage, a Riverside City Landmark. The crazy-quilt pattern of eleven basic colors on the shingles is rare, since the labor is so painstaking, but Chuck Vedder's painting crew specializes in whimsical, difficult jobs. This house reminds him of a music box— "and if you open the lid you can hear player–piano music."

David G. Mitchell built this home for himself in 1893, at about the time he was helping to create Riverside County, and the same year he was elected county treasurer, a post he held until 1927, when he was succeeded by his daughter Alice M. Mitchell.

Mitchell's life reads like an Edna Ferber novel. The son of an Erie, Pennsylvania, cooper, he served in the Union Army from age fifteen to nineteen and fought at the Battle of Gettysburg. Then he was a store clerk in Rockford, Illinois; a farmer; a construction-gang man on the Chicago, Milwaukee & St. Paul Railway; a rancher; and a businessman. At one time, there were three other Riverside houses based on the same stock plans. Only this one has been restored to its original single-family charm.

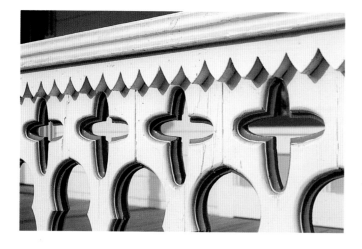

(*Opposite, above, and below*) 3255 Mulberry. Lacy gingerbread and quilt-like patterned shingles endow this embellished 1888 Stick dwelling with a magical air. Notice the lacy cutouts on the bargeboards and the porch trim and the painted panels over the windows. The detailing on the doorway and in the cutouts of the porch railing took many hours and lots of care. Chuck Vedder's scheme of twelve capering colors—lavender, plum, yellow, pale peach, Chinese red, deep tan, light and medium and dark green, light blue, ivory, and deep blue-gray—create an irresistible dollhouse for all ages. Owner Lee Stevens uses the Painted Ladies books to teach her five children about color, architecture, and history. It was difficult for Chuck and Lee to choose the right yellow. While they were poring over paint chips and catalogs, her brother-in-law came in eating a burrito. The yellow of the wrapper was the exact shade they were searching for.

David and Lee Stevens and preservationists in the city worked together to move the house twelve blocks to Riverside's Heritage Square Historic District. 3209 Mulberry and 3121 Mulberry are also in the District. Like the Stevenses' home, others have been saved by a coalition of local preservation heroes: the city council, the city's Cultural Heritage Board, and the local nonprofit Old Riverside Foundation. These groups collaborate to relocate historic houses that are no longer in context with their neighbors and are threatened with demolition.

Villa Montezuma, 1925 K Street. In 1887, the citizens of San Diego built Villa Montezuma for $19,000 for the famous musician Jesse Shepard in an effort to lure culture to the town. Architects Comstock and Trotsche followed Shepard's guidelines in designing this massive, eclectic Queen Anne mansion with its interior of dark, polished redwood and walnut walls and silvery Lincrusta Walton on the ceiling. In 1889, the *San Diego Sun* prophetically described it as "the most ornately finished and artistically furnished house in the city...itself a museum."

By that time, economic hard times had sent Shepard to Europe, and the town had to take over this regal, towered Moorish fantasy, eventually turning it into a cultural center that failed. Today, Villa Montezuma has been rescued by the San Diego Historical Society and is one of the most artistically designed house museums in the country. A fire in 1986 set back restoration, but now the house is remarkably alive, and rooms are being restored to their original design with the help of photographs taken during Shepard's stay. Large blowups of the original black-and-white photos on easels show the "before" so you can appreciate the "after."

(Overleaf and above) In the music room, the largest room in the house, stained-glass windows depict Sappho, Beethoven, Mozart, Rubens, Raphael, and allegorical representations of the Orient and the Occident. The handsome face of the Oriental knight is Shepard's. Shepard's life was as romantic as his novels. His fiancée, a Russian princess, died just before the wedding. He himself died in 1927 at the piano. He had just played the first piece at a benefit given on his behalf.

The interior, with original and period furnishings, glorious woodwork, and made-to-order stained-glass windows, is a marvel. The floors are polished fir, and this magic carpet was created with tiles. It reminds us both of a Bradbury & Bradbury wallpaper frieze and the traditional Victorian tiles in front doorways across the country.

Each of the house's five fireplaces is different, with elaborate overmantels and handmade tiles in the surrounds. The dining-room fireplace, with its beautiful blue tile, is a lasting tribute to the woodcarver's art.

(Overleaf) The eighteen-foot-wide bay window in the drawing room, with polychrome portraits of Shakespeare, Goethe, and Corneille in art glass created for Shepard by John Mallon of San Francisco, is dazzling in the afternoon light. The portraits are enamel, painted on single pieces of glass, and the surrounding decoration is made of brilliantly colored leaded glass interspersed with bevel-edged "jewel" pieces.

The second floor was used by Shepard as a gallery, a use it retains today, although the room was more cluttered then. A "designers' showcase" raised funds to reproduce the five lavish wallpapers used on the ceiling and walls of this upstairs drawing room.

(Opposite) The kitchen in the basement has been restored, with funds raised by preservation-society luncheons, as a turn-of-the-century "below-stairs" kitchen, right down to the filled spice rack. Like all wooden structures, the house does have to be painted every ten years or so. We look forward to the day when Villa Montezuma will be the gold-and-burgundy symphony envisioned by Jesse Shepard.

NATIONAL CITY

1515 L Street. The cacti in the garden surrounding this 1887 Steamboat Gothic mansion are indicative of the climate in National City, a town just south of San Diego that has more than three hundred historical homes. The bayfront is now being designed with a Victorian theme reflecting the city's heritage.

George Kimball was one of five brothers who purchased a former thirty-thousand-acre Spanish land grant, the Rancho de la Nación, and worked to make National City the leading community on San Diego Bay. He built his home in 1887. The woodwork is predominantly heart redwood and sugar pine, with Douglas-fir floors planed and milled at his brother Warren's planing mill. Bricks came from his brother Frank's brickyard. Unfortunately, the Transcontinental Railroad stopped coming to town, but Laura Kimball lived in the house even after it was sold for taxes in 1941. To empty the house so other tenants could move in with her, Kimball possessions were tossed into the cistern, which was sealed.

The cistern yielded a treasure trove of history, waterlogged after forty-five years but still useful: pictures, jewelry, china, pottery, medicine bottles, and furniture. The house is open to the public on the last Sunday afternoon of each month just to show all of the Kimball memorabilia.

(*Opposite*) Bruce Coons and his sister Alana are restoring the home, using as guides copies of old photographs of the rooms in their floor-to-ceiling wallpaper treatments. In the parlor, the Bradbury & Bradbury wallpaper treatment on the walls and ceiling complement the remarkable original polychrome treatment on the pipes of the 1880 reed organ. Each year, Bruce and Alana host a home tour to benefit a different historical or preservation group. In 1991, they were chosen San Diego's "Preservationists of the Year."

Bruce is a Victorian-design consultant who worked on Villa Montezuma. He feels that "It is extremely important to preserve as much of the original fabric of the house as possible inside and out. Beware of the gut-and-replace set. Repair and conserve, rather than replace. If you wanted a new Victorian, you could have built one."

WHAT'S NEO

In a cartoon in *The New Yorker* magazine, a husband-and-wife team are standing in front of Hansel and Gretel's gingerbread cottage, complete with candy canes, marzipan bargeboards, and sugarplum frills, and the wife says to the real estate broker, "Is it from a mix or from scratch?"

"Neos" are new Victorians, that is, houses built today from Victorian floor plans or from new plans with the features of a Victorian home. They're springing up all over the country as single-family "dream homes" or rows of townhouses used as condominiums or apartments. Even apartment-dwellers prefer the polychrome and gingerbread that provide the comfort of "grandmother's house."

While it's true that shortcuts such as aluminum windows and squared bay windows shout their "newness," remember the roots of these faux Victorians. A century ago, homeowners purchased their floor plans and architectural designs from the catalogs of such designers as A. J. Downing, George Barber, A. J. Bicknell, or George Palliser. Later, Sears & Roebuck and Montgomery Ward offered precut houses. Today, you can buy the same patterns—or the same patterns modified for modern use—from people like Home Planners and Larry Garnett.

You can buy a gazebo by mail. Hammacher Schlemmer once featured one on the cover of a catalog. Tin ceilings in century-old patterns can still be ordered from W. F. Norman. Spindles, cornices, brackets, and medallions designed one hundred years ago are available from dozens of woodwork-and-plaster dealers.

If farmers could transform their homes into lacy Carpenter Gothics or bristling Eastlakes by ordering gingerbread from a catalog and applying a new façade, Victorian homeowners can do the same today. Here are the most exciting Neo-Victorian houses we found, eleven homes in seven states. One thing's for sure; these are the original colors!

VIRGINIA
GREAT FALLS

204 River Park Drive. Patent attorney Rodger Tate planned his house for five years using old floor-plan books such as Bicknell's *Victorian Buildings*. He built the ten-room, 6,000-square-foot house in 1984 and filled it with antiques that he and his wife Alice had collected over the years. It's designed for modern living, but the shapes and proportions are Victorian. Brass hinges, four mantels, eight period windows, antique-glass doorknobs, and a hundred-year-old front door with Eastlake hinges—all came from auction houses and salvage firms.

The cherry staircase came out of a hotel in downtown Washington that was built in the 1880s and torn down in the 1980s. Four different parts of the staircase were found at four different salvage dealers after the main section had been discovered at an auction center. In the front entryway, the Tates used the Christopher Dresser collection of wallpapers in sets configured by Paul Duchscherer at Bradbury & Bradbury. The front parlor is done in Bradbury & Bradbury's Aesthetic series. Local master craftsman Patrick Shields put up the paper in the hall and did some of the wood graining. All the millwork on the first floor was custom-made to the Tates' specifications based on designs from Victorian pattern books.

Rodger and Alice, a watercolorist, did the color scheme with four custom-made colors: plum, raspberry, mauve, and cream. Bob Buckter has also provided a color scheme in grays. The Tates may stay with these colors or add some, using "Dr. Color's" ideas for placement for the home they call Secondhand Rose.

CHARLOTTE

5940 Millbury Court off Rama Road. In 1902, the Miller family built an amply proportioned Queen Anne home. In 1983, the home was restored, then sold to Frank and Peggy Dearien, who turned it into the popular Homeplace Bed and Breakfast Inn. At the same time, the rest of the property behind Sardis and Rama Road was subdivided, and twenty-four Neo-Victorians were built along several beautifully landscaped cul-de-sacs.

This delightful Queen Anne was built in 1983 and sold to Cindy Gray, a nurse who collects Italian ceramics. She chose the color scheme of yellow with white and green, copying a downtown lawyer's office because she likes these colors. Doug's photo captures the comfortable design of the home with the lush spring greenery surrounding it.

GEORGIA
ATLANTA

80 Waddell Street. The symbol on Atlanta's Inman Park banner is a butterfly, the symbol of transformation from ugliness to beauty, a fitting symbol for the transformation the neighborhood has been undergoing. In 1969, this area of five hundred Victorian homes had deteriorated into an oak-shrouded slum. Dozens of homes had been razed for a highway, and more were doomed. Young preservationists moved into the district and started one of the first successful inner-city projects in America.

But there were empty lots among the flowering Queen Annes and Eastlakes, and builder Kathleen Day, who already lived on the block with her family, decided that she wanted a big "old" house that would be exactly right for her. Her neighbor, architect Richard Dagenhart, designed her dream house, and Kathy and her husband, Bruce Gunter, moved in in 1988. She has built six houses on vacant lots surrounded by Victorians and has won awards for in-fill housing from the Atlanta Urban Design Commission. The Historic Inman Park District is now on the National Register.

When it was time to paint her house, Kathleen chose a pale aubergine as a contrast for some of the pinks she and the painters were testing. But she liked the pale aubergine so much, she scratched the pink theme and decided to build on the

aubergine instead, using a dusty blue trim, beetroot on the soffits, and "charisma lilac" on the trim. Now people call it the Purple House.

Kathleen reported that "One of the greatest compliments we've received from anyone was from an elderly woman who was raised on our street and had been away for thirty years. She pointed to our house and said, 'The Smiths used to live there.'" I told her that the house was new, and she replied that the original house was a large two-story with an intricate front porch trim just like ours. Without knowing it, we had repeated history."

This wonderful story makes us appreciate that homeowners of Victorians who love and care for their homes, whether they are new or old, are repeating history and are creating their own ways of doing it.

FLORIDA
ISLAMORADA

220 Atlantic Street. Roy and Jean Murphy wanted a large oceanfront Victorian. They wanted it to be light and airy with lots of porches and luscious colors, and they spent three years planning and building it. The property had been a coconut plantation, then a mobile home court. They got rid of the mobile homes, but transplanted twenty-eight coconut palms and kept a nineteenth-century conch-style cypress cottage on the edge of the property as a caretaker's cottage.

Jean worked with architects Tom Davies of Annapolis, Maryland, and Alan Green of Islamorada on plans and then with Michael K. Dooley of Long Key Constructors when they built the house in 1987 of tidewater cypress siding from Louisiana over concrete and stucco. The tin roof has storm-proof glass in the fifteen skylights, and there are ten thousand square feet of quarried Mexican tile flooring.

Jean wanted tropical gingerbread, so she drew a palm tree design, and Doug Mason of Islamorada made templates so that the pattern could be repeated around the two verandas. The shell pink exterior is punctuated by vibrant fuchsia rose, white, and a French blue that sometimes matches the color of the sea. Boxes with pretty gingerbread will hide the aluminum hurricane shutters that protect the seventy-eight windows because, alas, the coral reef that protects the white sand beach can't keep hurricanes at bay.

Although the house has modern conveniences, the unusually shaped rooms, gingerbread proch railings and trim, latticework, old-fashioned wicker furniture, and chintz-covered sofas add up to a home with Victorian charm and feeling.

(*Overleaf*) The center of the house is the two-story living room, which houses part of Jean's eclectic collection of antique furniture and toys. An automatic plant-watering system was designed by Michael Dooley to keep the plants green when the owners are away. The partly hidden two-story "dollhouse," a minibookcase created by San Francisco's Eric Landsdowne in 1988, inspired the colors used on the inside of the house.

The old carriage is filled with antique lace and teddy bears. The oldest teddy bear is Henrietta Paxford from Oxford. In the high chair, a doll named Victoria sits in front of the old English table and mirror on the back wall. Balustrades from a balcony on a castle in Granada, Spain, support the coffee table in front of the sofa. The writing desk is a family heirloom. And the fluffy hatbox on the footstool is made of antique lace and ribbons. The French doors open onto the spacious veranda looking out on the Atlantic. This house is a fantasy come true, a tropical beachfront made-to-order Victorian.

104 Odessa. John and Carrie Raeburn have three houses at Seaside, but they designed this "Caribbean cottage" for themselves. The pale pink body with blue doors and turquoise-green shutters is a typical Caribbean color combination. The soupçon of turquoise in waves on the gate is pure Carrie. The waves are a recurring theme on other sides of the house, and also inside on one of the walls and on a bookcase. The code at Seaside requires that all the picket fences and gates be white. But no neighbors complained and even the architectural commission couldn't resist. Carrie designs fabric and furniture. She told us, "I work with color all the time, and I like color play and the playfulness of color. Seaside is a wonderful place to promote a lighthearted look at buildings."

SEASIDE

(*Opposite*) Seaside is a dream come to life, the vision of one man who wanted to create something he was nostalgic for: a Victorian village by the sea. Robert Davis worked with Miami architects Andres Duany and Elizabeth Plater-Zybergk to plan a community of cottages built off the ground, so breezes could flow under as well as through them. *Time* magazine called it "a real old-fashioned small town, built from scratch since 1981."

The planned eighty acres (which Davis had inherited) turned out to have a quarter-mile radius, the distance a person can walk comfortably to go to work, to shop, or to eat. Streets were laid out to be comfortable for pedestrians—and in a straight line to encourage a feeling of neighborliness. Ronald Lee Fleming, a Cambridge, Massachusetts, historical preservationist has observed that "There's a search for a community and a civility that is seen as part of life one hundred years ago. People want that back." In the planning of Seaside, providing a sense of comfort and encouraging a spirit of neighborliness were just as important as the architecture.

Each charming painted wooden cottage has gingerbread deep roof overhangs, a tin roof, ample windows, front porches at least eight feet deep to make them comfortable to use, and a Victorian sense of play. Each home is required to have a picket fence sixteen feet from the porch (closer would be intrusive; farther away is too far for conversation), painted in one of thirteen shades of white; no fence can be identical in shade to any other fence on the same block. Some of the cottages, large and small, are permanent homes, some are vacation homes, and some can be rented by the night. The town is also a resort and a cultural center.

These two cottages exemplify the sense of whimsy found throughout this town, which calls itself "the Florida you dream about."

Ecstasy, at 124 Forest Street, is a Charleston-style house. In Charleston, the houses are turned so the side faces the street, not the front, because they used to be taxed based on the footage of the front of the house. This towered cottage has three stories. The first story is truest to the Charleston style: You walk in a narrow door, and when you're through the door, you step onto a huge, long verandah. The second story is transitional, with the porch off to the side and open to the third floor. The third floor is a straight shotgun cottage.

Owners John and Deborah Lynn Usher wanted to have the windows in front extend in a bay, but the architectural commission insisted that all the houses on that street be flat against the street. Since they couldn't have projecting elements or three kinds of siding on the façade, the Ushers decided to compensate with color.

Deborah Lynn Usher and her partner, Deborah Schafer, who have their own design business, used the Pantone Matching System chart to match colors and chose four greens, yellow, and white. Instead of a bay, they opted for painted quoins, and they used a darker turquoise to give them dimension. Purple and orange add pizzazz to the most colorful house at Seaside.

OHIO
CINCINNATI

---

502 Tusculum Avenue at Sachem. Just a few blocks from the row of newly restored and brightly painted Queen Annes built in the 1880s, shown earlier, this newly created Queen Anne echoes them in its peaked gables, rippled shingles, corner tower, and use of vibrant polychrome. Architect Timothy R. Jeckering and builders Jim and Pat McGoff built this dashing new princess in 1991. Pat is an artist, and she chose the happy colors.

COLORADO
TELLURIDE

(*Opposite*) 260 North Davis at Galena. Telluride, nestled in the shadows of the jagged San Juan Mountains, has been a historical landmark since 1964. A sense of the past is always present, and the old blends with the new. This flowery peachy castle was built in 1977 by Jack Para, who followed the designs of Telluride artist Ed Werner. Ed also cut some of the gingerbread designs and created the color scheme of peach, orange, beige, and black, with yellow and green accents. The town calls it the Peach House.

OURAY

Anna's Castle, 316–318 6th Street. When David and Kristi Westfall were building what is now David's law office, in "Westfall Victorian" style, their daughter Anna kept calling it a castle, so they named it Anna's Castle.

The original buildings on 6th Street were built in the mining heyday of the 1800s and have been destroyed by fire or time, so all of the buildings on the block were built after 1980. Turn-of-the-century photographs show a photography business on the site, but hundreds of horse and mule shoes in the land underneath indicate that a blacksmith shop or stable was also there.

The Westfalls built a retail store on the first floor and an FM radio station on the second in 1986. The tower originally supported the FM antenna bays. Then they took over both floors with David's law office. In 1989, a second stage of construction created the owners' quarters: a garage on the first floor; two bedrooms and a bath on the second; a family room, kitchen, and bath on the third; and a planned sun room and roof garden on the fourth floor.

Anna's Castle is a richly detailed fantasy blend of Victorian and Bavarian in smashing colors. David likes copper and adopted the Victorian tradition of using it in plaques on the façade. David chose the four-color scheme, and he and Kristi placed them: gray, emerald green, and deep and light violet.

CALIFORNIA
MANHATTAN BEACH

400 Manhattan Avenue. This handsome new apartment building, one short block from the Pacific, glows with passionate grape bouncing off raspberry and white on a navy blue background. Bob Buckter created the color scheme several years before the building was finished. The ribbed and patterned shingles and careful detailing on the cornices and bandboards attest to the care shown in the construction, and the attractive landscaping completes a welcoming ensemble.

REDONDO BEACH

402 South Broadway. In 1978, this house was a simple 1880s Victorian cottage a few blocks from the Pacific Ocean. Over the next few years, the owner restored and refurbished the place inside and out. Then he decided he wanted something different—something that would give him room for his burgeoning collection of Victoriana. One of his collectibles was a Victorian tower from a home about to be demolished.

He hired David John Modell, a restoration designer in San Francisco, to raise the roof. David integrated the tower into the house and built a second floor, another octagonal bay, and an extension in back. He also put in a window for the third story and crowned it with a gable. A patterned shingled roof, spindles, porch railings and balusters, a stenciled bandboard, pilasters on the bay, and decorations on the new gable were polished off with a five-color scheme in historically authentic browns, greens, and cream. The zigzag handmade copper lightning rod protects the new owners.

MONROVIA

444 Concord Avenue. Dennis and Nancy Gloyd's enchanting cottage, an 1880s Carpenter Gothic, appeared in *Daughters of Painted Ladies*, so like the home in Redondo Beach, this is not a completely new Neo-Victorian. The basic cottage, painted in peach and greens, was said to have been built for the Knudsen Milk family, who installed a solar-heating system on their roof that was not discovered until Dennis, a carpenter, climbed on the roof to add the gingerbread he had carved for the bargeboards.

Since 1987, the Gloyds have been busy. They have designed and built the octagon-shaped turret, raised the roof in back to add another story, installed a swimming pool, designed and built a gazebo, and then painted the house in a yellow, gold, peach, brown, white, and green color scheme with gold leaf. Everything you see in this picture is new.

(*Opposite*) Inside, Dennis created the mahogany fireplace mantels and overmantels and the built-in bookcases. Dennis and his brother Doug have a cabinet-making firm called Jericho Cabinets. Dennis stained all the woodwork and furniture in the house to match the quarter-sawed oak pieces he has collected, creating a visual continuity. Glorious hand-carved and polished wood fills every room, from kitchen to bath, and many pieces are works of art created by the owner for his home, a work of art in progress.

Honorable Mentions

Northeast: 30 Belden, Dobbs Ferry, NY; 34 Circular, Saratoga Springs, NY; 102 Lincoln, Saratoga Springs, NY; 37 Maple, Addision, NY; 9 South Batavia, Batavia, NY; 304 West Center, Medina, NY; 2 Sinclair Drive, Sinclairville, NY; 152 Prospect, South Orange, NJ; The Merry Widow, 42 Jackson, Cape May, NJ; 850 Beech Avenue, Pittsburgh, PA; 209 Market, Bethlehem, PA; 115 North State, Dover, DE.

The South: 9829 Capitol View, Tacoma Park, MD; 7305 Maple, Tacoma Park, MD; 7137–7139 Maple, Tacoma Park, MD; 535 Cedar, Tacoma Park, MD; 2104–2106 Mount Royal Terrace, Baltimore, MD; Scoop's Grill, Alexandria, VA; 915 15th, Arlington, VA; 6464 Washington, Arlington, VA; Reed & Reed Marketing, 1316 West Main, Richmond, VA; 1203–1203A West Main, Richmond, VA; 180 West Main, Richmond, VA; Fulman Street B&B, Harper's Ferry, WV; Bonnington Place, Charlotte, NC; 1011 Hayward, Greensboro, NC; The Oaks, Saluda, NC; Worth House Inn, 411 South Third, Wilmington, NC; 325 Park, Raleigh, NC; 252 Westend, Winston-Salem, NC; 944 Euclid Avenue, Atlanta, GA; 155 Greenville, Newnan, GA; 29 College, Newnan, GA; The Bailey House, Fernandina Beach, FL; 206–208 Washington, Natchez, MS; 2225 Drummond, Vicksburg, MS; 2429 Drummond, Vicksburg, MS; 235 Lavergy, Algiers, LA; 1001 Dauphine, New Orleans, LA; 633 Exposition, New Orleans, LA; 941 St. Ann, New Orleans, LA; 325 North Lopez, New Orleans, LA.

The Midwest: 1003 Neil, Columbus, OH; 301 West 4th, Columbus, OH; 200 West Pearl, Coldwater, MI; 410 27th, Des Moines, IA; 318 Hill, Galena, IL; 124 North Eddy, Fort Scott, KS; 643 Indiana, Lawrence, KS; 425 Greenwood, Topeka, KS; 212 South 4th, Seneca, KS; 9905 Brank Oak, Lincoln, NE; 2336 Whittemore, St. Louis, MO.

The Southwest: 915 South Crockett, Sherman, TX; 414 Main, Waxahachie, TX; 1500 West Main, Waxahachie, TX; 2902 Swiss, Dallas, TX; 2140 South Clayton, Denver, CO; 132 East 8th, Leadville, CO; Delaware Hotel, Leadville, CO; 433 West Colorado, Telluride, CO; 320 West Main, Aspen, CO; 66 South A, Virginia City, NV; 404 West Temple, Salt Lake City, UT.

The Northwest: 1020 West Franklin, Boise, ID; 1403 North 15th, Boise, Idaho; 1504 Warm Springs, Boise, Idaho; 107 Northeast Skipanon, Warrenton, OR; 1014 Southwest Washington, Albany, OR; 35 Granite, Ashland, OR.

California: 111 5th, Eureka; 312 Trinity, Eureka; 904 G, Eureka; Madrona Manor, 1001 Westside, Healdsburg; 659 1st, Woodland; 350 South Eureka, Redlands; 111 Liberty, Petaluma; 579 Bridgeway, Sausalito; 1336 Sherman, Alameda; 1338 Sherman, Alameda; 893 Union, Alameda; 1021 Union, Alameda; 2225 Pacific, Alameda; 2038 Pacific, Alameda; 2130 Yale, Palo Alto; 1005 Main Street, Santa Cruz; 896 East Main, Ventura; 440 South Grand, Pasadena; 5905 El Mio, Highland Park; 3092 Lime, Riverside; 2978 Carlsbad Bl., Carlsbad.

Copies of the photographs taken of these houses, and of those illustrated in the book, can be obtained from Michael Larsen/Elizabeth Pomada, 1029 Jones Street, San Francisco, CA 94109. Museum shows are also available.

Resources

The resources are divided into the following sections:

Color Consultants and Painters; Architects, Craftspeople, and Suppliers; B&Bs, Restaurants, and Reception Houses; Museums; Associations.

COLOR CONSULTANTS AND PAINTERS

Steven T. Aardweg
Aardweg Color Landscaping
Design from the Ground Up
43 Franklin Avenue
Bryn Mawr, PA 19010
(215) 527-4510

Joe Adamo
934 Shotwell
San Francisco, CA 94110
(415) 821-3372

Louis J. Aubert
Interior Design/Exterior Colors
337 De La Ronde Street
New Orleans, LA 70114-1003
(504) 366-1576

Dennis Aufiery
Color
3717 Hamilton Street
Philadelphia, PA 19104
(215) 382-7233

Robin Cannell Baker, ASID
P.O. Box 1199
Telluride, CO 81435
(303) 728-6606

Dennis Brown
Painter, color consultant
806 Ohio
Lawrence, KS 66044
(913) 841-2460

Bob Buckter
Color consultant
3877 20th Street
San Francisco, CA 94114
(415) 922-7444

Don Buckter
Painter
1369 29th Avenue
San Francisco, CA 94122
(415) 664-9354

Detail, Stowe House, 77 Forest, Hartford, CT

Chris Bundy
505 North Main Street
Salem, IN 47167
(812) 883-6045

Dean Carbone
Colorist
160 Washington Boulevard
Springfield, MA 01108
(413) 788-7517

Paul Castle
Painter
Ouray, CO
(303) 626-5795

Errol Cerovski
Painter
908 East 20th Avenue
Denver, CO 80205
(303) 830-8871

J. Pierce Christie
Color consultant
41 West Bond Street
Astoria, OR 97103
(503) 325-8100

Classic Strokes
Douglas Ham
Painting, wallpaper, tile, color experts
1005 East Lloyd Street
Pensacola, FL 32503
(904) 432-5797

Deborah Cole
Colorist
1648 North Oakley
Chicago, IL 60647
(312) 489-6826

James Martin
1522 Blake Street
Suite 300
Denver, CO 80202
(303) 534-4600

Rick Corner
Painter
55 East 15th Street
Dubuque, IA 52001
(319) 583-2600

Merlyn Dahl
Painter, color
403 E. Wisconsin
Delavan, WI 53115
(414) 728-5645

Jay Gardner
Local Color
1563 Northland Avenue
Lakewood, OH 44107
(216) 521-3268

Michael C. Hall
Colorist
Holmlund's Wallpaper & Paint Co.
40 Berkeley Street
Jamestown, NY 14701
(716) 665-2220/484-1811

Neil Heidemann
Old House Company Design
& Restoration
699 Dayton Avenue
St. Paul, MN 55104
(612) 224-8324

Eric A. Hutchinson
Colorist
201 Bissell Avenue
Oil City, PA 16301
(804) 676-2131

David Irvin
Architect/builder/color consultant
124 North Eddy Street
Fort Scott, KS 66701
(316) 223-2564

James Jereb
Color designer/painter
1001 East Alameda
Santa Fe, NM 87501
(505) 989-8765

Lydia Littlefield
Colorist
P.O. Box 595,
North Egremont, MA 01252
(413) 528-0996

Doorway, 27 King's Highway, Haddonfield, NJ

Mike Lyster
612 Elmwood Avenue
Oshkosh, WI 54901
(414) 426-0321

Paula McConnell
Color consultant
3009 Fairfield Avenue
Cincinnati, OH 45206
(513) 751-8339

Paul R. Murphy
256 Park Avenue
Corning, NY 14830
(607) 524-6353/962-7981

Picky Painters
Jim Yoachem and Ray Dewhaele
Council Bluffs, IA
(712) 323-1945

Tracy W. Porter, Jr.
Painting and decorating
7305 Maple Avenue
Takoma Park, MD 20912
(301) 270-5529

Dave Ridenour
Color consultant
203 West 6th
Dover, OH 94622
(216) 343-8441

John Vincent Robinson
Color consultant
2400 Blackwood Road
Little Rock, AR 72207
(501) 661-1174

Carol Wells Shepard
Color designer
Saratoga Springs Foundation
Box 442
Saratoga Springs, NY 12866
(518) 587-5030

John L. Tripi
The Woodcrafters
Colorist/painter
Wabash County Home & Store
Rehabilitation Network
49 West Canal Street
Wabash, IN 46992
(219) 563-9831

Tripp Sargis
Tripp & Co. Decorating
P.O. Box 59822
Chicago, IL 60630
(312) 878-4441

Doni Tunheim
Fresh Façades
Architectural color consulting
(408) 426-6415

Chuck Vedder
P.O. Box 4448
Crestline, CA 92325
(714) 338-2582

Kathleen Wargny
Color consultant
627 North Main
Butte, MT 59701
(406) 723-6161

ARCHITECTS, CRAFTS-PEOPLE, AND SUPPLIERS

"I told Paul Duchscherer 'I want an Oh My God Ceiling,' and that's what I got."
—Lee Albright, Haddonfield, New Jersey

Artistic License
1925A Fillmore Street
San Francisco, CA 94115
(415) 922-2854
A group of artisans known for the highest standards of period architectural and decorative art restoration. A member listing is available.

Steven Baird
Restoration architect
678 East South Temple
Salt Lake City, UT 84102
(801) 328-2541

Bradbury & Bradbury
Fine Art Wallpapers
P.O. Box 155-C
Benicia, CA 94510
(707) 746-1900

J. R. Burrows & Co.
Nottingham lace curtains,
William Morris carpets
P.O. Box 1739
Jamaica Plain
Boston, MA 02130
(617) 982-1812

Cliff Carey
Carpenter
635 Bates Avenue
St. Paul, MN 55106
(612) 774-0218

The Christmas House
520 Maple Avenue
Elmira, NY 14902
(607) 734-9547

Cirecast
Restoration hardware
380 7th Street
San Francisco, CA 94103
(415) 863-8319

City Lights Antique Lighting
2226 Massachusetts Avenue
Boston, MA 02140
(617) 547-1490

Eugene Cizek
Education Through Historic
Preservation Program
2016-20 Burgundy
New Orleans, LA 70116
(504) 945-0322

Coastal Millworks
112 Plantation Chase
St. Simons Island, GA 31522
(912) 634-1300

Bruce Coons
Victorian Design Consultants
1515 L Avenue
National City, CA 92050
(619) 473-3448

Don Cooper
Architect
442 West Kennedy, Suite 320
Tampa, FL 33606
(813) 253-2616

Bob Crane & Associates
Realtor
7676 Sunset Boulevard
Los Angeles, CA 90046
(213) 874-3311

Chris Craven
Architect
906 East 20th Avenue
Denver, CO 80205
(303) 839-1911

Cumberland Woodcraft
P.O. Drawer 609
Carlisle, PA 17013
(717) 243-0063

Custom Ironwork, Inc.
Iron fencing and gates
P.O. Box 99
Union, KY 41091
(606) 384-4486

Tom Davies
Architect
14–16 College Avenue
Annapolis, MD 21401
(410) 267-8424

Kathleen Day & Assoc.
Builders
80 Waddell
Atlanta, GA 30307
(404) 525-8728

Kim DeStiger
Architect
515 Madison Avenue SE
Grand Rapids, MI 49503
(616) 454-8734

Don Tedeschi
Don's Garden Center
Paving
2800 West Montrose
Chicago, IL 60618
(312) 252-7708

Michael K. Dooley
Long Key Constructors
Box 835
Long Key, FL 33001
(305) 852-2806

Keith Downing
Downing & Association
Architects
5115 McKinney, Suite B
Dallas, TX 75205
(214) 521-1390

Dreamscape by the Sea
Carrie Raeburn
Fabric and furniture design
and interiors
Rte. 1, Box 60,
Coffee Springs, AL 36318
(205) 347-1590

Paul Duchscherer
Designer
Bradbury & Bradbury
1925A Fillmore Street
San Francisco, CA 94115
(415) 922-4948/922-2989

Ed Eck
Eck Enterprises
Architectural restoration
1405 West Main
Richmond, VA 23220
(804) 359-5781

Education Through Historic
Preservation
Eugene D. Cizek, Ph.D.,
Professor of Architecture,
Tulane School of Architecture,
New Orleans, LA 70118
(504) 865-5389

Jon Eklund Restorations
Kitchens
80 Gates Avenue
Montclair, NJ 07042
(201) 746-7483

Addison Rose B&B, 37 Maple Avenue, Addison, NY

George and Mary Erickson
Construction/color
222 West McClane
Osceola, IA 50213
(515) 342-6151

Dieter Fahrenback
Cerwe Construction
Carpentry and contractor
2249 West Belmont Avenue
Chicago, IL 60618
(312) 525-6665

Douglas Fifield
Stained glass
715 Dayton Avenue
St. Paul, MN 55105
(612) 291-9251

Bernardo Fort-Brescia, AIA
Arquitectonica
2151 LeJeune Road
Suite 300
Coral Gables, FL 33134
(305) 442-9381

Larry Garnett & Assoc.
Building Designers
4710 Vesta Road
Pasadena, TX 77505
(713) 487-5182

Denis Gauthier
Wallcoverings
New Orleans, LA
(504) 734-8771

M. Brett Gladstone
Gladstone & Vettel
Attorneys at law, specializing in
preservation law and land use
177 Post Street
San Francisco, CA 94108
(415) 434-9500

Alan Green
Architect
Mile Marker 83
Islamorada, FL 88511
(305) 664-9250

Governor's Antiques
6240 Meadowbridge Road
Mechanicsville, VA 23111
(804) 746-1030

Len Gundy
Benchmark Construction
2422 East Highland Avenue
New Philadelphia, OH 44663
(216) 339-6882

Haas Wood & Ivory Works
64 Clementina Street
San Francisco, CA 94104
(415) 421-8273

Joel S. Herzel
Contractor
915 3rd Street
Santa Cruz, CA 95060
(408) 426-0810

Hess Forest Products
Moldings, etc.
501 Harbour Court
Pittsburg, CA 94509
(415) 427-1454

Terri Holliday
Victorian seamstress
P.O. Box 583
Ouray, CO 81427
(303) 235-4065

Home Planners, Inc.
Rickard D. Bailey, President
House plans
3275 West Ina Road, Suite 110
Tucson, AZ 85741
(602) 297-8200

Paul Hook
Contruction
115½ Walnut Lane
West Newton, PA 15089
(412) 872-4127

Paul Horan
Renovator
11 Miller Avenue
Cambridge, MA 02140
(617) 868-8970

Hubbard Brothers Hardware
335 East Main
Medford, OR 97501
(503) 773-7777

Jackson Tuckpointing Co., Inc.
28th and Pinard
Dubuque, IA 52001
(319) 556-8542

Janovic/Plaza
Paint supplies
30-35 Thomson Avenue
Long Island City, NY 11101
(718) 786-4444

Jericho Cabinets
Dennis Gloyd
243 West Maple
Monrovia, CA 91016
(818) 357-4412

Linda Kalzymarek
Restoration
2115 Scotwood
Toledo, OH 43620
(419) 244-9095

John W. Kearney
Sculptor
542 West Grant Place
Chicago, IL 60614
(312) 472-4004

Karen Kinnane Antiques
P.O. Box 212
Main Street
Shartlesville, PA 19554
(215) 488-7792

Bill Klein & Hoffman Interior Design
4105 West Bank Drive
Austin, TX 78746
(512) 327-5275

Mark Landsberg
Architect and planner, teacher of
Victorian house painting
371 Newtonville Avenue
Newton, MA 02160
(617) 969-1191

Little/Raidl Design Studios
Custom Art Glass
49 Hartford Street
San Francisco, CA 94114
(415) 552-3557

Mac The Antique Plumber
885 57th Street
Sacramento, CA 95819
(916) 454-4307

Steve Maher
Victorian consultant
New Berlin, NY
(607) 529-8865

Mainstreet Architects
Michael Faulkoner, AIA
468 East Main Street, Suite A
Ventura, CA 93001
(805) 652-2115

Thom McNamee
Restoration
Rte. 2, Box 240
Dundee, IL 60118
(708) 426-3299

Foster Meagher
Architectural design
1836 Courtney Terrace
Los Angeles, CA 90046
(213) 874-9773

Michael's Classic Wicker
8532 Melrose Avenue
Los Angeles, CA 90069
(213) 659-1121

Matthew J. Mosca
Historical paint research
2513 Queen Anne Road
Baltimore, MD 21216
(410) 466-5325

Paul Murphy
MPC, Inc.
Restoration and renovation construction, authentic historical color selec-
tions, historical registry assistance
22283 Clarks Mountain Road
Rapidan, VA 22733
(703) 854-4924

New York City Architectural
Salvage Program
337 Berry Street
Brooklyn, NY 11211
(718) 388-4527

W. F. Norman Corp.
Tin ceilings
P.O. Box 323
Nevada, MO 64772
(800) 641-4038

Old Home Supply House
1801 College Avenue
Fort Worth, TX 76110
(817) 927-8004

Old House Gardens
536 Third Street
Ann Arbor, MI 58103
(313) 995-1486

Ole Fashion Things
Architectural Antiques
405 Southwest Evangeline Thruway
Lafayette, LA 70501
(800) 228-4967

Period Details
Decorative painting and teaching
16841 Kercheval Place
Grosse Pointe, MI 48230
(303) 885-9237

Charles Pomada
Architectural salvage
85 Stark Road
Newfield, NY 14867
(607) 564-7930

Charles Prentiss Architect
89-D Spring Valley Road
Watsonville, CA 95076
(408) 724-8528

Preservation Associates
Consulting, educational and
rehabilitation services
207 South Potomac Street
Hagerstown, MD 21740
(301) 791-7880

Mark Primack
Architect
517 Mission Street
Santa Cruz, CA 95060
(408) 426-9340

Renovator's Supply
6283 Renovator's Old Mill
Millers Falls, MA 01349
(413) 659-2241

Bryce Reveley
Gentle Arts Textile Conservation
P.O. Box 15832
New Orleans, LA 70115
(504) 895-2628

River City Restorations
1221A Market
Hannibal, MO 63401
(314) 248-0733

Lynn Robinson
Design Forum
Denver, CO
(303) 770-6486

Roth Commercial Art Design
P.O. Box 55
Vermillion, OH 44089
(216) 967-5534

L. J. Ruschke & Co.
Clock shop
302 South Main Street
Algonquin, IL 60102
(312) 658-7755

Joedda Sampson
Allegheny City Restorations
939 Western Avenue
Pittsburgh, PA 15233
(412) 231-4948

Entrance, 126 Pope, Louisville, KY

San Francisco Victoriana
2076 Newcomb Street
San Francisco, CA 94124
(415) 648-0313

Scalamandré Silks
950 Third Avenue
New York, NY 10022
(212) 980-3888

Schumacher Textiles
79 Madison Avenue
New York, NY 10016
(212) 213-8100

Sepp Leaf Products
Gold leaf
381 Park Avenue South
New York, NY 10016
(212) 683-2840

Shady Lady
418 East 2nd Street
Loveland, CO 80537
(303) 669-1080

Sign of the Crab
Brass, protective coatings
3756 Omec Circle
Rancho Cordova, CA 95742
(916) 638-2722

Silk Surplus
37-24 24th Street
Long Island City, NY 11101
(718) 361-8500
Scalamandré discontinued and
discounted textiles

Silverton Victorian Millworks
P.O. Box 2987
Durango, CO 81302
(303) 259-5915

Sink Factory
240 San Pablo Avenue
Berkeley, CA 94702
(510) 540-8793

Patrick Shields
Paperhanger
Great Falls, VA
(703) 425-2461

Stephen P. Smith, Jr.
Historic real estate brokering
77 Parade
Providence, RI
(401) 942-7000

Smith Cornell
National Register and other plaques
711 Hazel Street
P.O. Box 686
Auburn, IN 46706
(800) 325-0248

Souvenirs of Yesteryears
William Gamble, Proprietor
208 West Chicago
Coldwater, MI 49236
(517) 278-8034

Steptoe & Wife Antiques
322 Geary Avenue
Toronto, Canada M6H2C7
(416) 530-4200

Anna Dale Sullivan
Interiors and renovations consultant
1506 North Nicholas Street
Arlington, VA 22205
(703) 536-5363

Sunrise Specialty
Baths
5540 Doyle Street
Emeryville, CA 94608
(415) 654-1794

James Swafford
Restoration carpenter
4735 Winton Road
Cincinnati, OH 45232
(513) 591-0842

Richard E. Thibaut
Fabrics and wallcoverings
706 South 21st Street
Irvington, NJ 07111
(201) 399-7888

Vic Torianhaus
Restoration and preservation
34 Derby Street
Oyster Bay, NY 11771
(516) 922-2127

Charles Uhl
Historic Preservation Services
P.O. Box 77080
Pittsburgh, PA 15215
(412) 492-9000

United House Wrecking
535 Hope Street
Stamford, CT 06906
(203) 348-5371

Deborah Lynn Usher
Dux Dlux
Graphic design
510 University Drive
Starkville, MS 39759
(601) 323-1503

Manuel Valesquez-Aceves
Artist
1641 West Pratt
Chicago, IL 60626
(312) 274-5277

The Victorian House and Shop
600 North Main Street
Mount Vernon, OH 43050
(612) 399-2400

Vintage Valences
Box 43326
Cincinnati, OH 45243
(513) 561-8665

Doorway, 281 East Chicago, Coldwater, MI

Dan Wagner
Albert J. Wagner & Sons
Tin restoration and roofing
3762 North Clark Street
Chicago, IL 60613
(312) 935-1414

Steve Waller
Restoration and construction
11505 Pedee Creek Road
Monmouth, OR 97361
(503) 838-4095

Jonathan Wallick
Construction
8216 Birch Street
New Orleans, LA 70118
(504) 861-4357

Don Walls
Interior decoration
52 College Street
Newnan, GA 30263
(404) 253-5100

John Waycaster
Architect
112 Main Street
Natchez, MS 39120
(601) 442-3649

James Webb
Architectural restoration and
color planning
327 Howard Street
Petaluma, CA 94952
(707) 762-3444

Christopher Winslow
Artist
3120 St. Paul Street, Apt. 3-E
Baltimore, MD 21218
(410) 243-1842

Becky Rogers Witsell
Studio-Werk
Faux finishes, *trompe l'oeil*, stencil-
ing, wall hangings, color, fabric, and
wallpaper design
P.O. Box 164646
Little Rock, AR 72216
(501) 376-3534

Charles Witsell
Restoration architect
101 East Capitol Avenue
Little Rock, AR 72216
(501) 372-1408/374-5300

Yestershades
3824 Southeast Stark
Portland, OR 97214
(503) 235-5645

B&Bs, RESTAURANTS, AND RECEPTION HOUSES

The Abbey
606 Columbia Avenue
Cape May, NJ 08204
(609) 884-4506

Addison Rose B&B
37 Maple Avenue
Addison, NY 14801
(607) 359-4650

Allyn Mansion Inn
511 East Walworth Avenue
Delavan, WI 53115
(414) 728-9090

Angel of the Sea
5 Trenton Avenue
Cape May, NJ 08204
(609) 884-3369/(800) 848-3369

Belle of the Bends B&B Inn and
Tour House
508 Klein Street
Vicksburg, MS 31980
(601) 634-0739/(800) 844-2308

Blue Violet Mansion
443 Brown Street
Napa, CA 94559
(707) 253-2583

The Captain Gilchrist Guest House
5662 Huron Street
Vermilion, OH 44089
(216) 237-1237

The Carriage House Inn
Rte. 1
Searsport, ME 14974
(207) 548-2289

Coleman House
A historical bed-and-breakfast inn
323 North Main Street
Swainsboro, GA 30401
(912) 237-2822

Colours Key West
410 Fleming Street
Key West, FL 33040
(305) 294-6977

Combellack-Blair House
2059 Cedar Ravine
Placerville, CA 95667
(916) 622-3764

Crescent Cottage Inn
211 Spring Street
Eureka Springs, AR 72632
(501) 253-6022

Eastern View B&B
22283 Clarks Mountain Road
Rapidan, VA 22733
(703) 854-4924

Eastlake Inn
1442 Kellam Avenue
Los Angeles, CA 90026
(213) 250-1620

The Martin and Lilli Foard House
B&B
690 17th Street
Astoria, OR 91013
(503) 325-1892

The Gables
4257 Petaluma Hill Road
Santa Rosa, CA 95404
(707) 585-7777

Garth Woodside Mansion Bed and
Breakfast
Rte. 1
Hannibal, MO 63401
(314) 221-2789

The Gatehouse Inn
225 Central Avenue
Pacific Grove, CA 93950
(408) 649-1881

Georgetown-Baehler Resort Services
Historical rentals
P.O. Box 247
Georgetown, CO 80444
(303) 569-2665

The Gingerbread House Reception
Home
1921 Bull Street
Savannah, GA 31401
(912) 234-7303

The Goff House Inn
506 South Evans
El Reno, OK 73036
(405) 262-9334

The Grape Leaf Inn
539 Johnson
Healdsburg, CA 95448
(707) 433-8140

The Charles R. Hart House
1046 Windsor Avenue
Windsor, CT 06095
(203) 688-5555

Heritage House
305 Pierce Street
Port Townsend, WA 98368-8138
(206) 385-6800

Homeplace B&B
5901 Sardis Road
Charlotte, NC 28270
(704) 365-1936

Linda Lee
725 Columbia Avenue
Cape May, NJ 08204
(609) 884-1240

Natalia's 1912 Family Restaurant
1161 Blair Street
Silverton, CO 81433
(303) 387-5300
May–October

The National Historic Bed and
Breakfast
936 East 1700 South
Salt Lake City, UT 84105
(801) 485-3535

The Queen Anne Guest House B&B
200 Park Avenue
Galena, IL 61036
(815) 777-3849

Rosewood Inn
Main Street, Rte. 14
Williamstown, VT 05679
(802) 433-5822

Russell-Cooper House
115 East Gambier Street
Mount Vernon, OH 43050
(614) 397-8638

Saracen Restaurant
141 East Bay Street
Charleston, SC 29401
(803) 723-6242

Ann Starrett Mansion
Victorian inn
744 Clay Street
Port Townsend, WA 98368
(206) 385-3205/(800) 321-0644

Stone Cliff Manor B&B
195 17th Street
Dubuque, IA 52001
Closed in winter; phone number
changes yearly (319)

The Towers
101 Northwest Front Street
Milford, DE 19963
(302) 422-3814

Union Hotel and Victorian Annex
362 Bell Street
Los Alamos, CA 93440
(805) 344-2744

The Victorian Bed and Breakfast
602 North Main
P.O. Box 761
Coupeville, WA 98239
(206) 678-5305

Victorian Corner Restaurant
541 Lighthouse Avenue
Pacific Grove, CA 93950
(408) 372-4641

The Victorian Rose Wedding Chapel
896 East Main Street
Ventura, CA 93001
(805) 648-3307

The White House Berries Inn
Restaurant and B&B
Box 78, Rte. 8
Bridgewater, NY 13313
(315) 822-6558

MUSEUMS

Alameda Historical Museum
2324 Alameda Avenue
Alameda, CA 94501
(510) 521-1233
Wednesday through Friday, 1–4;
Saturday, 11–4: Sunday, 1–4. Free.

Billings 1890 Farm and Museum
Rte. 12, P.O. Box 489
Woodstock VT 05091
(802) 457-2355
Daily, May to October, and on
Thanksgiving weekend. Fee.

Doorway, 426 Broad Street, Oneida, NY

Bowman-White House
9th and Rose
Georgetown, CO 80444
(303) 674-2625

The Castle
70 South B Street, Box 48
Virginia City, NV 89440
(702) 847-0275
Summer months

The 1890 House Museum and Center
for Victorian Arts
37 Tompkins Street
Cortland, NY 13045
(607) 756-7551

Grier Musser Museum
403 South Bonnie Brae Avenue
Los Angeles, CA 90004
(213) 413-1814
Wednesday–Saturday, 11–4. Fee.

Herald Democrat Newspaper
and Museum
717 Harrison Avenue
Leadville, CO 80461
(719) 486-0641
Friday and Saturday, 10–6; Sunday,
12–6; and seasonally. Fee.

Historic Pensacola Village
120 East Church Street
Pensacola, FL 32501
(904) 444-8905
A complex of museums, homes, and
an archaeological trail. One ticket
serves for all. Monday–Saturday,
10–4:30; Sunday, 1–4:30; between
Easter and Labor Day.

Historic Rugby
P.O. Box 8
Rugby, TN 37733
(615) 628-2441
Historical Victorian village.

Jack House
536 Marsh Street
San Luis Obispo, CA 93401
(805) 549-7300
First Sunday of month, October–
May; 1–4; Wednesday and Friday
in summer. Fee.

The Lace House Museum
161 Main Street
Black Hawk, CO 80422
(303) 582-5382
Memorial Day–Labor Day, 9–4, or
by appointment. Fee.

The Mark Twain House and Harriet
Beecher Stowe House
77 Forest Street
Hartford, CT 06105
(203) 525-9317
Daily June 1–Columbus Day and
December; Tuesday–Saturday,
9:30–4, and Sunday, 12–4, the rest
of the year. Fee. Museum shop.

Olana State Historic Site
Rte. 9G
Hudson, NY 12534
(518) 828-0135
Wednesday–Saturday, 10–4; Sunday
12–4; mid-April to November 1. Fee.

Rosalie House Tour Home
282 Spring Street
Eureka Springs, AR 72632
(501) 253-7377
Open daily. Fee.

San Francisco Plantation
La Reserve
P.O. Box Drawer AX
Reserve, LA 70084
River Rd., State Rte. 44, Garysville
(504) 535-2341
Daily, 10–4. Fee.

Toy and Miniature Museum of
Kansas City
5235 Oak
Kansas City, MO 64112
(816) 333-2055
Wednesday–Saturday, 10–4;
Sunday, 1–4. Fee.

Victoria Mansion
109 Danforth Street
Portland, ME 04101
(207) 772-4841
June 1–September 30, Tuesday–
Saturday, 10–4; Sunday, 1–4. Fee.

Villa Montezuma
1925 K Street
San Diego, CA 92102
(619) 239-2211
Wednesday–Sunday, 1–4:30. Fee.

Wing Museum
27 South Jefferson Street
Coldwater, MI 49036
(517) 278-2871
Wednesday–Sunday, 1:10–5:10. Fee.

ASSOCIATIONS

Baltimore Historical Society
409 West Cold Springs Lane
Baltimore, MD 21210
(410) 467-6424

Boise Historic Preservation Office
210 Main Street
Boise, ID 83702
(208) 334-3861

Galveston Historic Foundation
2016 Strand
Galveston, TX 77550
(409) 765-7834

Georgetown Historical Society
305 Argentine
Georgetown, CO 80444
(303) 569-2840

The Heritage Hills Foundation
126 College Avenue Southeast
Grand Rapids, MI 49503
(616) 459-8950

Historical Properties Commission
P.O. Box 829, Century Station
Raleigh, NC 27602
(919) 832-7238

Historic Dayton's
Bluff Association
732 Margaret Street
St. Paul, MN 55106

Historic Preservation League
of Oregon
26 Northwest 2nd Street
Portland, OR 97209
(503) 243-1923

Jefferson County Historical Society
City Hall
Port Townsend, WA 98368
(206) 385-1003

The Meadows Foundation
2922 Swiss Avenue
Dallas, TX 75204
(214) 826-9431

National Trust for Historic
Preservation
1785 Massachusetts Avenue
Northwest
Washington, DC 20036
(202) 673-4000
Publishes *Historic Preservation
Newsletter* and *Historic Preservation*.

Preservation Resources Center of
New Orleans
Louisiana State Historic Preservation
Office LSHPO
604 Julia Street
New Orleans, LA 70130
(504) 581-7032
Publishes *Preservation in Print
Newsletter.*

Providence Preservation Society
21 Meeting Street
Providence, RI 02903
(401) 831-7440

Riverside Cultural Heritage Building
Old Riverside Foundation
1510 University Avenue
Riverside, CA 92507
(714) 683-2725

San Diego Historical Society
P.O. Box 81825
San Diego, CA 92138
(619) 232-6203

Santa Cruz Historical Trust
1543 Pacific Avenue
Santa Cruz, CA 95060
(408) 425-3499

Telluride Historical Society
317 North First Street
Telluride, CO 81435
(303) 728-3344

Victorian Preservation Association of
Santa Clara Valley
265 North 13th Street
San Jose, CA 95112

Victorian Society of America
East Washington Square
Philadelphia, PA 19106
(215) 627-4252

Porch of Memory House B&B, 6404 Washington Boulevard, Arlington VA

Thanks to Everyone Who Mailed Photos

Thanks to those who submitted notes and photographs. You showed us the way. Michael, Doug, and Elizabeth looked at every one we received, and we "weeded out" any suggestions that one or more of the three of us did not like. We have kept our notes and pictures you wanted us to keep, and we'll look again before we do another national book. If you make changes such as adding another color or more gingerbread, please send us another picture. Please keep us posted on new discoveries for our next book. We're at 1029 Jones Street, San Francisco, CA 94109.

Maine: Candy Rogers, Kezer Falls; Ronald and Clyda Gagnon, Portland; Dr. Thomas B. Johnson, Auburn.

Vermont: Billings Farm & Museum, Woodstock; Northfield Inn, Northfield.

New Hampshire: Lawrence Leonard, Laconia; Betsy Paterman, Ashland; Nicholas Coniaris, Hollis.

Rhode Island: Tom and Michele Keister, Newport.

Massachusetts: James Laurence, Northborough; Bernard Flavhan, Hudson; Mrs. Richard Wallis, Holyoke; Elizabeth and Michael Gauthier, Lexington; Margaret Klein, Cape Cod.

Connecticut: Art and Pat Salvo, Tolland; Roger and Kay Haedicke Lowlicht, North Haven; Janice and Jeff Ruhloff, Shelton; Charles Irving, Essex; Mr. and Mrs. Samela, Ansonia; Antoinette Schmitt, Branford; Steve Harrod, Hartford.

New York: Steve Maher, Wisteria Gardens, New Berlin; Patricia Ackley, Sinclairville; Carol Z. Holcberg, Buffalo; Kathleen Rowe, Flushing; Kay Cocozza, Katonah; Lila Weinberg, Grand View; Thomas and Ronda Pollock, Port Jervis; George and Judith Knoll, Leeds; Ivar and Cheri Anderson, Hudson; Daniel Brown, Glen Falls; Robbie Smith, Port Lewis; Leonard and Jacqueline Lawton, Mexico; Shari and Douglas Reynolds, Penn Yan; Jo Ann and Paul Kloc, Weedsport; Gail Caye, Green Gables, Tupper Lake; Judy and Bill Pantl, Stittville; Patty Paul, Gansevoort; Sandy and George Green, Plumbush, Mayville; Lynne and Paul Argentieri, Howell; Charles Unger, Dobbs Ferry; Bill and Mary Ann Peters, Addison Rose, Addison; Mary Westering, Freeport; Betty Campbill, Octagon House of Camillus, Camillus; Janice Parietti, Altamont; Richard Leonardi, Woodhaven; Sheila and Samuel Speidel, Warrensburg; Michael and Joyce Mattes, Mattetuck; Michele Erceg, Saratoga Springs; W. S. Whiting, Cortland; Robert Selkowitz, Rosendale; Stephanie Melvin, Saratoga Springs; James Condon, Amsterdam; Steve and Marta Vultaggio, Setauket.

Pennsylvania: Steve Aardweg, Rosemont; Audrey Walters, Philadelphia; Dick and Kim Fornof, Oil City; Carl and Nadine Glassman, Wedgewood Inn, New Hope; Wayne and Barbara Harris, Oakmont; Carol Carlson, Smethport; Kathy Gullstired, Susquehanna; Greg and Colleen Jurau, Glenshaw, Lorraine Ezbiansky, Old Forge; Mrs. William Ortmann, Lancaster; Dick and JoAnne Diebert, Woolrich; Rev. and Mrs. Dale Timco, Tichoute; Shirley Lovcik, Williamsport; James Magee, Pittsburgh; Jim Kilby, Quarreysville; Michael Hardy, The Woodlands, Philadelphia;

Gersil Kay, Philadelphia; April Ryan, Washington; Karen Alleman, Newville; Wanda Berman, Adamstown Inn, Adamstown.

New Jersey: Tom Overall, South Orange; Joseph Clark, Jr., Haddonfield; Linda Caywood, Linwood; Jeanette Turnbull, Cape May; Bruce and Sylvia Wilson, Merchantville; Debbie and Chris Corbett, Montclair; Nancy Jessen, Metuchen; Sharon Specht, Mays Landing; Francine Cohen, North Plainfield; David Lipman, Springfield; Nancy Strathearn, Morristown; Merry Widow, Cape May; Fred and Joan Echevarria, Gingerbread House, Cape May; Keven Cordes, Cape May; Sea Holly Inn, Cape May; Dan Wells, The Queen Victoria, Cape May; Normandy Inn, Spring Lake; Michele Arman, Rutherford; George Wagner and Roberta Mayer, Hopewell; Shirley Dobbs, Vincentown; Mrs. Joyce Garrett, Plainfield.

Delaware: D. Coffey, Dover; Ellen Richardson, Dover; John Stevens, Dover; David E. Hargraus, Milford; Dorothy Davis, Newcastle: Anne and Brinton Seldonridge, Townsend.

Maryland: Tracy Porter, Jr., Takoma Park; Caroline Alderson, Takoma Park; James Wannamaker, Baltimore; Ray Zeleny, Perry Hall; The Inn at Buckeystown, Buckeystown; Peter Rivek, Silver Spring; Mr. Channon, Silver Spring; Jacqueline Brooks, Crisfield.

Virginia: The Hidden Inn, Orange; John and Marly McGrath, Memory House, Arlington; Nancy Freeman, Arlington; Kathi and Steve Walker, Culpepper; David and Judi Medwedeff, Vienna; Mary Bladon House, Roanoke.

North Carolina: Jack Wheatly, Raleigh; Yolanda Shimpock Miller, Greensboro; Marge Turcot, Asheville; Rick and Lois Cleveland, The Aerie, New Bern.

South Carolina: Lake E. High, Jr., Columbia; Rutledge Victoria Guest House, Charleston; The Painted Lady, Abbeville; Bruce Andrews, Sumpter.

Georgia: Dottie McCord, Shellmont B&B, Atlanta; Magnolia Place Inn, Savannah; Captain's Quarters B&B, Fort Oglethorpe; The Culpepper House B&B, Senoia; Gerald and Jennie Lewis, Bainbridge; Tony and Ann Ianaurio, Jefferson; Brandon Lewis, Newnan; Parrott Camp-Soucy Home; Newnan; Gloria Sampson, Columbus.

Tennessee: Patricia Mynott, Harriman; Kevin Smith, Fayetteville; Kathryn Newton, Knoxville; Newbury House, Rugby; Edith Sellers, Memphis.

Florida: Lynette J. Egelson, Pensacola; The Bailey House, Fernandina Beach; Gibson Inn, Apalachicola; Beverly Beske, Sanford; Chalet Suzanne, Lake Wales; The Artist's House, Key West; Roger Grunke, Tampa; Betty Doherty, Lake Helen; Fran Ames, Miami; Linda Everson Kasicki, Archer.

Alabama: Anne Sieller, Mobile.

Mississippi: Barry Burke, Meridian; Doug Jones, Vicksburg; Millsap Buie House, Jackson; Robert Jenson, Vicksburg; Jean Moffett, Natchez.

Louisiana: Louis Aubert, New Orleans; Bougainville House, New Orleans; Lawrence Jennings, New Orleans; Ann Wilkinson, Port Allen; Betty Reed, Houma-Terrebonne,

Tourist Commission, Houma; Eric Brock, Shreveport; Billy and Vicki LeBrun, Vivian; Jane Wadsworth, New Iberia.

Arkansas: Ethel and Fred Ambrose, Little Rock; John Vincent Robinson, Little Rock; Ferrell Johnson, Little Rock; Charles Ray, Little Rock; The Hearthstone Inn, Eureka Springs; The Piedmont House, Eureka Springs; Sunnyside B&B, Eureka Springs; The Edwardian Inn, Helena.

Ohio: Craig Bobby, Lakewood; Nancy Hanford, Springfield; Victorian House, Millersburg; Troy and Suzanna Kahler, Warren; Joe and Donna Mason, Munroe Falls; Curt Corvin, Coshocton; Sue and Jim Ptak; Shreve; Terri Dearth, Miamisburg; Chris Woodyard, Beaver Creek; David Dowty, Columbus; Bob and Dodie Liebcckc, Bellbrook; Charlie McGraw, Centerville; Dan Livesay, Dayton; Denise Wilson, Dayton; Craig Borts, Piqua; Charlotte Agrone, Athens; Patricia Lasswell, Centerville.

Michigan: The Garfield Inn, Port Austin; Dunn Homestead, Troy; Joanne Messina, Holly; John Collins, Marshall; Ken and Rita Tabor, Marshall; Emily Jaeperse, Hastings; Larry Gordon, Fenton; Alan Smith, Ann Arbor; Rhonda Allen, Watervliet; Reena Liberman, Detroit; Cyndi Sinnett, East Tawas; Lynda Pratt, Williamstown; Rick Drugger, Romeo; Mrs. Betty Otto, Cheboygan; Mary Powers, Kalamazoo; Ruth Anne Lomas, Grand Rapids; The Inn on Mackinac, Mackinac; Sheri Worm, Manistee.

Indiana: Chris and Jennifer Bundy, Salem; Kevin and Shelly Baumgartner, South Bend; The Book Inn, South Bend; Mr. and Mrs. Kenneth David, South Bend; The Queen Anne Inn, South Bend; Ronetta Curry, Martinsville; Karen Golden-Dibble, Attica; Cathy Bray, Newcastle; James Henry Ballard-Bonfitto, Fort Wayne; Bob Golden, Oxford; Jody Hemphill Smith, Fort Wayne; Don Orban, Fort Wayne; Jim and Mary Jo Daugherty, Fort Harrison.

Illinois: Athan Yugao Chilton, Urbana; Richard Vaughan, Plainfield; Barbara Cross, Ottawa; Elizabeth Miller, Chicago; Fran Sears, Chicago; Carol Kosterka, Chicago; Philip Pappas, Chicago; A. LaVonne Brown Ruoff, Oak Park; Polly and Jim Groll, Oak Park; Bonnie Beck, Oak Park; Gary Schwab, Oak Park; Judy Gyland, Oak Park; Don Callignon, Hinsdale; Hellman Guest House, Galena; Diane Peterson, Geneseo; Maureen and Bill McWaid, Elgin; White Rock House, Elgin; John and Deborah Heydicky, Aurora; Don Miller, Elgin; Stuart Wasilowski, Elgin; Jeff White, Elgin; Mrs. Heledy, Glen Ellyn; James and Denyse Thiller, Fox Lake; Mary Ann Langston, Springfield; Marcia Batastini, Frankfort; The Octagon House, Barrington; Joyce Crawford, Princeton; Jan and Doug Larson, River Forest; Drs. Gregory and Sandra Kane, Petersburg; Jill M. Dwyer, Joliet; Joseph Marconi, Batavia.

Wisconsin: Dallas Weekley and Nancy Arganbright, LaCrosse; Kurt and Barb Zipp, Darien; Steve and Kathy Liszewski, Cudahy; The Scofield House, Sturgeon Bay; Ann Short, Elm Grove; Judith Knuth, Milwaukee; Rob Mickalski, Marshfield; Tom Burton and Barbara Powers, Waukesha; Lucile Ann Short, Kewaunee; Raymond and Mary Joe Meier, Neilsville; James and Barbara Fett, Kiel; Julie Ann Jagemann, Wauwatosa; Denis Nichols and Judith Laitman, Madison; Mike Lyster, Oshkosh; Dreams of Yesteryear B&B, Stevens Point; David Thomson, Madison; Peg and Gary Wardall, Manitowoc; The Gables B&B, Kewaunee; Old Rittenhouse Inn, Bayfield; Jean Cecil, Racine.

Minnesota: Scott and Debi Nelson, Fergus Falls; Sharon Mohan, Winona; Sarah Kinney, St. Paul; Bill and Althea Sell, St. Paul; Teddy Miller, Northfield; John Trostle, Minneapolis; Isabel Meyer, Minneapolis; Victorian Lace Inn, St. Charles; Diana Hanger, Barnesville; Marlyn Bjorklun, Mankato.

Iowa: Lorraine Fullerton, Dacorah; Connie and Dale Lynch, Tipton; Kathy Heizberg, Afton; Hanna Marie Country Inn, Spencer; The Hancock House, Dubuque; Jackson Tuckpointing, Dubuque; Rick Carner, Dubuque; Jeff and Terri Jensen, Boone; Devorah Wilson, Davenport; Patrice Beam, Des Moines; Hotel Fort Des Moines, Des Moines; Mont Rest B&B, Bellevue.

Missouri: Patricia Arnold, Lebanon; Loretta Paris, Kansas City; Kay Kirkman, Kansas City; Claudia Palazola, Kansas City; Christy Ohrenberg, Independence.

Nebraska: Bob and Carol Workman, Waverly; Tony Mueller, Freemont.

Kansas: Robert Whitten, Pittsburg; D. L. and Betsy Salsbury, Ottawa; Louise Dietz, Ottawa; David Lauer Funeral Home, Seneca; Elly Fitzig, Wichita; Trix Fasse, Riley; Paul Buller, Newton; Jerry Palmer, Topeka; Jim Robertson, Topeka.

Oklahoma: Mary Ann Benham, El Reno; Karen Ley, Ponca City.

Texas: Randy Pace, Galveston; R. M. Roberts, Austin; Peter F. Maxson, Austin; Becki Novak, Duncansville; Jim and Judy Buckingham, Nagadoches; Alan Sheeley, Houston.

New Mexico: The Red Violet Inn, Raton; Susan Berry, Silver City; Judee Gay Williams, Las Vegas.

Colorado: Ellen Van Ness Seymour, Denver; Chuck Hunker, Boulder; Boulder Victoria B&B, Boulder; Doris Butler, Palisade; Sandie Elder, Denver; Queen Anne Inn, Denver; Richard Carter, Denver; The Hearthstone Inn, Colorado Springs; Sardy House, Aspen.

Wyoming: Michael Parson, Cheyenne; Ernest Halle, Cheyenne; George Taplin, Cheyenne.

Utah: Barbara Murphy, Salt Lake City; Mark and Susannah Nillson, Ephraim; Hugh Daniels, Park City.

Montana: Mr. and Mrs. Stan Cohen, Missoula; Allan Mathews, Missoula; Always Antiques, Bozeman; Willows Lodge, Red Lodge; Kathy Macefield, Helena.

Idaho: Pat Derbridge, Boise; Diana Cook, Boise.

Washington: Raymond and Zita Hachiya, Seattle; Sally and Jerry Alves, Camas; Sue Aran, Eden Wild Inn, Lopez Island; Capital Hill Inn, Seattle; Bob Parker, Seattle; William Love, Spokane; Bill and Mary Anne Phipps, The Portico, Ritzville; Charlene Majurski, Tacoma; Richard and Dale Beuttenmueller, Tacoma; The Inn at Pennycove, Coupeville; Holly Hill House, Port Townsend; Old Consulate Inn, Port Townsend; The Castle, Bellingham; North Garden Inn, Bellingham; Joanne and Paul Falandipz, Bellingham.

Oregon: Annie Oliver, Astoria; Ed and Marie Whittington, Astoria; Pat Perlson, Ashland; Kathleen Kimball, Haines; Mrs. Alice Myers, Warrenton; Marcyne and Bill Bell, Baker City; Steve Austin and Kathy Hitchcock, Portland; Annie's Guest House, Corvallis.

Alaska: Mike Dunham, Anchorage; Karen Stanley, Ketchikan.

Arizona: Dottie and Harold Viehweg, Prescott; Jim Grosskopf, Bisbee; William Kozar, Casa Grande.

Kentucky: Debra Richards, Louisville.

North Dakota: Ron Matties, Fargo; Royce Yeater, Fargo;

DeMores Historic Site, Medora.

South Dakota: John E. Ran, Vermillion; The Adams House, Deadwood; Jim and Mary Glenski, Sioux Falls; Elaine Pawley and Alexis Kenakes, Sioux Falls; R. Fred Thurston, Rapid City.

West Virginia: Alden and James Addy, Harpers Ferry; Cathy Cunningham, New Martinsville.

Nevada: Paul Yondre, Virginia City; Jim and Kathy McCarthy, Virginia City.

California: Mrs. Juanita Benson, San Francisco; Pria Graves, Palo Alto; Mary Hernandez, Fremont; Betty Mathieson, San Jose; Jeanne Lazzarini, San Jose; Anne Grassel, Berkeley; Alan and Pamela Nudelman, Los Gatos; Wallace J. Lourdeaux, Ross; Dave Sullivan, San Mateo; Doris Nello, Livermore; Pat Eisenhart, Oakland; Linda Townsend, Chico; Nina Jacobs and Fred Miller, Napa; Deborah Coffee, San Mateo; Todd Gracyk, Petaluma; Mare Matteoli, Eureka; Renee De Laney, Eureka; Robert and Eileen Korjenek, Gilroy; Pat Elemo, Tracy; Stephanie Coury, San Leandro; Ed and Marla Schroeder, Benicia; Jean Bennett, Santa Ana; Constance Gabrisch, Santa Ana; Ruth Filipelli, Alameda; Cindy and Andy Goldsmith, Alameda; Carol and Robin Dyer, Redlands; Rose Victorian Inn, Arroyo Grande; Ken Constantino, San Diego; Herb and Teresa Nelson, Glendora; Jim Gibson, San Diego; Joyce Oblow, Monrovia; Beverlee McGrath, Oxnard; Debbie McEwen, Santa Ana; Lacy Gage, Los Angeles; Patrick Dorfsmith, Redlands; James and Tracy Youden, Riverside; George Geis, Pasadena; Adele and Willey Stone, Healdsburg.

Glossary

Acroteria: A lacy decorative structure that stands up from the top of a roof, pinnacle, or gable. A finial is usually a long, narrow, decorative "topnote."

Baluster: A small post, one of a row that supports a handrail on a stairway.

Balustrade: A row of balusters.

Bandsaw: A long band of blade that runs on two wheels and is used to cut wood into curved or triangular shapes, such as shingles, dentils, or gingerbread.

Bargeboard: An elaborately designed flat board attached to the edge of the roof or placed against the side of a gable to hide the carpentry. Frequently lacy and used on Gothic Revival style buildings.

Board and batten siding: A wooden wall that shows all its ribs on the outside, frequently making decorative stripes. The vertical boards are nailed to the frame of a house and narrow boards, or battens, are applied over the joints between the boards. Batten can also mean rows of vertical planks nailed or pegged onto horizontal planks.

Bracket: A plain or decorated angled support placed under the roof eaves and other overhangs.

Chamfered: Beveled, grooved, or fluted on the edges.

Cornice: A horizontal projecting molding at the top of a building on the exterior. Inside the building, the cornice is a molding placed at the meeting of a wall and ceiling.

Cove or **coved:** Concave in shape. A cove ceiling is the curve, or concave surface, between a wall and ceiling.

Dado: A decorative border or paneling covering the lower part of a wall and topped by a piece of trim called a dado rail.

Dentils: A molding of small toothlike squares.

Façade: The front, or face, of a building.

Fishscale shingle: A shingle with curved edges that looks like the scale of a fish.

Gable: The triangular part at the end of a building formed by the two sides of a sloping roof, or by sloping roofs that meet over windows.

Gingerbread: Decorative elements applied to the exterior trim made of intricately turned or sawn wood.

In-fill housing: Homes built or moved onto vacant lots that take the place of houses that have been destroyed.

Lincrusta, Lincrusta-Walton: An embossed, linoleum-like wall covering. When it was invented by Frederick Walton, it was made of linseed oil. Today's version is plastic-based.

Molding: A strip of wood used for decorative purposes, with regular channels, curves, or projections, which provides a transition from one surface or material to another.

Parquet floor: A floor covering made of hardwood blocks laid in geometric patterns.

Pediment: A triangular section of molding over porticos, windows, and doors.

Pocket doors: Doors that slide into pockets in the walls.

Porticos: A structure of columns, usually around a door.

Quoin: An ornamental stone or wooden block treated to look like stone, set in vertical rows at the corner of a building.

Shotgun cottage: A simple cottage with rooms laid out so that a person could stand in the front door and shoot a shotgun out the back door without hitting anything.

Spoolwork: Decorative gingerbread that looks like an empty spool of thread.

Steamboat Gothic: A Carpenter Gothic style structure so loaded with gingerbread trim that it looks like a steamboat, rather than a house.

Stencil: A thin sheet of metal or paper with decorative cutouts that form a pattern when paint is rubbed over it.

Tongue-and-groove: A way of joining the edges of boards so the tongue of one fits into the groove of the next, usually without nails.

Valence: Fabric arranged in vertical folds hung from a pole or cornice above a window.

Wainscoting: Woodwork, frequently paneled, that covers the lower portion of the wall of a room.

Witch's cap: A shingled conical tower roof—an upside-down ice cream cone shape attached to the top of a tower.

Bibliography

Armitage, Katie, and Lee, John. *Nineteenth Century Houses in Lawrence, Kansas.* Spencer: University of Kansas, 1987.

Arrigo, Joseph. *Louisiana's Plantation Homes: The Grace and Grandeur.* Stillwater, Minn.: Voyageur Press, 1991.

Barber, George F. *George F. Barber's Cottage Souvenir Number Two.* With a new Introduction by Michael A. Tomlan. Watkins Glen, N.Y.: The American Life Foundation, 1982.

Barth, Gunther. *Instant Cities: Urbanization and the Rise of San Francisco and Denver.* Albuquerque: University of New Mexico Press, 1988.

Benham, Jack. *Ouray.* Ouray, Colo.: Bear Creek Publishing, 1976.

Benham, Jack. *Silverton.* Ouray, Colo.: Bear Creek Publishing, 1981.

Bird, Allan G. *Bordellos of Blair Street: The Story of Silverton, Colorado's Notorious Red Light District.* Grand Rapids, Mich.: The Other Shop, 1987.

Blair, Edward. *Everybody Comes to Leadville.* Gunnison, Colo.: B & B Publishers, 1981.

Blumenson, John J. G. *Identifying American Architecture: A Pictorial Guide to Styles and Terms, 1600–1945.* New York: W. W. Norton, 1981.

Brolin, Brent C., and Richards, Jean. *Sourcebook of Architectural Ornament: Designers, Craftsmen, Manufacturers, and Distributors of Exterior Architectural Ornament.* New York: Van Nostrand Reinhold, 1982.

Brown, Georgina. *Victorian Nostalgia: A Look at Leadville's Homes of Fortune.* Gunnison, Colo.: B & B Printers, 1988.

Calhoun, William G. *Fort Scott: A Pictorial History.* Historic Preservation Association of Bourbon County Inc., Fort Scott, Kans.: 1981.

Casewitt, Curtis. *Colorado: Off the Beaten Path.* Chester, Conn.: Globe Pequot Press, 1987.

Chapman, William. *The Madison Historic Preservation Manual: A Handbook for Owners and Residents.* Athens, Ga.: University of Georgia, 1990.

Claflin, Mary Ann: *Bon Air: A History.* Richmond, Va.: Hale Publishing, 1977.

Clark, Rosalind. *Architectural Oregon Style.* Portland, Ore.: Professional Book Center, 1983.

Crocker, Mary Wallace. *Historic Architecture in Mississippi.* Jackson, Miss.: University Press, 1973.

Cudworth, Marsha. *Victorian Holidays: Self-Guided Architectural Tours, Cape May, N.J.* New York: Lady Raspberry Press, 1985.

Dallas, Sandra. *Gaslights and Gingerbread: Colorado's Historic Homes.* Athens, Ohio: Swallow Press, 1984.

Dolkart, Andrew S. *This Is Brooklyn: A Guide to the Borough's Historic Districts and Landmarks.* Brooklyn, N.Y.: The Fund for the Borough of Brooklyn, Inc., 1990.

Dulaney, Paul S. *The Architecture of Historic Richmond.* Charlottesville, Va.: University Press of Virginia, 1976.

Edeline, Denis P. *Ferndale: The Village 1875–1893.* Eureka, Calif.: Eureka Printing Co., 1987.

Eisenhour, Virginia. *Galveston: A Different Place.* Galveston, Tex.: Eisenhour, 1989.

Ferro, Maximilian L. *How to Love and Care for Your Old Building in New Bedford.* Prepared for the City of New Bedford, Mass., 1977.

Gebhard, David, and Winter, Robert. *Architecture in Los Angeles.* Salt Lake City, Utah: Peregrine Smith, 1985.

The Georgetown Society. *Georgetown: Guide to the Silver Plume Historic District.* Evergreen, Colo.: Cordillera Press, 1990.

Gilliatt, Mary. *Period Style.* Boston: Little, Brown, 1990.

Gleason, David King. *Plantation Homes of Louisiana and the Natchez Area.* Baton Rouge: Louisiana State University Press, 1982.

Green, Harvey. *The Light of the Home: An Intimate View of the Lives of Women in Victorian America.* New York: Pantheon Books, 1983.

Gunn, George C. *Buildings of the Edwardian Period: City of Alameda, 1905 to December 31, 1909.* Alameda, Calif.: Alameda Historical Museum, 1988.

Gunn, George C. *Documentation of Victorian and Post Victorian Residential and Commercial Buildings: City of Alameda 1854 to 1904.* Alameda, Calif.: Alameda Historical Museum, 1988.

Haas, Irvin. *Historical Homes of American Authors.* Washington, D.C.: Preservation Press, 1991.

Haglund, Karl T., and Notarianni, Philip F. *The Avenues of Salt Lake City.* Salt Lake City: University of Utah, 1980.

Handlin, David P. *The American Home: Architecture and Society, 1815–1915.* Boston: Little, Brown, 1979.

Harris, Bill. *Great Homes of California.* New York: Crescent Books, 1990.

Hayna, Lois. *Gold in the Hills.* Central City, Colo.: Eureka Valley Publishing, 1983.

Holmes, Kristin, and Watersun, David. *The Victorian Express.* Wilsonville, Ore.: Beautiful America, 1991.

Howard, Hugh. *How Old Is This House: A Skeleton Key to Dating and Identifying Three Centuries of American Houses.* New York: Farrar, Straus & Giroux, 1989.

Howard, Hugh. *The Preservationist's Progress: Architectural Adventures in Conserving Yesterday's Houses.* New York: Farrar, Straus & Giroux, 1991.

Jackson, Hal, with Ted Loring, Jr. *A Guide to the Architecture and Landscape of Eureka.* Eureka, Calif.: Hal Jackson, 1983.

Klein, Marilyn W., and Fogle, David P. *Clues to American Architecture.* Washington, D.C.: Starrhill Press, 1986.

Landmarks Heritage Preservation Commission. *A Comprehensive Program for Historic Preservation in Omaha.* Omaha, Neb.: Omaha City Planning Department, 1980.

Lavender, David. *The Telluride Story.* Ouray, Colo.: Wayfinder Press, 1987.

Lentz, Lloyd C., III. *Guthrie: A History of the Capital City, 1889–1910.* Guthrie, Okla.: Logan County Historical Society, 1990.

Leopold, Allison Kyle. *Cherished Objects: Living with and Collecting Victoriana.* New York: Clarkson Potter, 1991.

Lewis, Arnold, Turner, James, and McQuillan, Steven. *The Opulent Interiors of the Gilded Age.* New York: Dover Press, 1987.

Lewis, Betty. *Watsonville: Memories That Linger*, Vol. 1. Santa Cruz, Calif.: Otter B. Books, 1986.

Logan, William Bryant, and Ochshorn, Susan. *The Smithsonian Guide to Historic America: The Pacific States*. New York: Stewart, Tabori & Chang, 1989.

Logan, William Bryant, Ochshorn, Susan, and Muse, Vance. *The Smithsonian Guide to Historic America: The Deep South*. New York: Stewart, Tabori & Chang, 1989.

Maass, John. *The Gingerbread Age: A View of Victorian America*. New York: Bramhall House, 1957.

Maddex, Diane. *All About Old Buildings: The Whole Preservation Catalog*. Washington, D.C.: Preservation Press, National Trust for Historic Preservation, 1985.

Maddex, Diane. *Architects Make Zigzags: Looking at Architecture from A to Z*. Washington, D.C.: Preservation Press, National Trust for Historic Preservation, 1986.

Makinson, Randell L. *Greene & Greene: Architecture as a Fine Art*. Salt Lake City, Utah: Peregrine Smith, 1987.

Malone, Lee and Paul. *The Majesty of the River Road*. Gretna, La.: Pelican Publishing Company, 1988.

McTighe, James. *Roadside History of Colorado*. Boulder, Colo.: Johnson Books, 1989.

Mitchell, Robert, Jr. *Classic Savannah: History, Homes and Gardens*. Savannah, Ga.: Golden Coast Publishing, 1987.

Moss, Roger W. *Century of Color: Exterior Decoration for American Buildings 1820–1920*. Watkins Glen, N.Y.: The American Life Foundation, 1981.

Moss, Roger W., and Winkler, Gail Caskey. *Victorian Exterior Decoration: How to Paint Your Nineteenth Century American House Historically*. New York: Henry Holt, 1987.

Naverson, Kenneth. *West Coast Victorians*. Wilsonville, Ore.: Beautiful America, 1988.

Naverson, Kenneth. *East Coast Victorians*. Wilsonville, Ore.: Beautiful America, 1990.

Old-House Journal Catalog. Brooklyn, N.Y.: Old House Journal Corp., 1990.

Payne, Richard, and Leavenworth, Geoffrey. *Historic Galveston*. Houston, Tex.: The Herring Press, 1985.

Pearce, Sarah J., and Eflin, Roxanne. *Aspen and The Roaring Fork Valley*. Evergreen, Colo.: Cordillera Press, 1990.

Pearce, Sarah, Eflin, Roxanne, and Pfaff, Christine. *Central City and Blackhawk*. Evergreen, Colo.: Cordillera Press, 1987.

Phillips, Steven J. *Old House Dictionary: An Illustrated Guide to American Domestic Architecture, 1600–1940*. Lakewood, Colo.: American Source Books, 1989.

Pomada, Elizabeth, and Larsen, Michael. *The Painted Ladies Guide to Victorian California*. New York: Dutton Studio Books, 1991.

Quapaw Association. *The Quapaw Quarter: A Guide to Little Rock's 19th Century Neighborhoods*. Little Rock, Ark.: 1976.

Reiter, Beth Lattimore. *Coastal Georgia*. Savannah, Ga.: Golden Coast Publishing, 1988.

Rohrbough, Malcolm J. *Aspen: The History of a Silver Mining Town, 1879–1893*. New York: Oxford University Press, 1986.

Rybczynski, Witold. *Home: A Short History of an Idea*. New York: Viking, 1986.

Rybczynski, Witold. *The Most Beautiful House in the World*. New York: Viking, 1989.

Sakech, Tim and Deborah. *The Official Guide to American Historic Inns*. Dana Point, Calif., 1991.

San Francisco Plantation House. *Return to Elegance*. Reserve, La.: Franklin Printing Co.

Schwin, Lawrence, III. *Old House Colors: An Expert's Guide to Painting Your Old (or Not So Old) House*. New York: Sterling, 1990.

Scully, Vincent. *American Architecture and Urbanism*. New York: Henry Holt, 1988.

Secretary of the Interior's *Standards for Rehabilitation and Guidelines for Rehabilitating Historic Buildings*. U.S. Department of the Interior: National Park Service, 1983.

Seale, William. *The Tasteful Interlude: American Interiors Through the Camera's Eye, 1860–1917*. Nashville, Tenn.: American Association for State and Local History, 1981.

Sherman Preservation League. *So You Own An Old Building?* Sherman, Tex.: 1988.

Smith, Reid, and Owens, John. *The Majesty of Natchez*. Gretna, La.: Pelican Publishing Co., 1986.

Thomas, Jeannette A. *Images of the Gamble House*. Pasadena, Calif.: The Gamble House, University of Southern California, 1989.

Waldhorn, Judith Lynch, and Woodbridge, Sally B. *Victoria's Legacy: Tours of San Francisco Bay Area Architecture*. San Francisco: 101 Productions, 1978.

Warren, Scott, and Warren, Beth. *Victorian Bonanza: Victorian Architecture of the Rocky Mountain West*. Flagstaff, Ariz.: Northland, 1989.

Weber, Rose. *A Quick History of Telluride*. Colorado Springs, Colo.: Little London Press, 1974.

Wellikoff, Alan. *The American Historical Supply Catalogue*. New York: Schocken Books, 1984.

Williamson, Roxanne Kuter. *American Architects and the Mechanics of Fame*. Austin, Tex.: University Press of Austin, 1991.

Wilmington Historic District Commission. *District Guidelines*, Wilmington, N.C., 1988.

Wilson, Chris. *Architecture and Preservation in Las Vegas, Vol. 2*. Las Vegas, N.M.: Citizens Committee for Historic Preservation, 1982.

Wilson, Mark A. *A Living Legacy: Historic Architecture of the East Bay*. San Francisco: Lexikos, 1987.

Winkler, Gail Caskey, and Moss, Roger W. *Victorian Interior Decoration: American Interiors 1830–1900*. New York: LCA Associates/Henry Holt, 1986.

Zimmerman, H. Russell. *The Heritage Guidebook: Landmarks and Historical Sites in Southeastern Wisconsin*. Milwaukee, Wis.: Heritage Banks, 1978.

Periodicals

Architectural Digest, P.O. Box 10040, Des Moines, Iowa 50340; 5900 Wilshire Blvd., Los Angeles, Calif. 90036.

Franklin Historical Review, 51 Milwaukee Street, Malone, N.Y. Vol. 27, 1990.

Historic Preservation and *Historic Preservation Newsletter*, National Trust for Historic Preservation, 1785 Massachusetts Avenue, N.W., Washington, D.C. 20030.

The Old-House Journal, Old-House Journal Corp., 435 Ninth Street, Brooklyn, N.Y. 11215. (718) 636-4514.

Preservation in Print, Preservation Resources Center of New Orleans, 604 Julia Street, New Orleans, La. 70130.

Victoria Magazine, The Hearst Corporation, 1700 Broadway, New York, N.Y. 10019.

Victorian Homes, Renovator's Supply, Inc., Miller Falls, Mass. 01349.

Victorian Sampler, P.O. Box 546, 707 Kantz Road, St. Charles, Ill. 61744.

Notes on the Photographs

Ah, the road. That slithering steaming ribbon of asphalt weaving the geography of America together. New England, the Rocky Mountains, the Deep South, the East and West Coasts, the Southwest, and the Heartland. All await the turn of the ignition key and the forward lurch into the great unknown.

With Elizabeth in San Francisco serving as Mission Control and Michael navigating, I piloted my 1989 crimson Isuzu Trooper through forty-seven states. The journey has always been part of mythology and folklore, so with a mind toward adventure and an eye on the horizon, we began the quest for finding and photographing America's Painted Ladies. Michael was fueled with that strange inner fire that drives all visionaries, but alas, the Trooper and I subsisted on more conventional propellants. The Trooper gobbled up 1,729 gallons of unleaded regular while logging 29,433 miles on the odometer. My quest to become a New Age health-food guru had to be once again postponed as I fell under the spell of Peets 101 Blend French Roast Coffee for a jump start in the morning, followed by ample doses of Smarties™, an etheral confection of dextrose, citric acid, calcium stearate, artificial flavors and colors, and FD&C yellow #5. Our 104 nights on the road were spent at sixty-six Super-8 motels, six Econ Lodges, four Day's Inns, three Ramadas, two Motel 6's, five bed and breakfasts, three private homes, and fifteen miscellaneous motels.

Super-8 motels were by far the most consistent in quality and price. Many times we went out of our way to stay in a Super-8, and they are to be commended for providing comfortable lodging for many a night. The days always went a little smoother when I knew there was a Super-8 awaiting me that night.

This photographic assignment was by far the longest and most involved of my career, and it required equipment that would not fail under intense daily use. All of the photographs, with the exception of a few detail shots, were photographed on Ektachrome 6105 4X5 transparency film. This film, introduced by Kodak a few years ago, has a bit of a red boost, which gets rid of some of the blueness of other Ektachrome films. In addition, I used a Tiffen 812 filter when photographing back-lit houses or on cloudy days. During periods of extreme overcast, I used an 81A filter.

With the exception of a few detail shots, all of the photographs were taken with my Sinar F 4x5 camera. I used 65, 90, 120, 135, and 180 mm lenses. The Sinar system is a marvel of Swiss engineering with all parts interchangeable with all of the Sinar 4X5 cameras made in the last thirty years.

The F's compactness, lightness, and durability make it an excellent choice for any large-format photographer who needs to transport equipment. The Sinar system is also backed by an excellent service staff. When I overzealously broke a rail clamp, they Federal-Expressed me a new one the next day. It might also be noted that Federal Express has many "drop shipment" stations throughout the country that are a boon to any traveler to whom items need to be shipped. Bill Andrews at Sinar helped out with the loan of some accessories—most notably a binocular reflex housing, which made the composition of the photographs much easier. Sinar has long been dedicated to serving the professional community in projects such as this, and I thank them for their assistance and generous loans.

All of the exterior photos were taken with the aid of a ladder tripod loaned by Norm Fisher of Fisher Photo. All of the processing was also done by the lab at Fisher Photo, supervised by Laverne Fisher, with Al Stewart keeping the soup pumped up and film running.

Interior photographs were illuminated with Novatron flash equipment. For large areas 1600w/s, 1000w/s, and 400w/s powerpacks were required to light the dark Victorian interiors. I usually used the 1600 pack with a bare tube head and a photoflex whitedome as the main light, with various combinations of other heads and ambient light to complete the lighting scheme. I have been a fan of Novatron equipment almost from the company's beginning. The powerpacks deliver more punch for the dollar than anything else on the market, and more important, they are backed by a friendly and knowledgeable service staff headed by Charles Donald. When Michael and I were in Dallas, we stopped by the factory. Charles did a tune-up on a couple of pieces of my equipment and, along with company president, Jim Gaskin, gave us a tour of the plant.

When we photographed exteriors, Michael would set up the tripod, and while I was selecting a lens and a camera angle, Michael would work with the homeowner to adjust window shades, turn on lights if necessary, and generally spruce up the house. Michael then took a light reading, and I shot a sheet of Polaroid Type 59. If the Polaroid looked good, we then shot the Ektachrome and moved on to the next location.

Interiors were, of course, more involved. Furniture had to be moved, proper mixtures of ambient and artificial lighting needed to be achieved, and large boxes of equipment had to be moved in and out. For these shots, Michael and the homeowner acted as art directors, while I kept busy figuring out F-stops, shutter speeds, watt seconds, rises, falls, shifts, reciprocity factors, and reflection control. We generally shot three or four Polaroids before exposing final film.

Even with the most wonderful equipment in the world, I would not have been able to keep up the grueling pace of this job if it hadn't been for my friends back in California and some friends I met along the road. Michael took care of the basics of life: making motel reservations, taking care of the meals, calling ahead to homeowners, art directing, assisting on the photos, and providing the enthusiasm that kept us going. Every evening, I would call or write to my friends, and together they would keep track of my travels and bolster my spirits. So here's to Andrew Moran, Doug Boilesen, Sharon Orlando, Brenda Belden, Lawrence Brown, Wendy Wallace, Lisa Murphy, Maryellen Murphy, Raye Lynn Jacobs, Bob and Nancy Terrebonne, Joanna Crowell, Karl Grossner, R. T. Newt, Wisal Fare, Connie Bond, Bruce Jaffe, Debbie Sours, Laura Martinez, Mark Davis, Hannah Sours, Kathleen Wargny, Joan Kiley, Andrea Bersson, Meagan Shapiro, Suzy Locke, Debra Richards, Judy Masten, Nancy Krueger, Carl and Katherine Keister, and Bill Wilson, who along with Dr. Bob Smith put together a way of life for people like me. Thanks to you all.

D. R. KEISTER
Desiree Isle
Black Rock Desert,
Nevada